Step-by
WATERCOLOUR

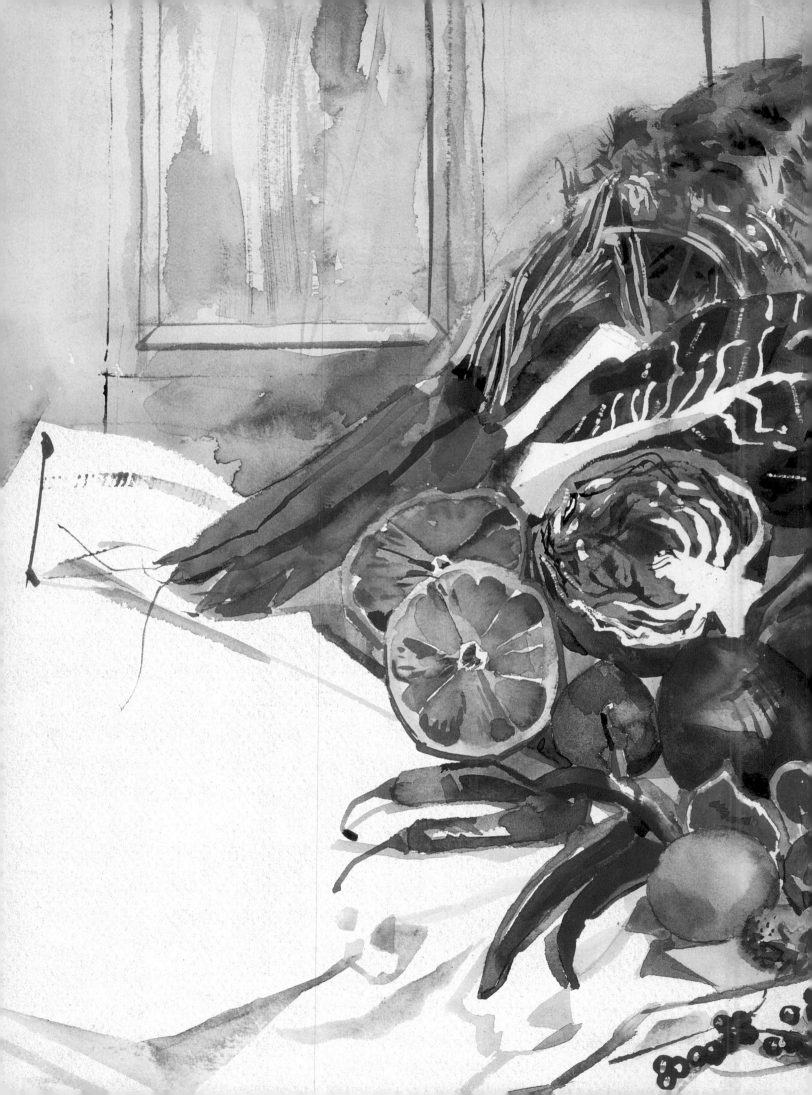

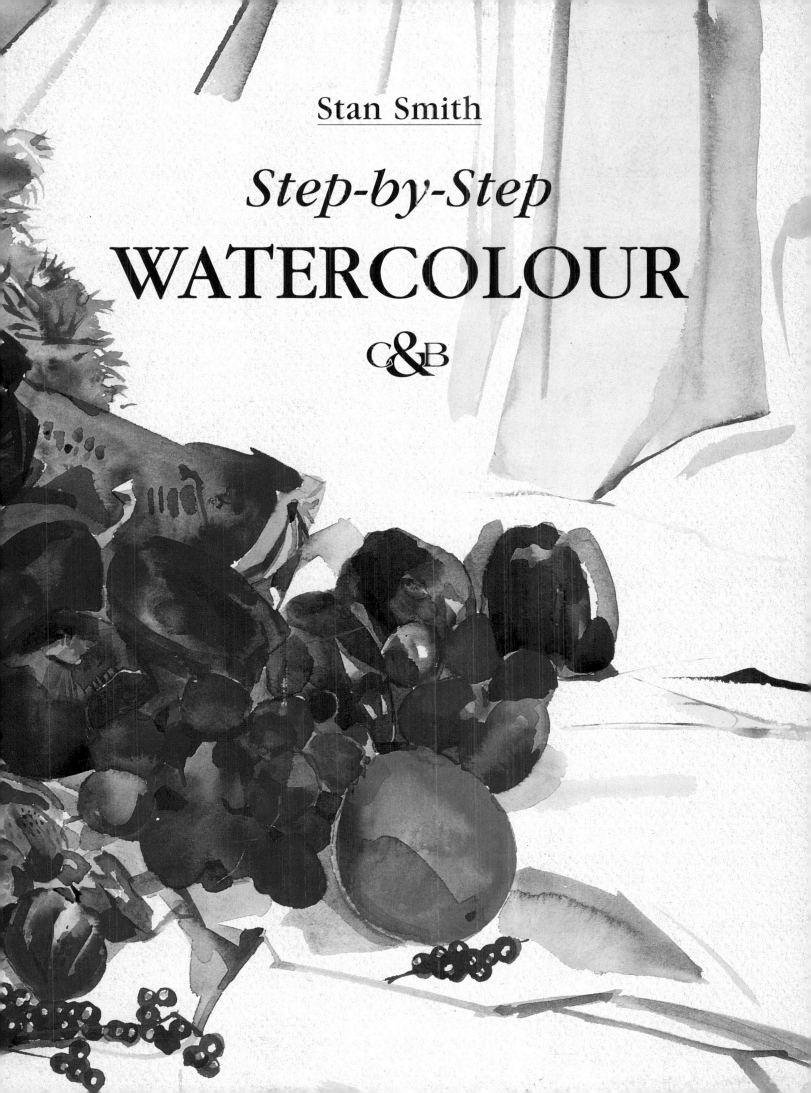

Stan Smith

Step-by-Step
WATERCOLOUR

C&B

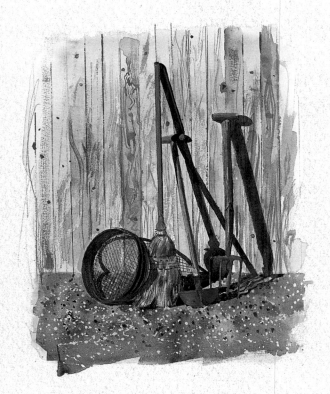

First published in Great Britain in 1995
by Collins & Brown
64 Brewery Road
London
N7 9NT

A member of the Chrysalis Group plc

3 5 7 9 10 8 6 4 2

British Library Cataloguing-in-Publication Data:
A catalogue record for this book is available from the British Library.

ISBN 1 85585 258 6

Managing Editor: Sarah Hoggett
Associate Writer: Miranda Fellows
Art Director: Roger Bristow
Art Editor: Sarah Davies
Designer: Suzanne Metcalfe-Megginson
Picture Researcher: Phillipa Lewis
Studio Photographer: Matthew Ward

Printed in Italy

Contents

Tools and Materials

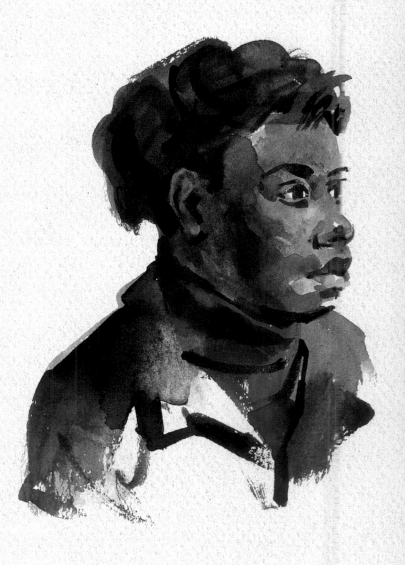

The Fundamentals of Watercolor

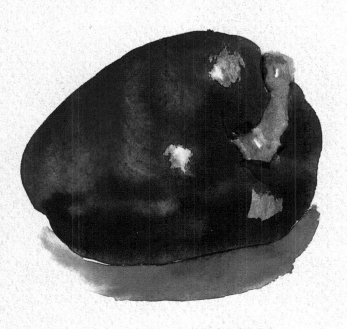

The Projects

Light

The Natural World

Still Lifes

Painting People

Introduction

WATERCOLOR IS ONE OF the most popular media for amateur painters today. One reason for its popularity is the fact that, compared to oil painting, watercolor equipment is relatively inexpensive. You need very little to start painting in watercolor: a few brushes of varying shapes and sizes, a small palette of paint colors, water, jars, paper, and a board or easel will be perfectly adequate for most purposes.

More important than such practical considerations, however, is the unique aesthetic appeal of watercolors. The medium is renowned for its translucency and the way the paper shines through the paint. As a result, good watercolor paintings can convey a feeling of light and airiness unmatched by

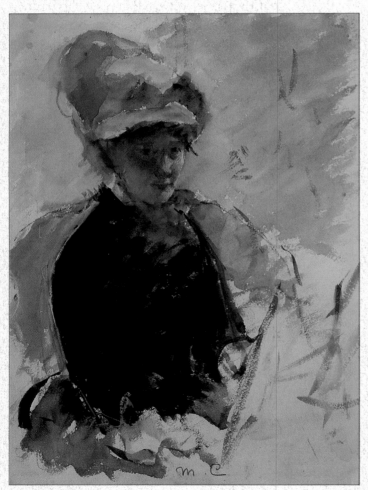

Self Portrait, Mary Cassat (1845–1926)
This charming painting embodies many of the most delightful qualities of watercolor: loose, almost impressionistic, washes; layers of color one on top of another; and carefully controlled wet-into-wet mixes in which the colors flow together in an apparently semirandom manner.

any other medium. Washes of color so delicate that they seem to float above the paper surface, subtle shifts in tone as one color merges into another: these are the qualities most frequently associated with watercolor painting. Yet watercolor is capable of a far more varied range of effects. Although it has at times been seen as a poor relation of oil painting, watercolor has a long and illustrious list of exponents. From exquisitely detailed studies of flora and fauna by the 15th-century German artist Albrecht Dürer (p. 112) to the color abstractions of Paul Klee in the 20th century (p. 33); from the wonderfully evocative paintings of English watercolorists Thomas Girtin and J.M.W. Turner (p. 102) to the intense works of the influential American artist Winslow Homer (p. 90); from the jewel-like miniatures of Hindu gods and legends by the Kangra School in India (opposite) to the fluent impressionistic paintings of figure and landscape in Europe and America by John Singer Sargent (p. 138): the range of styles, moods, and subject matter that can be tackled in watercolor is almost infinite.

Yet the very quality that attracts people to watercolor painting — the translucency of the paint — imposes certain technical constraints. If you apply a second color on top of paint that has already been laid down, for example, particles from the first layer will still show through. This means that you have to plan your watercolors very carefully before you pick up a brush and start to paint. You must always work from light to dark; you can overlay light areas with dark colors, but not the other way around. So — as well as thinking about composition, shadows, colors, and all the other things that artists have to consider — you need to begin by deciding where the light areas in your painting are going to be. Furthermore, there is no such thing as white paint in pure watercolor painting. You cannot paint on white highlights; you have to allow the white of the paper to do that job. This means you must train yourself to leave certain areas of paper free of paint, and either paint around them or protect them in some way so that they aren't splashed with unwanted color.

Another challenging thing about painting in watercolor is its unpredictability. Even after paint has been laid down, its quality can change. This is particularly apparent when one wash of watercolor is laid on top of another wash that is still wet: different-colored pigments and different strengths of washes blend together and create new colors and effects. And because some watercolor techniques and color mixes demand that you use a wet, sloppy paint mix, it is easy for paint to trickle into areas that you don't want it to touch.

For all these reasons, watercolor painting has acquired a reputation for being a difficult medium to master. But in fact, it is no more difficult to produce a good watercolor painting than it is to produce a good oil painting. The trick is to develop a good understanding of how the paint will behave in a given situation. You need to know, for example, that a wet mix of paint applied to damp or wet paper will bleed and spread, while the same mix applied to dry paper will have more clearly defined edges. You need to know what color will result if you lay one paint mix over another. And this knowledge needs to be so deeply ingrained in you that it is instinctive: if you have to spend time wondering which technique or color to use to achieve a particular effect, much of the spontaneity of your work will be lost.

All the theoretical knowledge in the world will not enable you to produce a good watercolor without

Right: Krishna
Painted by an artist of the Kangra school in India in the early 19th century, this jewel-like miniature of the Hindu god Krishna is a wonderful example of the precision and finely detailed renderings that can be achieved in watercolor paint.

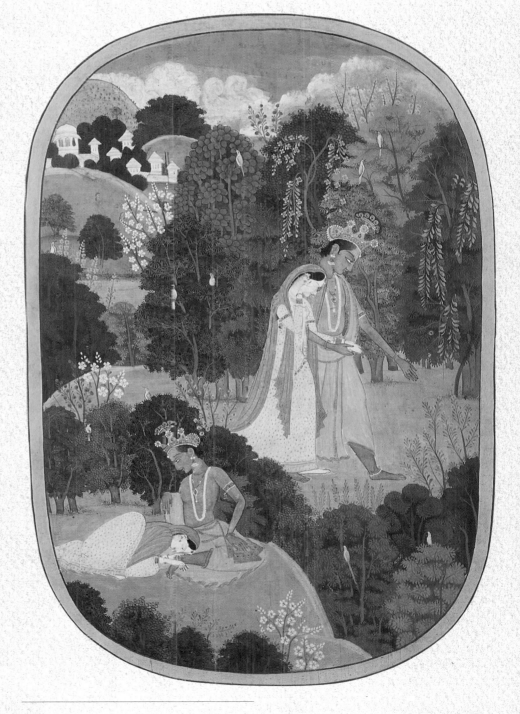

Below: Watercolor Brushes
The brushes shown here – a no. 2, 6, and 10 – will allow you to do everything from delicate detailing to laying a wash over a large area. You do not need to buy a huge range of brushes to begin with.

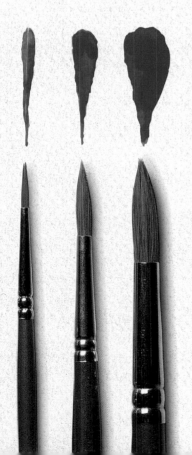

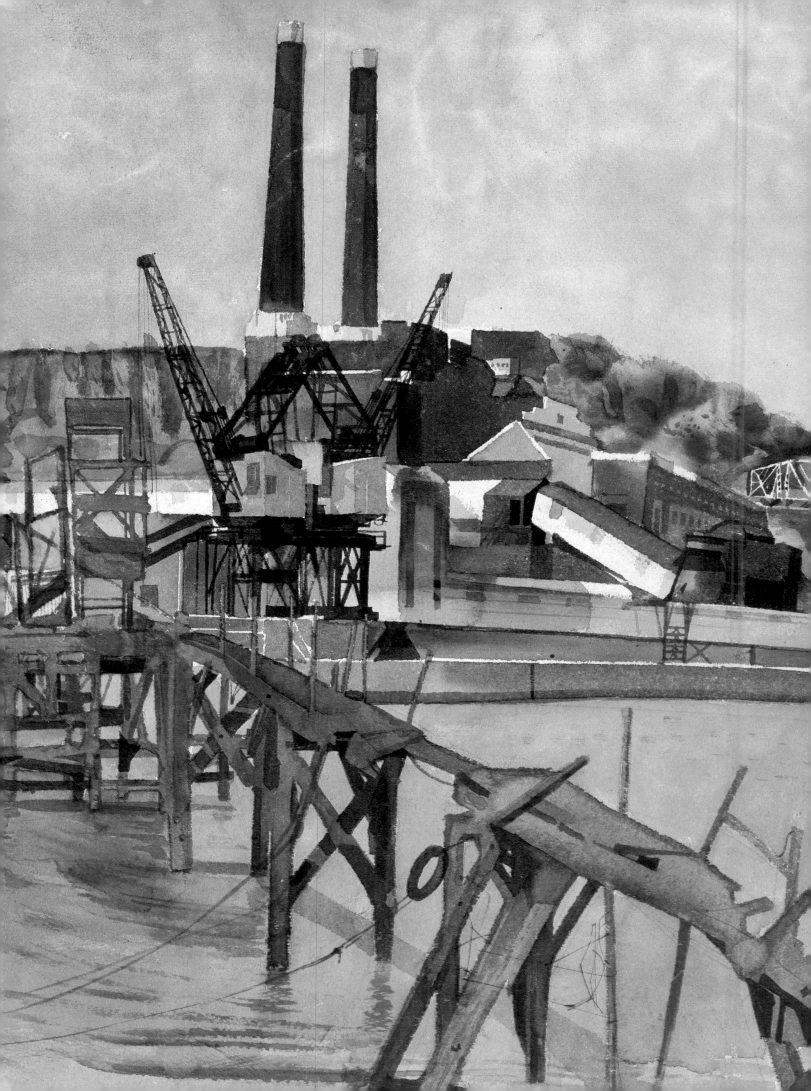

practice. To become a competent watercolorist you need to set up your easel, dip your brush into the paint, and make those first few brushstrokes. Get used to holding brushes at different angles and using them to manipulate paint on the paper. Experiment to find out just how much water you need to add to your paint to achieve a particular color or effect. Never be afraid to get your hands dirty.

This book is a carefully structured course that will take you from choosing equipment through basic watercolor techniques to developing the skills and artistic vision that you need in order to create compositions of your own.

Chapter 1, "Tools and Equipment," lists equipment that is essential for the aspiring watercolorist and provides details of more specialized equipment you might like to try. There are two suggested color palettes, one limited, one more extensive, which will prepare you for all the exercises in the book (pp. 32–33). There are many brushes to choose from, and this chapter explains the different types available as well as their uses. The chapter also looks at other watercolor tools, such as watersoluble pencils and crayons, to enable you to exploit the range of effects that each can produce.

Chapter 2, "The Fundamentals of Watercolor," introduces preliminary techniques that will enable you to gradually build up confidence in using your

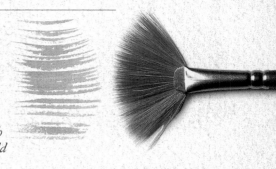

Right: Brushes to Experiment With
This fan brush makes a very different mark from the standard round brushes on p. 7. Experiment with unusual brushes to add variety to your work.

materials before you attempt to create an elaborate composition. The learning curve is a gradual one. Every exercise leads to a completed practice painting, so that you will feel a sense of accomplishment at every step of the way. In the early stages of the course, the exercises are kept simple so that you can hone your skills. Do not worry if your result looks different from the one reproduced on the page. Every mark you make with the brush will teach you something new about painting in watercolor, even if you feel that some of your early results don't turn out quite as you had expected.

To give you a chance to master each technique fully, after each group of basic skills there is a painting exercise entitled "Practice Your Technique." These exercises are a little more elaborate than the previous technique exercises, and enable you to combine several of the methods you have recently learned in a carefully planned full-scale painting.

Right: The Simplicity of Watercolor
Here a flat wash of just two colors is enlivened by spattering paint across the surface of the oranges. You will learn both these techniques in the early stages of this book – proof that you can produce an interesting and colorful painting with a few simple techniques.

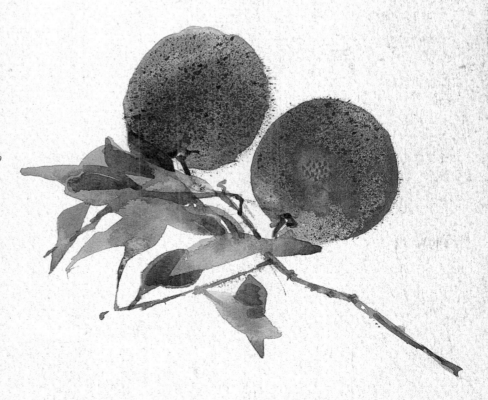

Left: Compositional Strength
Learning how to arrange elements within the picture area is as important a part of becoming a competent watercolorist as learning how to manipulate paint on the paper. The main technique used in this painting – applying washes – is very simple, but the strong composition has produced a dynamic work full of character.

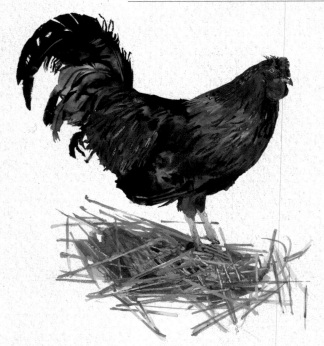

Above: Techniques in Combination
With experience, you will become more confident about combining several techniques in one painting. This deceptively simple-looking study combines washes and overlays of color, masking, additives, and various ways of creating texture to produce a vibrant, colorful image.

Later in the chapter you will find some more unusual techniques. This will give you a chance to have some fun and to experiment with such methods as bleach into ink and sgrafitto.

By the time you have completed all the exercises in "The Fundamentals of Watercolor," you should have a sound grasp of the main techniques for painting in watercolor as well as an understanding of the effect that each technique creates. But, if you feel that there are some gaps in your skills, you can do the exercises again or concentrate on a particular technique and use the relevant exercise as the basis for your own paintings. Keep any additional work simple at this stage. Remember: practice is the key to learning. Do not be afraid of doing a little more on each exercise than there is room to show in the book; it can only help you to improve.

Once you feel confident with the basic techniques, you are ready to move on to "The Projects." In this chapter, the exercises are led by subject rather than by technique. This is how competent artists approach their work. They begin by deciding on a subject such as a landscape or a portrait, and then they select the most appropriate techniques. Having worked through Chapter 2, you will already have

some idea of the potential applications for each technique. Chapter 3 opens your eyes to a much broader range of posssibilities. Rather than concentrating on one particular method and producing technical studies, you are now faced with the exciting artistic challenge of deciding which elements in a scene you want to concentrate on and running through your repertoire of skills to select the ones that will bring the result you're after. Furthermore, you will need to combine several techniques to produce a successful painting of your subject. You have already started to do this in the "Practice Your Technique" exercises in Chapter 2. In this chapter, you are constantly building on those principles, using perhaps a touch of drybrush work here, a deft overlay of color there, and a subtle wet-into-wet blending of paint colors somewhere else. It takes a lot of practice – and self-restraint – to limit your use of a particular technique to a small area of your painting, but this is often the most effective way of creating interesting contrasts. Once you are able to do this, you will find that your paintings will start to take on a character and style of their own.

Chapter 3 is divided into four sections: light (a proper understanding of which is crucial to all painting, whatever medium you choose to work in), followed by the three most popular subject areas for the amateur watercolorist – the natural world (landscapes, flowers, foliage, and living creatures), still lifes, and people. Some subjects may interest you more than others, but it is worth working through the course systematically from start to finish in the order that has been planned.

As in Chapter 2, each section ends with a practice exercise entitled "Combining Your Skills" which brings together a number of the subjects and

Right: Color Choices
One of the most satisfying things about painting in watercolor is learning how to mix colors to achieve the right one for the job. You will be amazed at how many hues you can mix from a carefully selected range of, say, six colors.

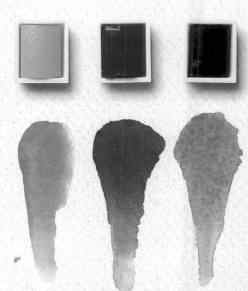

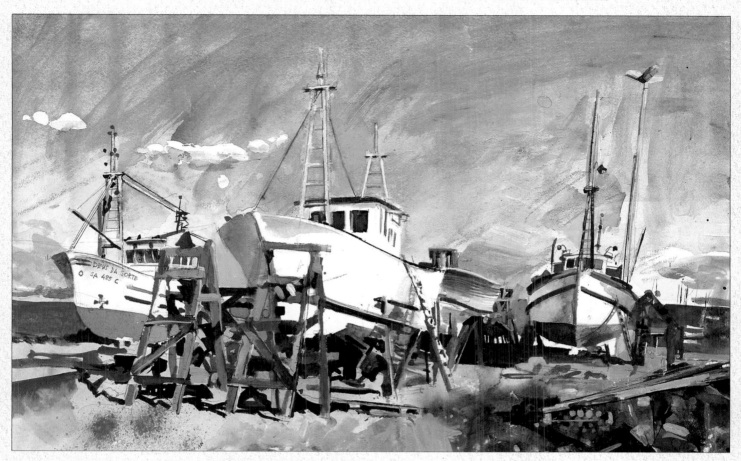

Above: Light and Translucency

The translucency of watercolor paint can be emphasized by leaving some areas free of paint and allowing the whiteness of the paper to play an important role in the painting. The result is a feeling of light that cannot be matched by any other medium – perfect for this sunny Portuguese harbor scene.

approaches you have studied in isolation. You should be prepared to revise "the fundamentals" as you go; you will need to employ all the basic techniques at some point in this part of the course.

If anyone tries to tell you that they never make a mistake in watercolor painting, don't listen to them! There are as many reasons for paintings going wrong as there are painters, and no one can expect to get everything right the first time. You may apply too heavy a color to an area of your work; the paint itself may behave unpredictably, dribbling into an area you didn't want it to touch; you may decide at an advanced stage in the painting that the balance of your composition is wrong. But don't give up! If you do that, you're simply wasting paint and paper – not to mention all the hard work and emotional energy that you've put into your painting. At the back of this book, you will discover a section called "Rescuing Lost Causes." If you do make a mistake

and cannot figure out how to correct it, have a look at this section. You will find a series of exercises demonstrating how you can turn a disaster into a success – even if that means throwing a wash of warm water over the entire paper surface and starting afresh. People are often afraid that if they try to fix a mistake they'll end up making matters worse. As a result they settle for something that they know is not up to standard. Why settle for second best? If your rescue attempt fails, try again – and again, if necessary, until you're sure you've exhausted all possible options. Even a minor alteration can make the difference between something that you hide away in a portfolio and a work that you can proudly hang on your wall for all to see.

This book sets out to introduce you to the world of watercolor painting and, through a series of carefully thought-out exercises, to instruct you in its methods of application. By the time you have completed the course, you should possess all the skills you need to create lovely, translucent pictures that you will be proud to frame and display. Watercolor painting is a hobby that you will be able to return to time and time again, whatever the season and wherever you are, and from which you will gain enjoyment for many years to come.

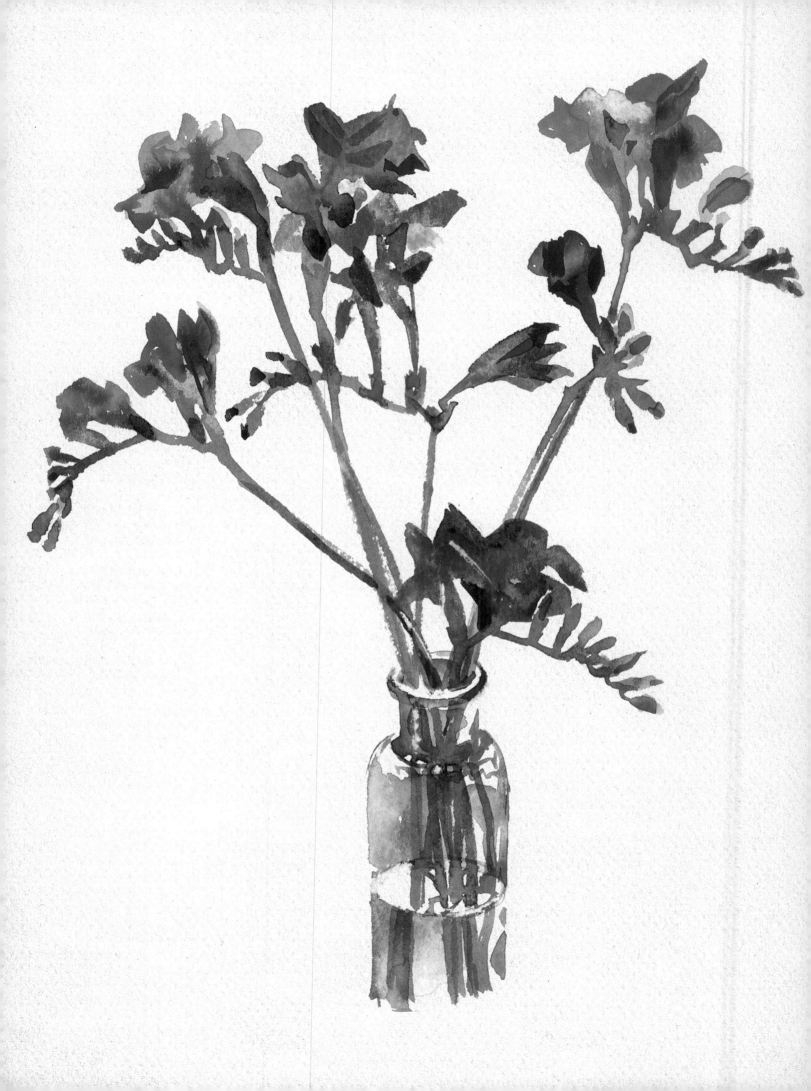

Tools and Materials

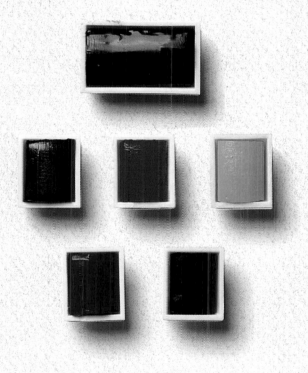

Watercolor Paints

WATERCOLOR PAINTS are available to the artist in three forms: pan, half pan, and tube. There is no difference between the ingredients used to manufacture the paints, but one form may suit you better than another. If you often work on location, you will find that pans are easier to transport than tubes. Most artists who use pans buy full pans of the colors that they use most frequently and half pans of colors they use less regularly. Tubes, however, are better for mixing large quantities of color – for a wash, for example.

The range of colors available is wide, but you should never need to keep more than 12 from which to mix a wide palette. Some artists only use four or five colors (see pp. 28–29). However, different colors dry to different finishes. In some, the particles spread evenly and the color either dries to a flat finish, like viridian, or produces a granulated effect as the pigment settles into the hollows of the paper, like raw umber. In others, such as French ultramarine blue, the paint particles may come together in clumps, creating a mottled effect. This happens when the particles of paint are drawn toward one another in clusters. Some watercolor paints stain the surface of the paper while others create a transparent wash. Those that stain are permanent and do not wash off if water is applied once they have dried. The others can be washed off. Check the paint label or refer to the manufacturer's catalog (available in your art supply store) for details.

Watercolor paints vary in their pigment quality and lightfastness. Look for those that are 100 per cent lightfast, as these should not fade or discolor over time. Watercolor paint comes in two categories: students' and artists' quality. Students' quality paints are manufactured with less pure pigment and more filler substances than the artists' equivalents and are much cheaper to buy. As a result they are not necessarily lightfast and do not mix to such subtle ranges of color. Artists' quality paints give you better results and you need less paint to achieve the same color density than with students' quality paints

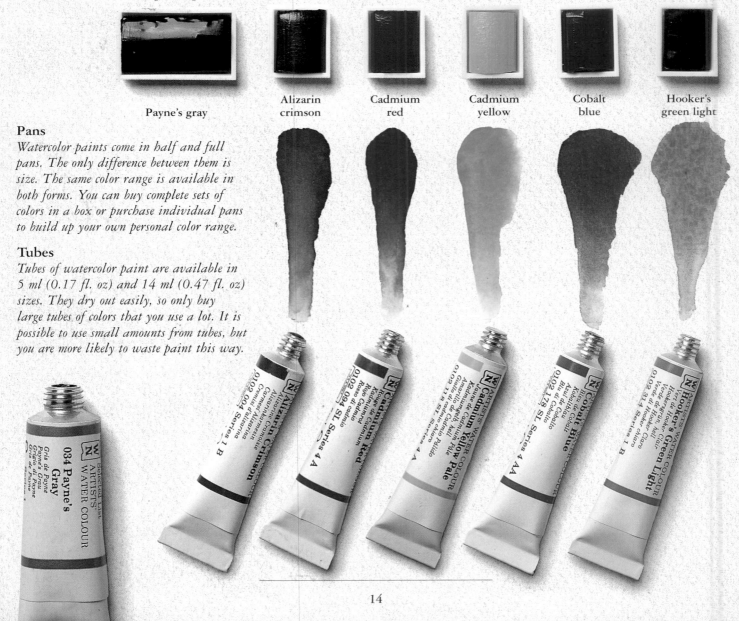

Payne's gray   Alizarin crimson   Cadmium red   Cadmium yellow   Cobalt blue   Hooker's green light

Pans
Watercolor paints come in half and full pans. The only difference between them is size. The same color range is available in both forms. You can buy complete sets of colors in a box or purchase individual pans to build up your own personal color range.

Tubes
Tubes of watercolor paint are available in 5 ml (0.17 fl. oz) and 14 ml (0.47 fl. oz) sizes. They dry out easily, so only buy large tubes of colors that you use a lot. It is possible to use small amounts from tubes, but you are more likely to waste paint this way.

Paint Containers

Field Box

Field boxes are designed specifically for use on location. They contain space for half pans of paint, a water bottle, mixing wells, and (usually) small brushes. Some are designed to fold away to half their length as a space-saving device. You could, of course, take a separate water bottle and palette on location. The advantage of a field box is that it provides you with everything you need in one compact, easily portable unit.

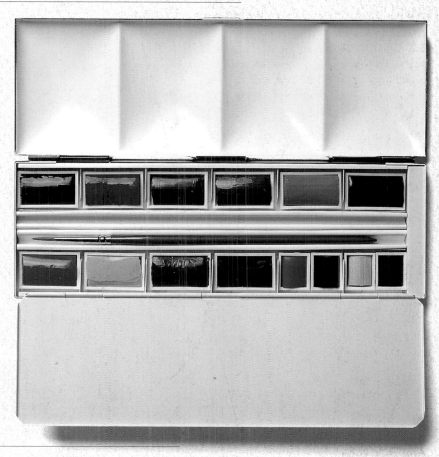

Painting Box

Lightweight metal boxes are common watercolor containers. You can also buy plastic versions. The boxes contain standard-sized spaces in which you place your paints. The model shown here is for pans only, but you can also buy painting boxes with spaces for tubes of paint. They have a hinged flap that lifts up to reveal an enamelled mixing surface.

Other Watercolor Media

WATERCOLOR PURISTS sometimes frown on the use of anything that is not a conventional watercolor paint, but there are a number of other watercolor media available that can extend your painting possibilities. There are no hard-and-fast rules, and you can experiment with whatever you choose. The following are examples of water-based media that can complement traditional watercolor techniques.

Watersoluble pencils come in a huge range of colors. They can be used dry on top of watercolor or laid down wet. Watersoluble crayons are softer than watersoluble pencils and produce a thicker, more textured line. They are best used for bold applications or for covering large areas of paper quickly.

You can buy dry pigments and mix them with gum arabic to create your own intense hues. Watercolor is also available in concentrated liquid form, sold in a bottle like an ink. These intensely pigmented paints are particularly popular with graphic designers and illustrators, as their finish is far more vivid than that of conventional watercolor paints. They can be watered down, but they still have a more potent color density than their conventional watercolor equivalents.

Gouache is an opaque medium so, unlike conventional watercolor paint, it can be painted light over dark. The most popular is Chinese white, which is listed and sold as a watercolor even though it is opaque. Watercolorists use it to paint highlights or white areas on top of watercolors that have already been laid down.

When you feel confident that you have mastered conventional watercolor paints, experiment with these other media to see how they can enhance your work.

Watersoluble Pencils

Watersoluble pencils are extremely useful for adding fine details, such as the delicate veins of a petal or the grain of a wood surface, to watercolor work. You can use them dry like ordinary pencils. Alternatively, you can go over the pencil marks on your paper with water and a brush to blend or soften colors. You can also make watersoluble pencil marks on scrap paper and then use the paper in the same way as a palette, diluting the colors with water and a brush before adding them to your work.

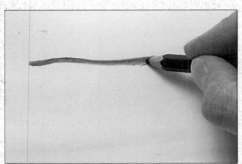

Fine Detailing Over a Wash
You can add watersoluble pencil marks over a conventional watercolor wash to create strong, consistent lines. Allow the paint to dry slightly: if it is still wet, the pencil mark will blur and spread.

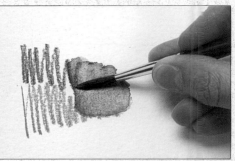

Blending Watersoluble Pencil Marks
Once you have made a mark on the paper, you can blend it by brushing over it with a damp brush. Use the same technique with watersoluble crayons.

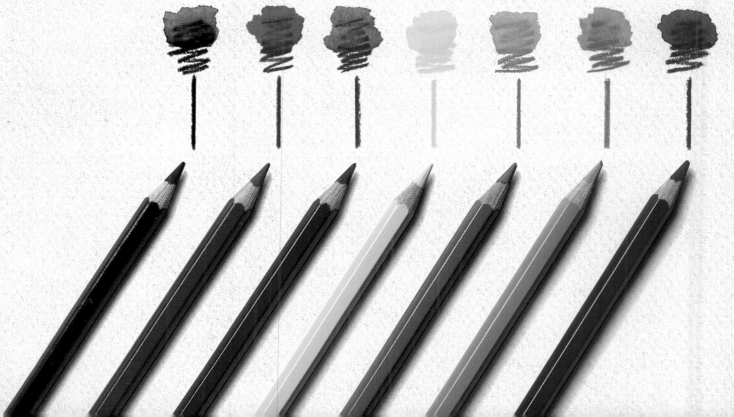

Watercolor Pigment

You can make your own watercolor paints, although it is time-consuming. Mix approximately one part liquid sugar, one part glycerin, and three parts gum arabic into a thick solution, and add a few drops of oxgall, a wetting agent that increases the flow of watercolor paint. Slowly add watercolor pigment with a palette knife until you produce a stiff paste. Finally, grind the mixture with a pestle in a mortar until it is smooth.

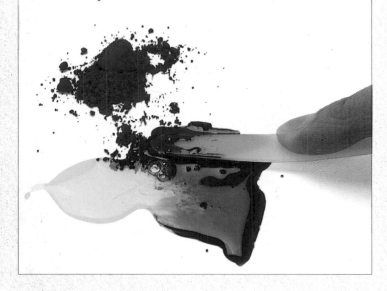

Watersoluble Crayons

Watersoluble crayons are an alternative to watersoluble pencils. They can be applied in exactly the same way as watersoluble pencils (see opposite), but because they are thicker and cannot be sharpened to a point, you cannot produce such fine detailing as you can with pencils. One advantage of crayons, however, is that because they are not encased in wood, you can use the side of the crayon as well as the tip. In this way, you can cover large areas more quickly than you can with a pencil.

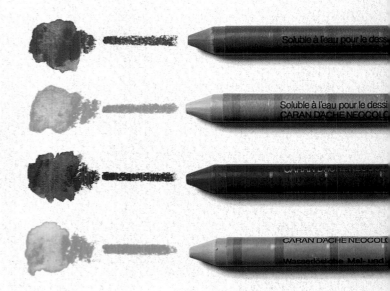

Concentrated Watercolors

Concentrated watercolors are very bright watercolor inks that dry to a more vibrant finish than conventional watercolor paints. They are often used by graphic designers because of their flat, even finish when dry. They are packaged in bottles and come with a dropper. You can squeeze a few drops into water to dilute them for painting washes, or you can use them directly from the bottle, without adding any water.

Chinese White Gouache

You can dilute Chinese white gouache to a milky consistency for pale washes over darker colors, or you can mix it with watercolors to create opaque, creamy colors. Another possibility is to apply it straight out of the tube for highlights and such subjects as foam on waves or clouds in the sky. Chinese white dries to a chalky and flaky finish, in contrast to the flat translucency of watercolor.

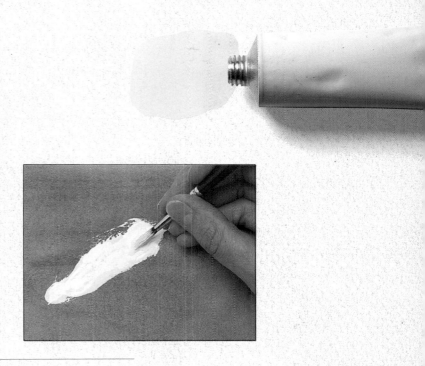

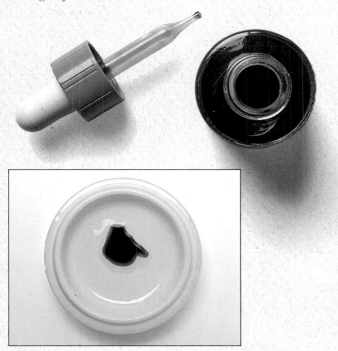

Papers

THERE ARE THREE TYPES of paper to choose from: hot-pressed (HP), cold-pressed (CP), and rough. The main difference between hot- and cold-pressed paper is the texture. Hot-pressed paper has a very flat, smooth finish and is useful for such techniques as pen-and-ink drawing and watercolor washes where it is important that the ink or paint is applied evenly. Cold-pressed paper is rough in texture, but the degree of roughness varies considerably. Rather confusingly, there are two types of cold-pressed paper. One is actually called cold-pressed; the other is known as rough paper. Rough paper is the more textured of the two.

Papers come in different weights, which are expressed in pounds. The weight refers to the weight of a ream (500 sheets) of paper. Sheets come in standard sizes, although paper can, of course, be cut to any size from large rolls. Generally, sheets of watercolor paper are manufactured in standard weights: 90 lb (185 gsm), 140 lb (300 gsm), and 300 lb (640 gsm). The heavier the paper, the thicker it is – and the more resilient it is to vigorous handling.

Unless otherwise stated, the paper you use for the exercises in this book should be medium-weight (i.e., 140 lb – see the table below) rough paper. It absorbs paint well and can withstand vigorous handling.

Paper Weights and Uses

Type and Weight	Characteristics and Uses
Hot-pressed 90–300 lb	• Stretch before use if 140 lb or less • Suitable for very wet washes, pen-and-ink work, line-and-wash work • Flat, smooth finish; slow absorption
Cold-pressed 90 lb, 140 lb	• Stretch before use • Suitable for most watercolor techniques except when using large amounts of wet-into-wet washes or scoring techniques that will damage the paper surface • Even finish with slight texture; absorbent
Cold-pressed 300 lb	• Does not need to be stretched before use • Suitable for techniques that require vigorous handling, such as sgraffito or bleach into ink • Slightly textured finish; slow absorption
Rough 90 lb, 140 lb	• Stretch before use • Suitable for most watercolor techniques, although pitted surface is not good for fine detail • Rough textured finish; absorbent
Rough 300 lb	• Does not need to be stretched before use • Suitable for techniques that require vigorous handling, such as sgraffito or bleach into ink • Rough textured finish; slow absorption

Stretching Paper

Lightweight papers need to be stretched before use; otherwise they are likely to buckle when water is applied to them. Any paper over 140 lb in weight should not need to be stretched.

1 Cut the paper to the size you want, then check that it fits when you lay it on a heavy board that will not warp when dampened. Leave a margin around the edge for paper tape.

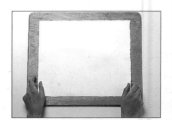

2 Soak the paper for a few minutes in a sink or flat tray of clean water, then remove it and allow any excess moisture to drain away.

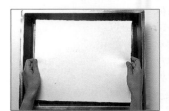

3 Cut four strips of paper tape, one for each side of the paper. Each piece should be slightly longer than the sides of the paper.

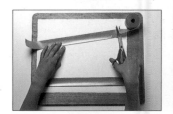

4 Lay the tape on a separate surface. Dip a clean sponge in water, then use it to dampen the adhesive side of the tape.

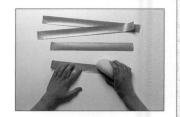

5 Lay the wet paper flat on the board, smoothing out any bubbles with a damp sponge. Tape the paper to the board, starting with the long sides, making sure the paper remains tight on the board.

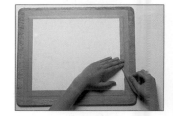

6 Let the paper dry completely before you start to paint. If possible, leave it overnight.

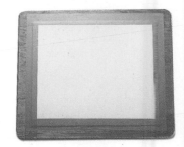

Papers

Watercolor paper is available in rolls, sheets, and various
sized pads or blocks. A roll of paper is the cheapest option
and you can cut it to the size you want. Pads are either
spiralbound or glued and come in small sizes for sketching
and larger sizes for studio work. In blocks the paper is
pulled taut, so you do not have to stretch it first. It
is glued along all edges, and you simply remove the top
sheet when a painting is finished.

140-lb HP
paper has a
smooth surface
and the paint is
absorbed slowly.

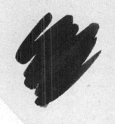

Tinted Papers

*As watercolor paint
is translucent, a hint
of the underlying
paper color always
shines through.
Although they are
sometimes frowned
upon by purists,
tinted papers can be
useful for creating
an overall color
temperature (see
pp. 94–97) and
atmosphere. Try
using a tinted paper
as an alternative to
laying an initial
flat wash.*

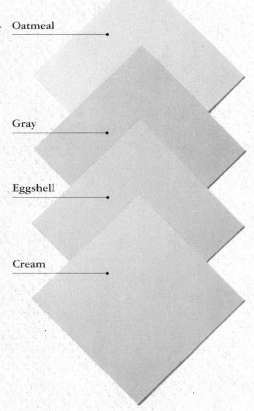

Oatmeal

Gray

Eggshell

Cream

300-lb CP paper
is semirough.
The texture of the
surface gives the
paint mark an
uneven quality.

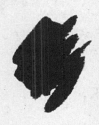

300-lb rough
paper has a pitted
surface. The paint
is absorbed quickly
but unevenly,
leaving a
textured finish.

Pads and Blocks

Pads and blocks, available in various sizes, are more
practical than sheets of paper for location work or
quick studio sketches.

Blocks of paper
come in many differ-
ent sizes. They are
glued together on all
sides to keep the
paper flat until a
sheet is required.

Spiral-bound pads
are useful for out-
door work. Buy thick
paper that does not
need to be stretched.

Brushes

WATERCOLORISTS have a wide choice of brushes – from large, flat wash brushes to fine-tipped ones for detailed work. Three factors influence the type of effect you can achieve with a brush: the material it is made from, its shape, and its size.

Brushes are made from natural hair, natural bristle, or synthetic fibers that are manufactured to copy the characteristics of the first two. Although hair and bristle are similar in most respects, a hair has a single, individual point while a bristle divides into a number of natural tips called flags. Bristle is less versatile but more durable than natural hair. Sable – the tail hairs of the Kolinsky, or Siberian, mink – makes the best-quality watercolor brush, as the hairs hold their shape the longest. But sable brushes are extremely expensive. Camel hair is a good

alternative. Some brushes are made from a combination of natural and synthetic hair, giving you some of the benefit of a natural hair brush at a much lower cost.

A good way of judging the quality of a brush is to examine its ferrule, the metal casing within which the hairs are contained. If the ferrule has no seam, then the brush hairs will be held tightly and evenly. There is nothing worse than buying a brush only to find that the hairs fall out onto your work. Cheap brushes are more likely to suffer from this problem than expensive ones.

The width of the ferrule at the point where the brush hairs leave it dictates the size of the brush. Most watercolorists rarely use the smallest brushes – those marked 000, 00, and 0 – although these can be useful for fine lines and adding minute details. The most commonly used brushes are no. 1, no. 4, and no. 8. These should offer you a wide range of possibilities. You don't need to buy a complete range. In fact, many professional watercolorists find that they only use two or three brushes for their work. Experiment with different brushes in order to discover which ones suit you best. Unless otherwise stated, the brushes used for the exercises in this book are good-quality round brushes. These general-use brushes are sufficiently versatile for most purposes.

No. 4 brush made from synthetic fibers

No. 4 brush made from a mix of sable and synthetic fibers

No. 3 brush made from sable

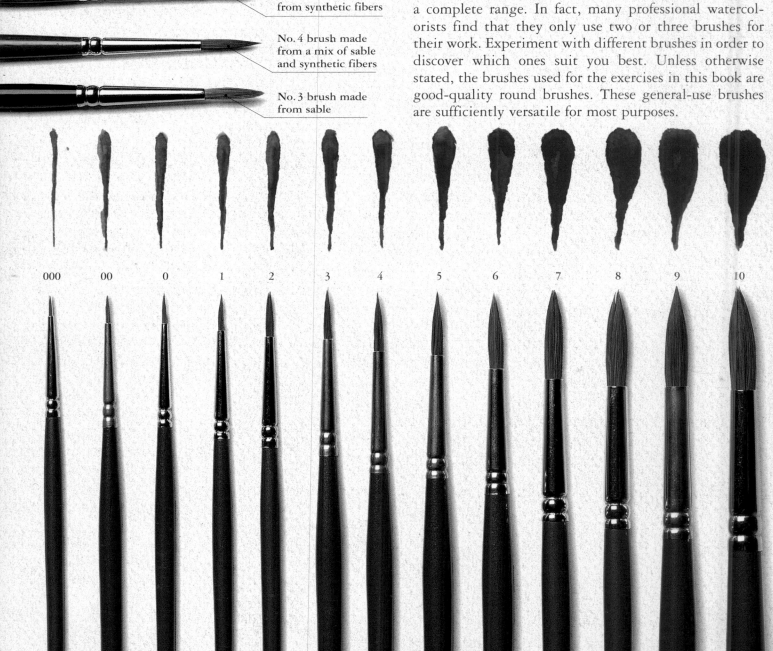

| 000 | 00 | 0 | 1 | 2 | 3 | 4 | 5 | 6 | 7 | 8 | 9 | 10 |

Caring for Brushes

The more you care for your watercolor brushes, the longer they will last. Always clean your brushes immediately after use. With your fingertips, gently tweak the hairs back to their original shape after washing. If you wish to store them for a long time, make sure they are completely dry before placing them in a box with a tight-fitting lid.

Washing Brushes

Hold the brush in your hand and gently massage warm, soapy water into the hairs, working right up to the ferrule, until you produce a foam. Hold the brush under warm running water and rinse it until the water runs clear.

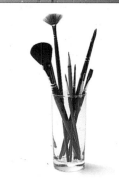

Storing Brushes

Always store brushes on their tips, otherwise you will blunt and break the hairs. Once you have cleaned your brushes, reshape the hairs and stand them upright in a glass or jar until you need them for your next painting session.

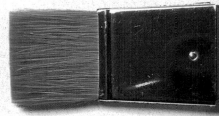
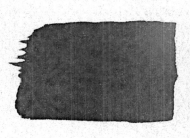

1-in (2.5-cm) Flat Brush

A large wash brush is the perfect choice for painting flat washes. It holds ample paint, and produces wide, flat marks, making it especially useful for one-stroke applications.

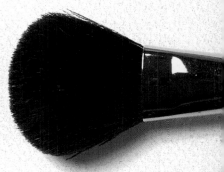

7/8-in (2-cm) Mop Brush

This big, fat brush is an excellent tool for laying heavy washes and softly blending large areas of damp paint.

No. 6 Round Brush

This medium-size round brush is good for general watercolor work. It can be used for broad strokes but will also form a sharp point. The brush shown here is made from a mixture of synthetic fibers and sable.

1/4-in (6-mm) Chisel Brush

This flat brush gives firm, sharp lines for lettering. Made from a sable-synthetic mix, the brush retains its shape well and is long-lasting.

Long-handled No. 4 Fan Brush

This brush is designed specifically to be used for fine feathering and delicate blending. The long handle enables you to hold the brush at a number of angles to the paper.

No. 3 Lettering Brush

Designed for fine lines and scroll work, the lettering brush is not used for general watercolor work. It can be useful when you want softer ink lines than you can create with a pen.

Chinese Brush

Chinese brushes, which do not contain a conventional ferrule, have great holding power and are shaped to perfect points. They are useful for calligraphic techniques. The largest sizes can be used for laying washes.

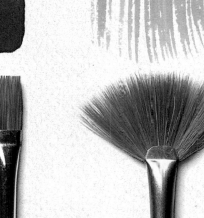
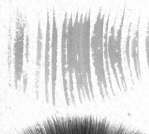
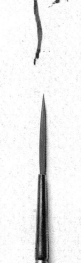
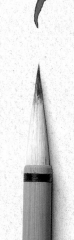

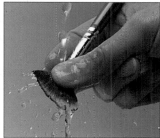

Other Useful Equipment

THERE ARE A NUMBER of additional pieces of equipment that you will find useful in your watercolor painting. The ones suggested here should all be kept close at hand while you are working. They are not expensive, and several are everyday items that can easily be found around the home.

There are no hard-and-fast rules in watercolor painting and, by experimenting, you may discover new ways of applying and mixing paint. To add texture to your paintings, try spattering paint onto the paper with a toothbrush, or scraping a plastic palette knife over wet paint to develop crosshatching, or pressing a piece of cloth, such as velvet, onto wet paint to leave an interesting pattern on the surface. Other domestic items that double as painting implements include sponges (used to dampen the surface of the paper for washes), and cotton rags, cotton swabs, blotting paper, and paper towels, all of which are used to blot off excess paint or paint that has run into an area that you did not want it to touch.

You will need palettes to mix your paint in, and these can be bought at an art supply store. The two main kinds are a round china dish with a matching lid (useful for keeping paint wet) and a rectangular partitioned china dish with wells at the bottom for holding water (good for mixing paint colors together).

You can buy special pastes and gums (additives) to mix with your watercolor paint in order to change its characteristics. Glycerin slows down the paint's drying time; others, such as oxgall, speed it up. Other substances, such as honey and Chinese white gouache, change the character of the paint (see pp. 68–69). These additives can be used for both small and large areas.

Finally, masking tape and masking fluid are useful materials for blocking areas of your paper to keep them free of paint, enabling you to produce highlights and crisp edges. Masks (see pp. 62–65) are often applied to an underdrawing to protect specific areas before the painting process begins and removed in the final stage.

Blotting Off

You can lift off paint or remove unwanted pools and runs of watercolor in a variety of ways. For small details cotton swabs are best; for larger areas blotting paper, sponges, paper towels, or a cotton rag may be more suitable, although their texture may show up on your painting.

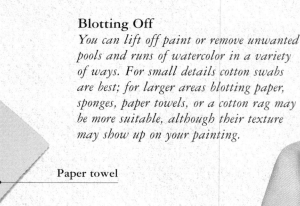

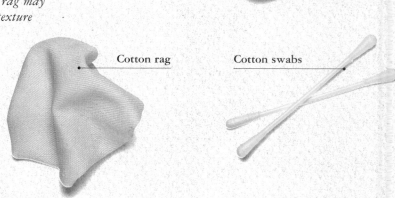

Sponge

Paper towel

Blotting paper

Cotton rag

Cotton swabs

Tools for Texture

To achieve unusual textures or surfaces, tools other than brushes are sometimes more suitable, both for applying watercolor paint and for manipulating it once on the paper. You can experiment with anything you have at hand, but toothbrushes and plastic palette knives are two of the most commonly used. Both create interesting textures: a toothbrush makes an excellent tool for spattering paint over the paper, while a plastic palette knife is useful for scraping into the surface of wet paint, developing lines, and crosshatching.

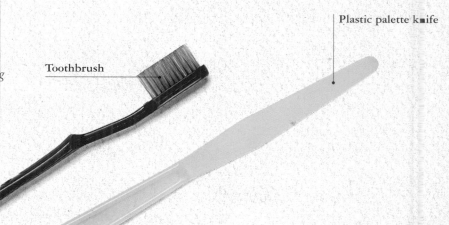

Plastic palette knife

Toothbrush

Palettes

Although you can mix watercolors on the surface of the paper, artists usually mix paint on a palette. There are many varieties. A round china dish with a lid (below left) enables you to cover and store paint, and it will keep the paint wet for longer than if it is exposed. A partitioned china dish (below right) is perfect for color mixing.

Water is placed in the round wells at the bottom of the palette.

Colors are mixed in the flat, slightly sloping sections. The mixed paint settles at the bottom of the sloping sections (see p. 38).

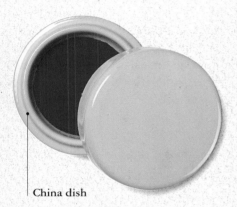
China dish

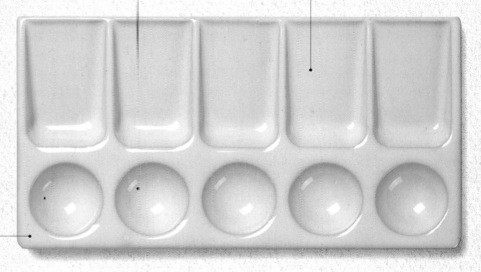
Partitioned china dish

Retardants and Accelerators

Retardants slow down watercolor's drying time. Glycerin makes it more gluelike and malleable; gum arabic gives it a varnished appearance. Honey mixed with water creates an effect similar to gum arabic and increases the intensity and luminosity of the watercolor. To accelerate the drying time, add either oxgall or rubbing alcohol to the paint.

Retardants
Glycerin
Gum arabic
Honey

Accelerators
Rubbing alcohol
Oxgall

All these retardants and accelerators should be mixed with the paint before you apply it to the paper.

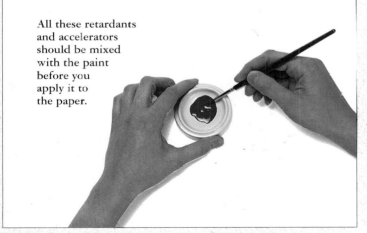

Masks

Masks are used to block out areas of your paper so that they remain free of paint (see pp. 62–65). There are three common masking materials: masking tape (use artist's masking tape rather than standard office tape), transparent masking fluid, and colored masking fluid. Any brush can be used to apply masking fluid, but you must wash it out with warm soapy water immediately after use.

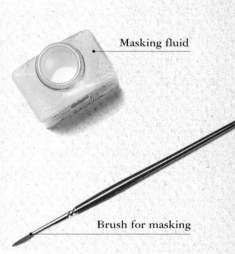
Masking fluid

Brush for masking

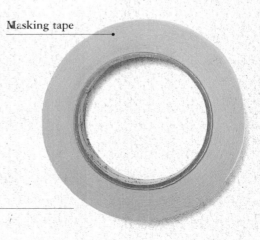
Masking tape

Easels

BEFORE YOU BUY AN EASEL, think carefully about how you intend to use it. There is a wide choice of easels, ranging from simple board-mounted surfaces to elaborate aluminum foldaways. Although some easels are freestanding, others have to be rested on your lap or on a tabletop. You can position most, but not all, at different angles: this is essential for watercolor work, as you will need to alter the angle of your paper for different watercolor techniques.

Some people tape the paper to a board and then set the board at an angle on their lap. There are, however, two main drawbacks to this method: you have to hold the board with one hand and paint with the other, and it is impossible to walk away and view your work from a distance to see how it is progressing without disturbing your original position. When you paint outdoors, this method is particularly unsatisfactory. An easel allows you to get around both of these problems.

For outdoor work, a lightweight collapsible easel is best, as it is easy to transport. Some easels even contain a compartment for paints and brushes. This is useful for outdoor work because you can carry everything you need in one compact unit.

When working in your studio or at your kitchen table, a table easel is the most suitable support as it is versatile and easy to move around.

The top clip holds the painting board in place.

The lower board support can be moved to allow you to alter the height of the painting board.

Table Easel
A table easel is the most versatile support for working at home or in the studio. It can be adjusted to lie flat or to rest at a variety of angles, allowing you to change the angle to suit the technique. Check before you buy: some table easels can be set only at very steep angles, which are unsuitable for watercolor work. Position stretched watercolor paper on the easel as shown below.

A table easel can be adjusted to a variety of angles.

Sketching Easel
Sketching easels are convenient for outdoor work, as they are lightweight and easy to transport. You can buy wooden or aluminum varieties, and some have a place for materials. You can alter the angle of a sketching easel slightly, but not to the same degree as a table easel. Always choose a sketching easel that has spiked legs, which you can push down into the ground to give additional support and prevent the easel from being blown over by the wind.

The legs can be adjusted to alter the height of the easel to whatever is most comfort-able for you.

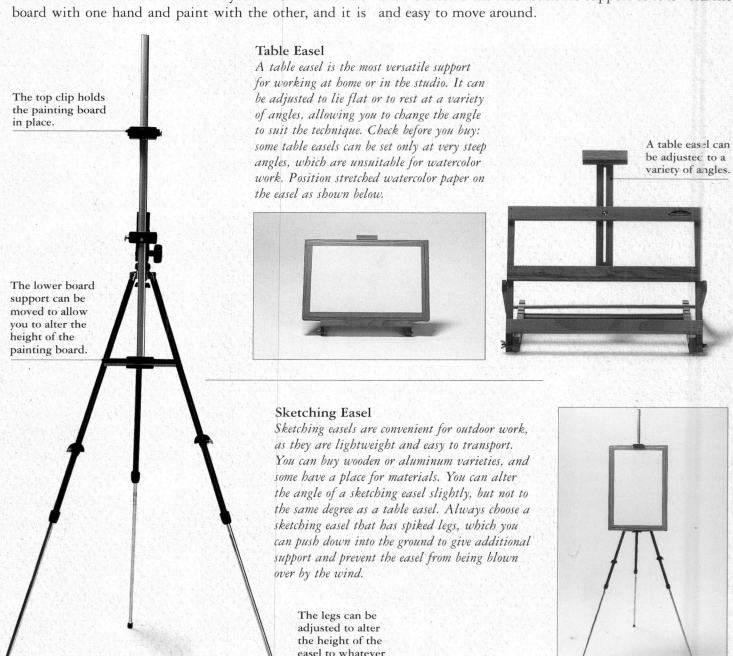

Box Easel

The box easel, like the sketching easel, can be taken out on location. It is heavier than a sketching easel, however, and is generally used in the studio. It is called a box easel because it contains a box underneath the main frame for you to store your art materials in. You can also adjust the frame so that you can work flat on the tabletop or at any chosen angle. As with the sketching easel, you can adjust the legs to give you the height you prefer.

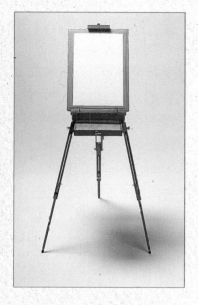

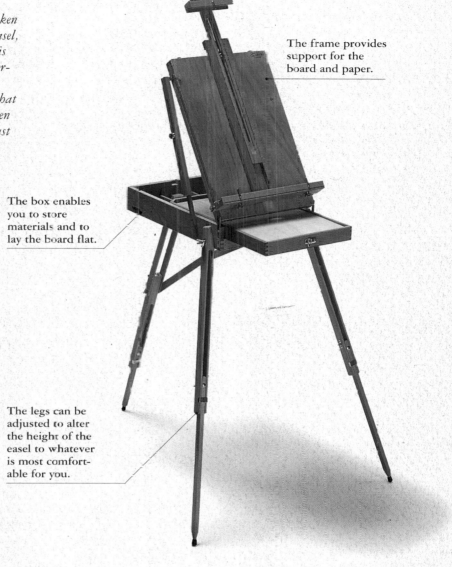

The frame provides support for the board and paper.

The box enables you to store materials and to lay the board flat.

The legs can be adjusted to alter the height of the easel to whatever is most comfortable for you.

Horse Easel

Sometimes called a drawing horse or a drawing bench, the horse easel is suitable for those who like to work sitting down, as it serves as both a seat and a support for your work. You sit astride the bench, as if on a horse's back. The frame can be adjusted up and down, from 180 degrees to flat, allowing you to work at a variety of angles.

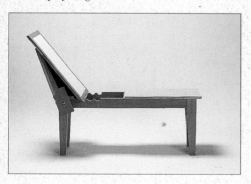

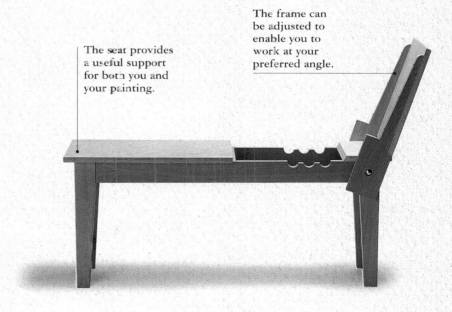

The seat provides a useful support for both you and your painting.

The frame can be adjusted to enable you to work at your preferred angle.

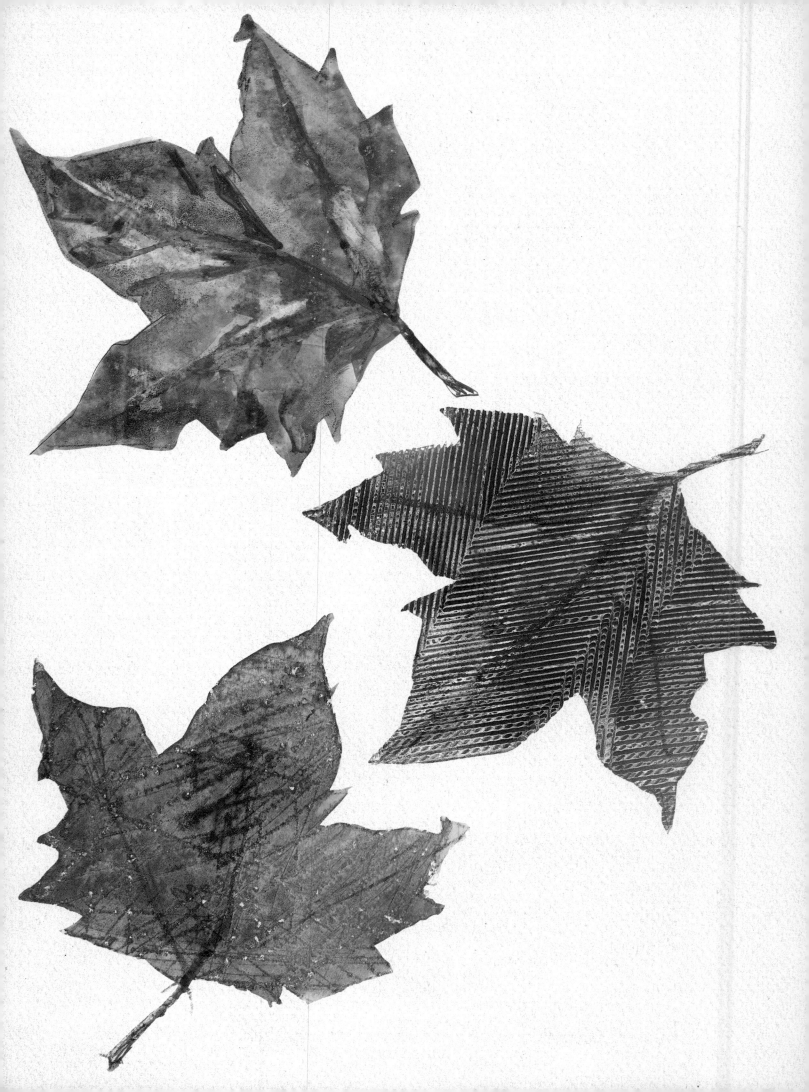

The Fundamentals of Watercolor

Choosing Your Colors

BEFORE YOU BEGIN TO PAINT, choose your palette of colors. The selection of paints in your art supply store may seem bewildering at first sight. You may even wonder why, with so many colors available, you should bother to learn how to mix colors together to obtain new ones. It is possible to produce a complete painting from ready-mixed paints – but learning how to mix your own colors is essential if you are to develop your skills as a watercolorist (see pp. 38–39). When you have mastered how to do this, you will be able to make subtle transitions in tone, as well as to create the exact color you want for a specific job.

You do not need many colors. Once you have learned to dilute individual colors to various strengths and to mix more than one color together, you will find that your palette holds more potential than you might at first have realized. Some great artists have achieved almost miraculous subtleties of color using a very limited palette. The British landscape painter Thomas Girtin (1775–1802), for example, used only five colors in his paintings, laying them on top of one another to develop sensitive gradations in hue and tone.

Before you begin painting you need to know a little about color theory (see pp. 32–33) and the mechanics of mixing and overlaying colors (see pp. 38–39). By experimenting you will find that you can vary the intensity of watercolor paint by altering the amount of water you add. Yellow ochre, for example, may appear as a deep caramel color when only slightly diluted but become a pale yellow when mixed with plenty of water. See how many hues you can obtain from one color. Then take one basic color and mix it with other colors one at a time to get a clear idea of what each color combination produces. It is a good idea to keep a record of successful mixes for future reference so that you can recreate them whenever necessary. To do this, simply paint a small square of the mixed color onto a piece of paper or cardboard, noting which colors (and, if possible, in what proportions) you used to create it, and keep it somewhere safe in your studio or workroom.

Basic and Extended Palettes

These two pages demonstrate the effect of using a basic and a more extended range of colors. A basic range might consist of as few as six colors: here, cobalt blue, Hooker's green light, yellow ochre, raw umber, burnt sienna, and alizarin crimson were selected. By using this palette, you will discover just how many color-mixing options watercolor paint offers. Sometimes you may want to extend your basic range. For the second painting on p. 29, sepia, cadmium red, cadmium yellow, viridian, cerulean blue, and Payne's gray were added to the basic palette.

Extended Palette

Basic Palette

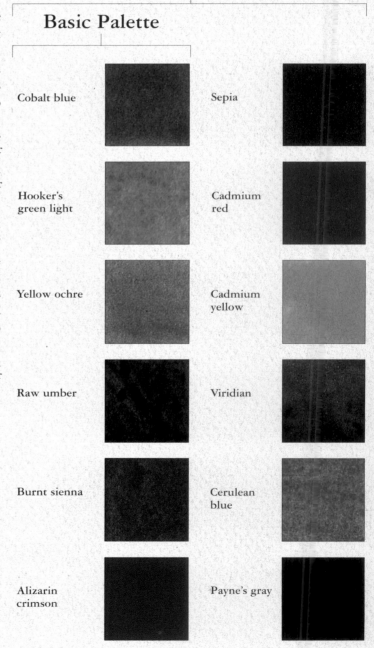

Cobalt blue

Sepia

Hooker's green light

Cadmium red

Yellow ochre

Cadmium yellow

Raw umber

Viridian

Burnt sienna

Cerulean blue

Alizarin crimson

Payne's gray

Using a Basic Palette

This landscape was painted only with colors from the suggested basic palette, yet a rich and detailed picture was produced. The effect is warm and subtle, with the wet-into-wet washes of the sky contrasting with the textured paint in the plowed field, produced by scraping a plastic palette knife through the wet color. To increase definition, pen-and-ink lines were added over the dried painting.

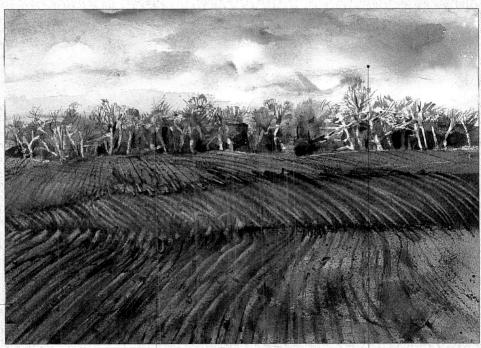

Hooker's green light, yellow ochre, and raw umber are overlaid wet over damp in the plowed field, before being partly scraped off with a palette knife.

Burnt sienna adds warmth to the trees on the horizon line, and alizarin crimson provides a change in tone in the foreground of the fields.

Cobalt blue is washed wet into wet into the sky to produce a subtle range of blue tones.

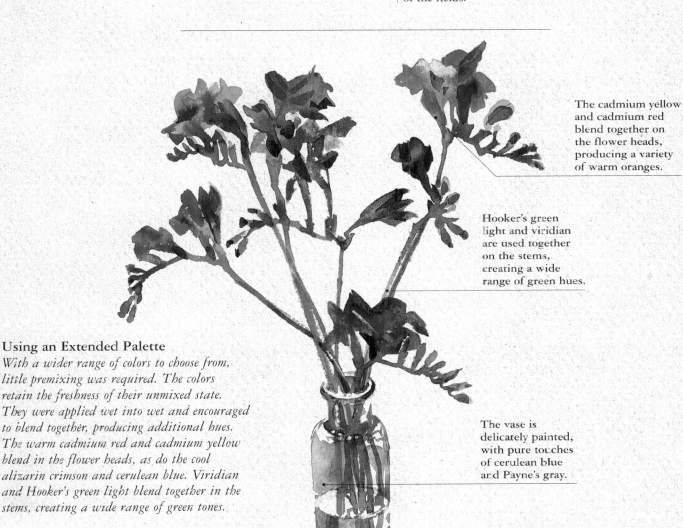

The cadmium yellow and cadmium red blend together on the flower heads, producing a variety of warm oranges.

Hooker's green light and viridian are used together on the stems, creating a wide range of green hues.

Using an Extended Palette

With a wider range of colors to choose from, little premixing was required. The colors retain the freshness of their unmixed state. They were applied wet into wet and encouraged to blend together, producing additional hues. The warm cadmium red and cadmium yellow blend in the flower heads, as do the cool alizarin crimson and cerulean blue. Viridian and Hooker's green light blend together in the stems, creating a wide range of green tones.

The vase is delicately painted, with pure touches of cerulean blue and Payne's gray.

Holding Brushes

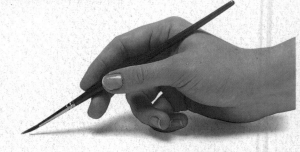

THERE ARE NO hard-and-fast rules about how to hold brushes, but the way you hold the brush affects the mark you are able to make with it. To make a small, tight brushmark, hold the brush close to the tip or by the ferrule and move it over the paper by moving your fingers. Small brushes are normally used for such detailed work.

The higher up the handle you hold the brush, the harder it is to control the length of the marks you make and to place them precisely. If you want to make a loose mark, for which you need to move your wrist, hold the brush about a third of the way up the handle. For broad, sweeping brushstrokes, where you need to move your fingers, wrist, and even the whole of your lower arm, hold the brush in the middle or toward the end.

Sometimes particular brush types or sizes are associated with particular techniques – a large, flat brush with washes, for example. Never make the mistake of thinking that a particular brush should always be held in a particular way. It is the character of the mark you are making that is important, not the tool you use to make it, and there may be times when you need to hold even a very large brush near its tip for precise brushwork.

Whatever type of brush you are using, always choose a grip that feels comfortable and enables you to make the type of mark you want. Don't worry if your grip isn't entirely orthodox. Your brushstrokes are as unique as your signature, and it is the result that matters, not the way you achieve it.

Moderately Broad Marks
For a moderately broad mark, hold the brush a third of the way up the handle (above) *so that you can move your wrist freely.* Right: *A small to medium-sized brush (no. 4) is good for general detail.*

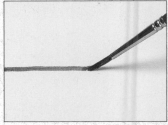

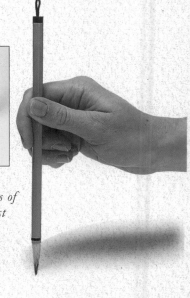

Calligraphic Marks
Hold the brush three-quarters of the way up the handle, almost perpendicular to the paper (above), *to produce flowing marks.* Right: *The Chinese brush shown here is designed specifically for calligraphy.*

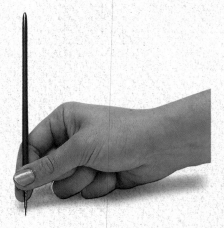

Fine Details
By holding the brush on the ferrule (above), *you can maintain tight control and keep a steady hand as you paint.* Right: *This fine-tipped brush (no. 000) is rarely used but is capable of making very delicate marks.*

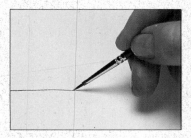

Broad Strokes
Broad, flowing strokes require movement from the lower arm, wrist, and fingers. Hold the brush near the end of the handle (above). Right: *A $^7/_8$-in (2-cm) mop brush is ideal for covering large areas quickly.*

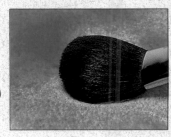

Different Grips for One Brush

Every brush can be held in a number of
different ways. Rather than buying a large range
of specialty brushes and disrupting the flow of
your painting by switching from one to another,
experiment with a small number to see what you
can achieve. The no. 8 brush, shown here, is of
medium size and one of the most versatile.

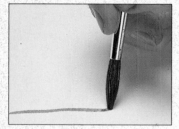

Detail and Fine Lines

*Hold the brush close to the
ferrule (top), and do not
overload it with paint.
Above: Used in this way, a
no. 8 brush can form a thin
tip and produce fine lines.*

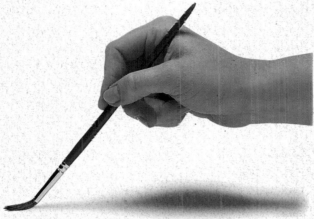

Broad Marks

*By gripping the brush halfway
up the handle (above), you can
press the bristles down onto the
paper and make broad flat
marks (right). This technique
is particularly suitable for
painting washes.*

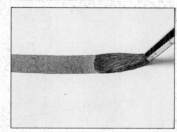

Feathering

*By pressing the bristles of the
brush between your thumb
and forefinger, you can splay
out the hairs into a fan shape
(top). Above: This technique
is useful for drybrush effects
(see pp. 56–57).*

Different Effects with a Chisel Brush

Chisel brushes come in many sizes, but they
all have a sharp, flat edge, making them useful for
edging, fine line drawing, and crosshatching.
They can also be used for broad, flat marks.

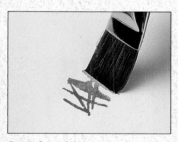

Crosshatching

*Hold the brush between your
thumb and forefinger, perpendicular to the paper, halfway
along the handle (right).
Use the flat edge of the brush
to make crisscross marks on
the paper (above). This is a
good way of implying loose
shading in your paintings.*

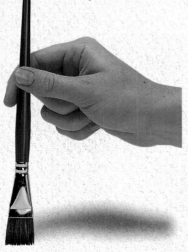

Broad marks

*Hold the brush two-thirds of
the way along the handle
(above). Right: Place the bristles on the paper at 45 degrees
to the handle. Pull the brush
across the paper, maintaining
pressure to create broad marks.*

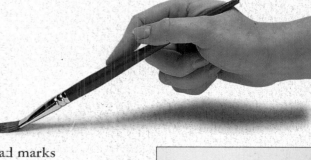
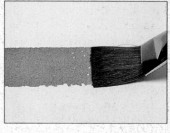

Color Theory and Value

COLOR IS CATEGORIZED by hue, value, intensity, and temperature. The term hue refers to the general color name – red, blue, green, and so on. Value, or tone, describes the relative lightness or darkness of a color. Intensity points to the brilliance or purity of the color, and temperature indicates whether the color is warm (tending toward red) or cool (tending toward blue). By using colors of similar value, temperature, and intensity, you will produce more harmonious compositions.

The best way to learn about the scientific relationships between colors is to consult a color wheel – a device that explains the relationships between the three primary colors of red, yellow, and blue. Primary colors are ones that cannot be mixed from any other colors. Mixing primaries together produces a range of secondary colors: blue mixed with yellow gives you green; red mixed with yellow, orange; and red mixed with blue, purple. A secondary color mixed with its complementary (the color that lies opposite it on the color wheel) gives a tertiary: orange (secondary) mixed with blue (primary), for example, produces a tertiary mix.

Color Wheel

A color wheel is based around the three primary colors: red, yellow, and blue. Between these appear the secondary colors – orange, green, and purple – produced when each primary is mixed with its neighbor.
The hue that you produce by mixing two colors together depends on which reds, yellows, or blues you choose. No color in your palette is pure: any red, yellow, or blue leans toward a related warm or cool hue. Cadmium red (a warm red) mixed with cadmium yellow creates a warm orange. Alizarin crimson (a bluish red) mixed with cadmium yellow gives a cool orange.
The complement of any color is the one that lies directly opposite it on the color wheel. The complement of red, for example, is green. When a secondary color is mixed with its complementary, the resulting color, which tends to be a neutral gray-brown, is known as a tertiary color.
When complementary colors are placed next to one another, they enhance one another's color.

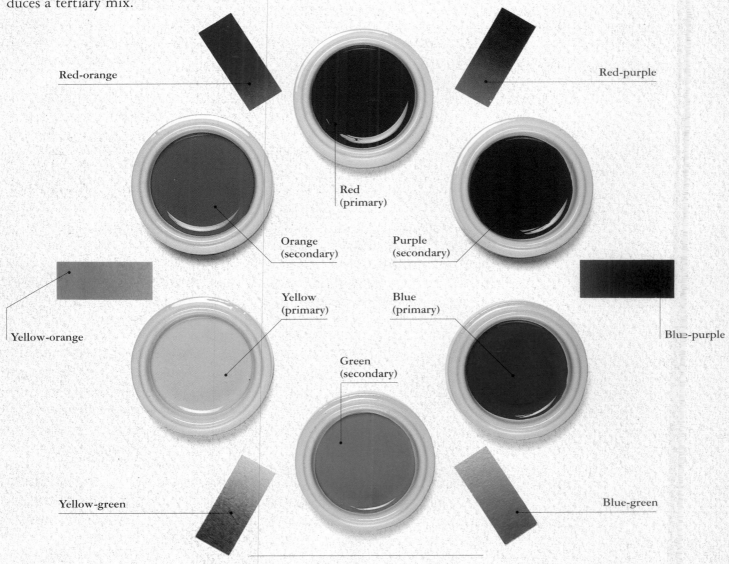

Red-orange

Red-purple

Red (primary)

Orange (secondary)

Purple (secondary)

Yellow-orange

Yellow (primary)

Blue (primary)

Blue-purple

Green (secondary)

Yellow-green

Blue-green

Tonal Strip

A good practical starting point for learning about color theory and value is to put one color in your palette and then experiment to see how far you can change it. Add water to the paint to lighten it, and add the appropriate complementary color – for example, raw sienna to cerulean blue, or alizarin crimson to Hooker's green light – to move it toward a neutral gray.

Hue
The basic color from which you start is known as a hue.

Shade
A shade is a hue that is darkened by the addition of a second color, usually its complement. Here, different amounts of Payne's gray are added to produce increasingly darker shades of Hooker's green.

Tint
A tint is a lighter tone of any hue. In pure watercolor painting, you lighten a hue by adding water to the paint. It is possible to produce a tint that is so pale as to be almost imperceptible – useful for producing a toned ground (see pp. 94–97).

Kairouan Departure, Paul Klee (1879–1940)
A Swiss painter and etcher, Klee taught at the Bauhaus, an art school in Germany, from 1922 to 1931. He was a theorist who experimented with the way colors relate when mixed or placed next to one another on paper.

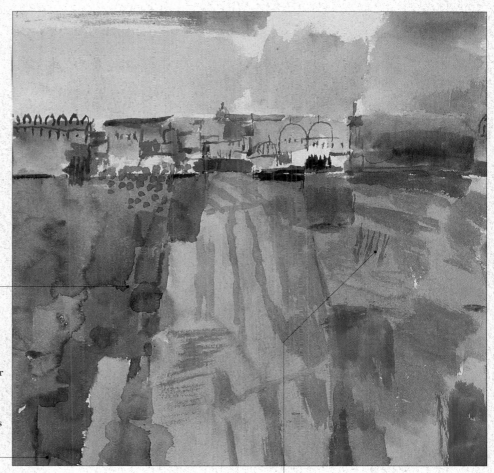

A tonal variation is created in the red area by laying dark greens over the paint while it is still wet. The two colors merge and separate to form a wide range of tones.

Red and green (complementary colors) are placed next to each other on the paper. Their proximity gives warm overtones to the painting, since the eye mixes the two colors optically.

Blue is normally a recessive color but here, laid on pale colors from the other side of the color spectrum (orange-brown and very dilute crimson), it comes to the fore.

Composition

COMPOSITION IS THE TERM used to describe the way different elements are organized within a picture. The best way to learn about composition is to look at other artists' work and then apply the same principles to your own paintings. The most important element in a picture – the part to which your eye is drawn – is called the center of interest. When you look at a picture, first decide what the center of interest is, and then think about how the artist directed your eye toward that point. Is it in the middle of the picture? Perhaps there is a pathway that leads you to it. Or maybe the colors become more vivid toward the focal point.

Always plan the position of the center of interest before you begin painting. Encourage the viewer's eye to explore the entire picture, rather than resting on one point. Place features on or near an imaginary line that runs through the picture – a curve that snakes through the picture area or a strong diagonal line that cuts straight to the center of interest, for example. Dividing the picture area into thirds, both horizontally and vertically, and placing important features at the points where these imaginary lines intersect, is another well-established practice, and

we instinctively recognize the result as a balanced and appealing composition. Balance does not necessarily mean symmetry, however, and placing the center of interest in the middle of the composition may render it dull and lifeless. Try creating tension by placing the center of interest toward one side of the work. This will also help to suggest that action continues outside the picture.

Space is another important factor in composition. Empty spaces can be as evocative and loaded with meaning as areas of intense activity; do not try to include too much in your picture.

Before you put paint to paper, look at your subject from several different angles in order to decide which one works best. Do not always go for the most obvious viewpoint. Sometimes the least likely approach – perhaps a high viewpoint or a very low one – will give you a more interesting composition.

With practice, you will develop a feeling for good and bad composition. Although many artists do not use formal theories to compose paintings, it is surprising how often they inadvertently adhere to one or another of the well-established principles described on these pages.

Low Horizon

When painting landscapes, your first decision should be where to place the horizon line. In this example, the composition is divided horizontally into thirds with the horizon line positioned on the bottom third. As a result, the wide open sky, which takes up the top two-thirds of the picture, dominates the composition. Diagonal lines across the field direct the eye toward the trees at the right corner of the horizon. From here, the clouds draw the eye up and across the large sweep of sky. These devices combine to create an impression of wide-open spaces.

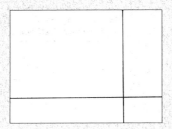

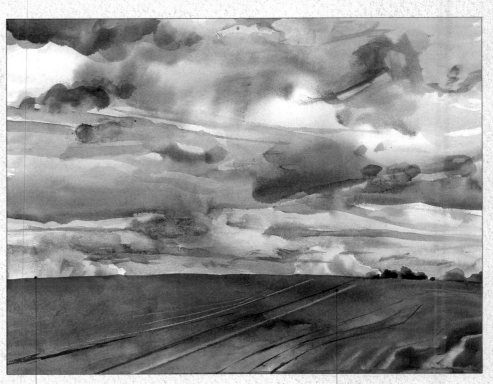

The low horizon line emphasizes the sky.

The diagonal lines of the field lead the eye through the composition to the center of interest (the trees) and up into the sky

Linear Composition

The center of interest – a house – nestles between the land and the trees, roughly one-third of the distance from the left edge of the paper. Although it is small by comparison with the amount of space devoted to the land, trees, and sky, all lines lead toward it. A touch of white on the building's wall contrasts with the rich surrounding tones and draws our attention to it. The fact that it is half-hidden is intriguing and further arouses our interest.

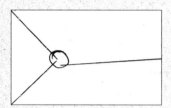

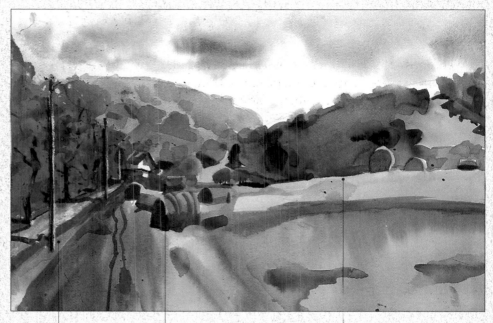

The telephone poles recede toward the center of interest, following the road.

The house and outbuildings are the focal point toward which all other lines in the composition lead.

The edge of the field curves downward and leads the eye gently and slowly toward the focal point.

Rhythmic Composition

This picture is painted from an unusually high viewpoint. First, we look down over the castle walls, then our eye is led back up over the mound to the painting's center of interest, the castle at its summit. The curved pathway around the mound is painted in pale grays so that it stands out from the darker areas on either side; our eyes follow the line of this pathway around the composition and then up into the distance. The white castle on the summit stands out against the receding dark hill, which in turn contrasts with the paler land in front of it. The receding colors help to create an impression of distance (see pp. 98–99).

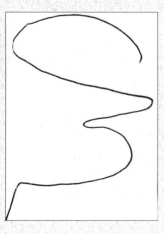

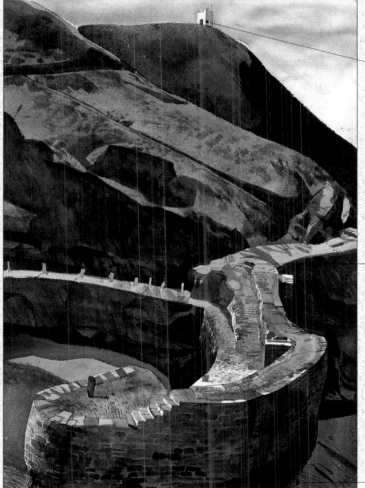

Our eyes are led through the foreground and up the hill to settle on the castle at the summit.

The light path leads up through the middle ground toward the solid mass of hills in the distance.

The dark shadow in the foreground does not hold the eye's attention; instead, it encourages it to move toward the lighter areas and explore the center of the composition.

DECIDING WHERE TO PLACE OBJECTS in a composition is essential to successful picture making. If you do not organize the elements well, your painting will be unsatisfactory. Before you start painting, try editing the scene in front of you to discover "hidden" views. You can learn a lot about composition by doing this. Frame the scene with a pair of L-shaped pieces of cardboard, framing first one part and then another, until you find an area that works. There is usually more than one potential picture in any scene. You may discover three or four different compositions within the scene that you initially selected, or even an abstract pattern that can become a successful painting in its own right.

In the following two pages you can see how the same scene can give rise to a number of alternative compositions, all of which work equally well. The same theory applies to any subject – landscapes, figure painting, or still-life compositions. You can organize any collection of objects to produce a harmonious composition. Take time to move around your subject, crouch down in front of it, or look at it from a high viewpoint, to see which options are available to you. You may find that you need to rearrange the lighting on a still life to emphasize the center of interest or to draw attention away from an object of secondary importance. If you are painting a figure from life, ask your sitter to change the angle of his or her legs or arms, or the tilt of the head, until you find the most successful pose. Even if you are studying nature, you are creating a piece of art and you can always alter what you see to produce a better picture. If, for example, a tree unbalances the scene, then leave it out. By the same token, if your composition lacks a central subject – a group of buildings or a figure, for example – there is nothing to stop you from adding them.

The Whole View

This elaborate composition is split roughly into thirds, both diagonally and horizontally: two-thirds land to one-third sky and one-third mountains to two-thirds valley. The small town nestling on the horizon provides the center of interest, with the steeple of the church adding a focal point. In contrast to the pale wet washes that constitute the sky, the buildings and foreground foliage are rendered in rich colors and fine detail. The scene is painted from a low viewpoint, from within the grasses and cacti that cover the foreground. As a result, the scene appears to stretch up and away from us into the far distance.

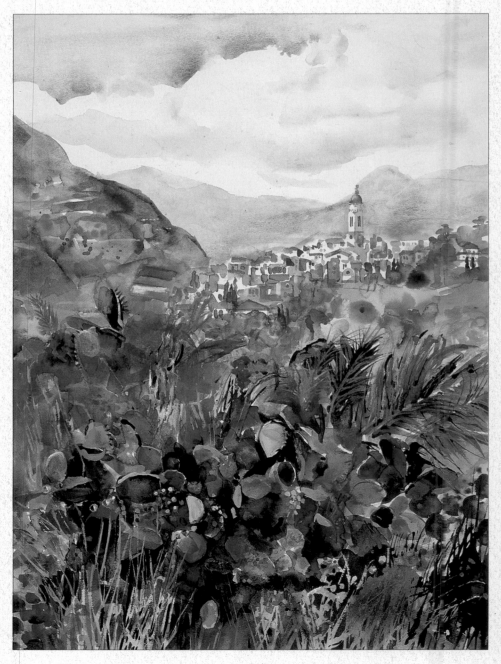

Low Horizon

By cropping the composition and getting rid of all the foreground detail, the scene takes on a different, but equally successful, aspect. The town now fills the foreground of the composition, and it is dwarfed by the large mountain to the left and the vast sky that engulfs it from above. As the horizon line is low, the emphasis shifts to the sky above it. The balance of colors has changed too, with the pale tones of the sky playing a more important role in this picture than they did in the original composition.

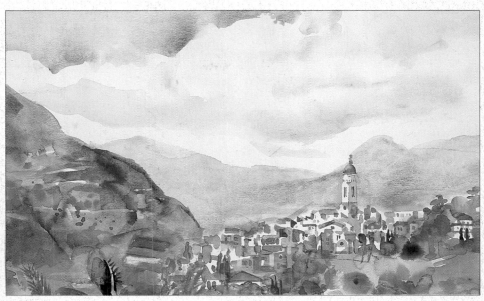

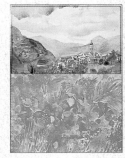

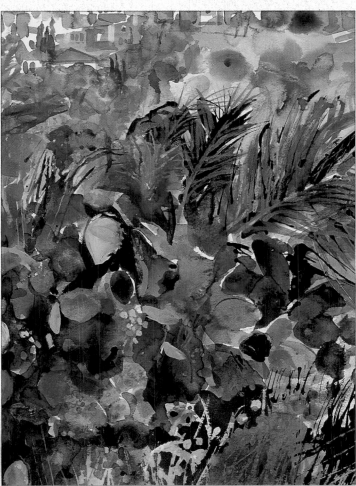

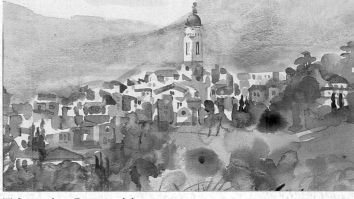

Triangular Composition

In this instance the picture has been cropped on the left and from above and below. The result is a triangular or pyramidal composition, in which the church steeple, in the center of the composition, is the pinnacle of the whole scene. Without the sky and the foreground detail, all our attention rests on the town itself.

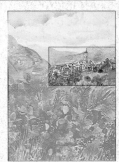

Abstracting the Scene

In a more daring crop, the representational detail is abandoned in favor of an inspiring pattern of shapes and colors. The horizon line has vanished, and the scene concentrates fully on the rich content of the foreground. The composition depends on form and color, rather than on recognizable objects, although you can still see that the subject matter is based on natural forms.

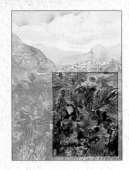

Mixing and Overlaying Colors

WATERCOLOR PAINTS can be mixed either on your palette or on the paper. Most watercolorists use both methods to achieve the widest possible range of effects. By mixing paint on a palette, you can be sure you have the color you want before you lay it down on the paper. Be sure, however, to prepare a little more than you think you are going to need. If you run out before you have finished a painting, it is always difficult to remix a color exactly.

There are two ways to mix paint on paper, although both involve overlaying color. You can paint one color on top of another while the first is still damp, allowing the colors to mix and blend together on the paper. Alternatively, you can allow the first color to dry before applying the second. This is a more predictable and controllable way of mixing colors; it is also the way to create a darker tone, by gradually building up layer upon layer of the same color until you achieve the shade you want.

Always remember, however, that paint will dry lighter than it appears on the palette or when it is wet on the paper. To compensate for this, mix a slightly darker color than you want for the final result.

Overlaying One Hue

In this example, layer upon layer of one hue – burnt umber – is built up to achieve a darker tone. The effect is similar to placing several layers of tissue paper over one another, as the translucent paint allows underlying layers to show through. A wide range of tones can be created from a single color. The translucency of the paint also allows the white of the paper to show through.

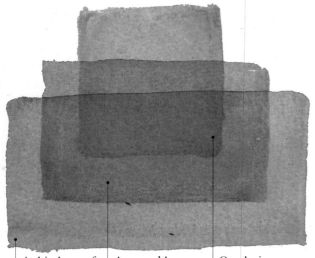

A thin layer of burnt umber produces an even, flat wash of color.

A second layer of color, overlaid, produces a deeper tint of the same hue.

Overlaying a third layer of the color strengthens its intensity.

Mixing Color on a Palette

You may have more control if you premix colors on a palette. A partitioned porcelain palette, like the one shown here, is useful for mixing colors. Place one color in the first trough, another in the second, and then mix the two in the third to create the color you want. Always mix more paint than you think you will need.

1 *Squeeze a little cerulean blue, a primary color, from a tube onto the first partition. Put some clean water into the round well at the bottom of the partition.*

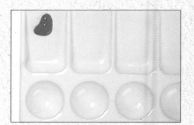

2 *Wet your brush in the well and touch it in the paint so that the paint dissolves slightly and begins to run down to the bottom of the slanted section. Pull down more paint with the brush.*

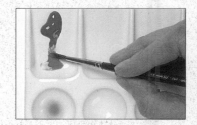

3 *When you have achieved the color intensity you want and have mixed the amount you will need for your painting, leave the paint and wash out your brush.*

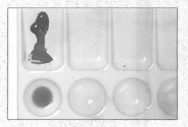

4 *Now repeat the exercise in the second slanted section, this time using another primary color – cadmium yellow. This is an intense, brilliant paint, so you may need to add more water to it than to the blue.*

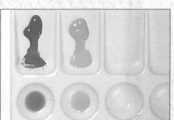

5 *Wash out your brush. Now dip it into the blue pool of paint you have mixed and then move to the third slanted section. Place the paint there, rinse your brush, then add yellow. Mix the colors together.*

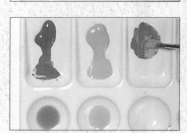

6 *As the two colors mix, green, which is a secondary color, will emerge. The color will vary as you change the relative amounts of blue to yellow or of water to paint.*

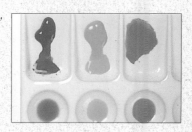

Mixing Color on Paper

In addition to mixing color on a palette, you can also mix color on paper by laying wet color over dry paint. This enables you to exploit the translucency of the watercolor paint. When dry, each layer allows the particles from the previous layer to show through. Bearing this in mind, always work from light to dark with watercolor. The more layers of color you put down, the darker the tone you will achieve. You can mix two colors in this way, to produce other hues, or put down consecutive layers of the same color to create subtle gradations in tone.

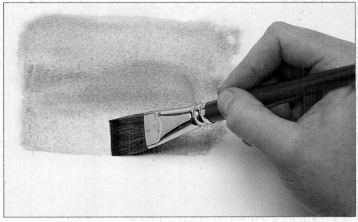

1 Brush cerulean blue onto the paper with a flat brush, using even strokes, then rinse out your brush. Allow the paint to dry completely. You can test that it is dry by feeling the paint with the back of your hand, which is more sensitive than your fingertips and enables you to detect any remaining dampness.

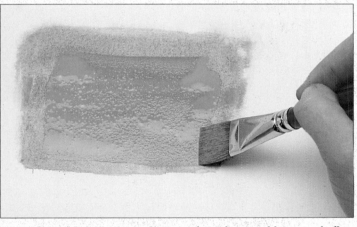

2 Dilute some cadmium yellow on the palette. Add a second, flat wash of cadmium yellow on top of the cerulean blue. Take care not to go over the same area of paper twice with this wash.

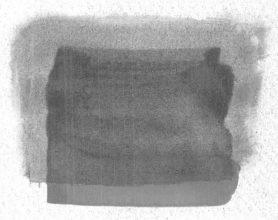

3 As the cadmium yellow begins to dry, it becomes translucent and allows particles of the blue paint to show through. Although both colors are apparent, they mix optically, producing a secondary green tone.

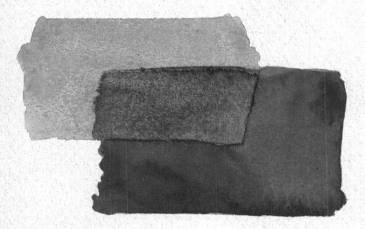

Blue on Crimson

A flat wash of alizarin crimson is painted over the surface of the paper and allowed to dry. Next, a flat wash of cerulean blue is painted to overlap the crimson. Where the colors meet, a secondary violet color appears.

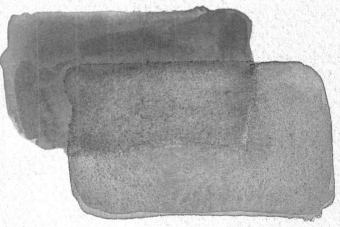

Yellow on Green

A flat wash of Hooker's green light is painted over the surface of the paper and allowed to dry. Next, a flat wash of cadmium yellow is painted to overlap the green. Where the colors meet, a yellow-green tone appears.

Laying a Flat Wash

A FLAT WASH is an even application of one color that dries with very little variation in the tone. Watercolor is a difficult medium to perfect, as the paint runs and spreads. Learning to control a flat wash will stand you in good stead for all other techniques.

Any paper that weighs less than 140 lb should be stretched before you lay a wash (see pp. 18–19).

The secret behind applying an even flat wash is to work quickly, touching each area of the paper with just one stroke of paint. If you hesitate or repeat a stroke, the paint will not dry evenly. The fewer strokes you use, the flatter or more even the wash will be, so use a large brush if you are intending to cover the entire paper. Angle the watercolor board slightly so that each brushstroke runs into the next without streaking.

To begin with, you may find it easiest to dampen the paper with a brush or sponge before applying the wash, so that the paint spreads quickly, leaving no hard edges. If you wet the paper too much, however, it will buckle and the paint will spread unevenly, so mop up any excess water with a sponge before you start to apply the paint. Premix lots of color so that you don't run out of paint halfway through the wash as you will find it difficult to mix a second wash to exactly the same shade.

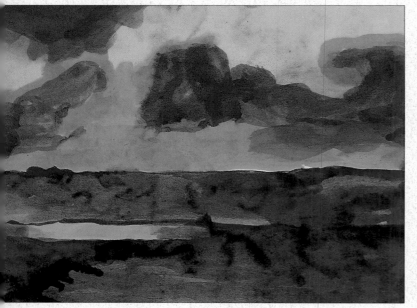

Sunset over Gotteskoog, Emil Nolde
(1867–1956)
German Expressionist painter Emil Nolde laid a series of flat washes onto dampened watercolor paper to produce this vivid sunset scene. As each color is laid, it blends into the surrounding wet paint in an atmospheric shock of colors.

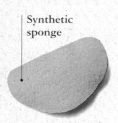

Synthetic sponge

Sponge on Dry Paper

A flat wash may be applied to dry paper with a sponge. Use a large, flat synthetic sponge with an unpitted surface. Mix up a large quantity of your color before beginning, and place your watercolor board at a slight angle. Dip the flat side of the sponge into the paint evenly to ensure an even covering of color.

1 *For the first stroke, work from left to right across the top of the area you want to cover. Applying even pressure, draw the sponge smoothly across the surface, leaving a flat wash of paint behind it. Try to work evenly and quickly.*

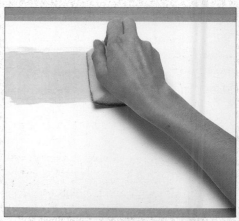

2 *When you have finished one stroke, dip the sponge into the paint again. Repeat the exercise, beginning once again from the left side, but lower down the paper. Overlap the first stroke of paint so that you pick up the previous paint edge.*

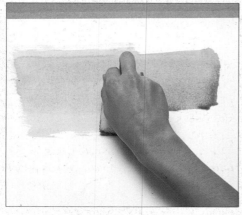

3 *With a wide sponge, you do not need to put down many strokes of color to achieve a flat wash. Once you have finished, let the wash dry before judging its color and smoothness. It will become paler and flatter as it loses moisture.*

Brush on Dampened Paper

Alternatively, you can lay a large flat wash on dampened paper. The paint will spread into the damp paper to give an even finish. You may dampen the paper with either a sponge or a brush, but take care not to make the surface too wet. Always prepare your paint for the wash before you dampen the paper surface.

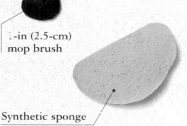

1-in (2.5-cm) mop brush

Synthetic sponge

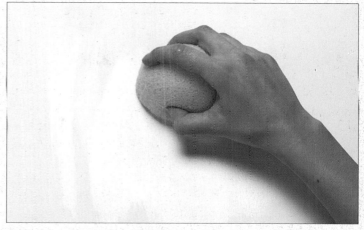

1 *Dampen the surface of the paper with a sponge, making sure that you mop up any droplets of water that develop on the surface of the paper. If the paper gets too wet, remove the excess with a dry sponge or brush.*

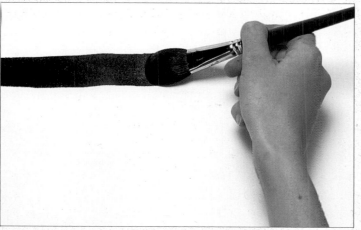

2 *Dip a 1-in (2.5-cm) mop brush into the paint, taking care not to overload it in case you drip paint onto the paper. Starting at the top left corner of the area you want to cover with a flat wash, paint an even stroke of color. Do not hesitate or falter or the wash will not dry flat.*

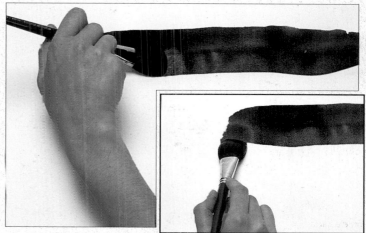

3 *When you reach the end of the stroke, pull the brush back across the paper to achieve a second stroke of color that overlaps slightly with the one above it. Inset: To turn the corner, leave the brush on the paper and swivel it around in one fluid movement so that it sits comfortably in your hand.*

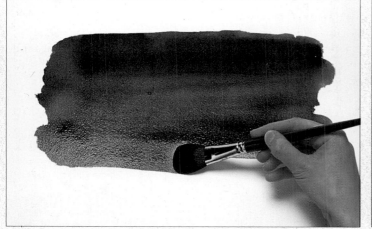

4 *Continue to work down the paper, from left to right, then back from right to left, until you have reached the bottom of the paper. If you need to refill your brush, wait until you have reached the end of a stroke before lifting it away from the paper.*

5 *Let the wash dry before you judge its color or the evenness. The particles ought to spread evenly as they dry. Don't be disappointed if your first effort looks uneven while wet: it will dry to a much flatter finish.*

Gradated and Variegated Washes

THE FLAT WASH is only one of a number of wash techniques. Two others that are equally, if not more, useful are gradated and variegated washes. A gradated wash is applied in exactly the same way as a flat one, but rather than using the same flat, even color, you lighten or darken the color as you work, or you reload your brush with water as you progress so that the color weakens and gets lighter. Gradated washes are especially useful for painting skies and landscapes, where you may want to use subtle changes of tone to convey an impression of distance.

A variegated wash does not grade from dark to light or from light to dark. It usually comprises various colors that randomly blend and merge into one another as they are dropped onto damp paper. A variegated wash can be made using as many colors of varying strengths as you choose. You can also use the same technique with just one color. The effects are hard to control, but such random marking creates interesting results, as the watercolor paint is allowed to bleed into different colors in different areas of the paper. The degree of control that you have and the way the paint reacts depends entirely on how damp the paper is. If it is very wet, the wash will spread and blend quickly so that it loses its edges; if it is only slightly damp, it will bleed a little but will not blend into an adjacent color. You can use any type of brush to apply a wash. Your choice will be dictated by the size of the area you want to cover.

Gradated Wash

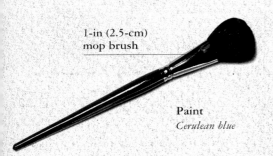

1-in (2.5-cm) mop brush

Paint
Cerulean blue

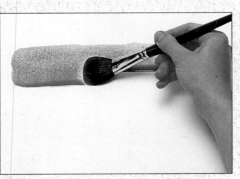

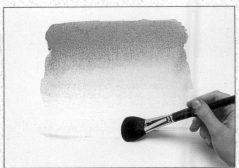

1 As *in the flat wash demonstration (see pp. 40–41), lightly lay the first stroke of color across the paper from left to right. It is not essential to dampen the paper with water first, though you may find it easier to lay the color evenly if you do so.*

2 *Continue working from left to right, then back from right to left, down the paper. When the paint runs thin, add more water to the brush, rather than more paint, so that the color gets lighter as you progress.*

The Result
When you have completed the wash, it should appear to gradate – in this instance, from dark to light. The wash should appear even: the paint should not dry in streaks.

Skyscape
Gradated washes provide you with a simple, yet effective method of creating an atmospheric sky. Here, the cool cerulean blue wash dominates two-thirds of the picture, yet it does not overwhelm this picturesque view of a typical French village.

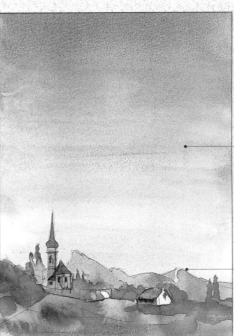

The gradated wash begins as a dark flooding of cerulean blue across the top of the paper. As the wash progresses, the brush is loaded with more water and less paint.

The color of the gradated wash is almost lost on the horizon line. This is a useful painting device, as a pale horizon draws the eye into the heart of the picture.

Variegated Wash

½-in (12-mm)
chisel brush

Paints
Viridian
Hooker's green light
Cadmium yellow

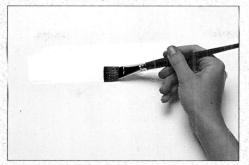

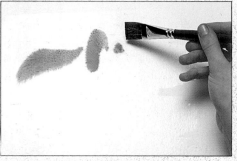

1 *Dampen the surface of the paper with a ½-in (12-mm) chisel brush. Work as quickly as you can so that the paper does not dry before you start applying the paint.*

2 *This simple variegated wash uses only two colors – viridian and a mix of Hooker's green light and cadmium yellow. Begin by making a few brushstrokes of viridian on the dampened area of the paper.*

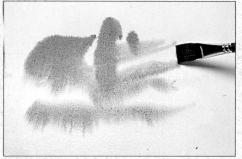

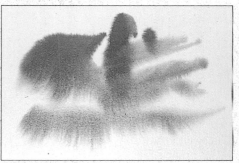

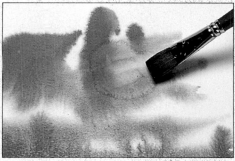

3 *Make more marks, using both viridian and a mix of Hooker's green light and cadmium yellow, varying the direction of the brushstrokes and the amount of pressure you apply. Pull the paint across the paper.*

4 *Stop and watch the paint as it moves and settles into the wet surface. Tip the watercolor board to encourage the paint to flow across the paper and merge with the paint already laid down.*

5 *Now reload your brush and add more paint to the variegated wash. There are no hard-and-fast rules: experiment with the paint and see what effects you can achieve.*

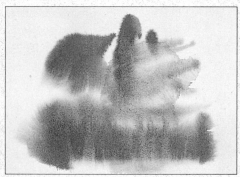

The Result
The paint blended and flooded across the paper in all directions. It created an uneven finish, with interesting textures and surfaces. The variegated wash may now be developed into an image – perhaps trees or foliage.

Here dark viridian blends over paler washes of Hooker's green light mixed with cadmium yellow, to create dark tones, providing form and substance.

The pale mix of Hooker's green light and cadmium yellow spreads thinly across the lower foliage and produces a light, clear surface of color, suggesting fresh growth.

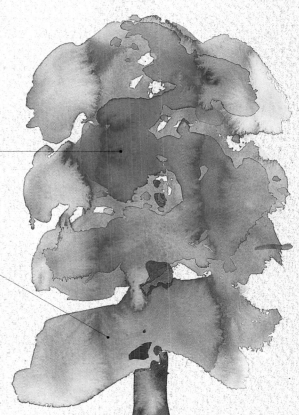

Tree in Summer
Variegated washes are particularly useful for natural subjects such as foliage, grasses, and water. Here, the artist used the technique to create a tree in summer splendor. The washes blend to produce an impression of three dimensions, and the use of different green hues enhances the contrasts between light and dark.

Wet into Wet

WET INTO WET means applying paint to damp paper – either paper dampened with water or paper on which previously applied paint has not yet dried – and allowing the paint to spread. The technique is unpredictable and semirandom: the paint reacts in different ways, depending on how wet the paper is and the proportion of water to paint in your mix. You can achieve a fine degree of control by learning exactly how different amounts of paint react to different dampnesses of paper. American artist Andrew Wyeth (born in 1917) is famous for his control with this method.

You can use more than one color when working wet into wet, allowing the paints to blend into one another and achieving soft, blurred results. Once the paint is laid down, do not work into it too much with a brush, as this makes the surface appear muddy. Paint applied wet into wet looks very different when it dries. The pigments shift and settle, and the colors always look lighter when dry than when they were first laid down.

When working wet into wet, use a heavy-grade paper that will not buckle under the weight of the water. If you use a lightweight paper, you will need to stretch it before you start painting (see pp. 18–19).

With this method, you can suggest atmospheric effects, such as rain or mist over a landscape. Let the paint run and blend on the paper, creating areas of color without any hard edges.

To achieve a degree of control when working with more than one color or layer of paint, allow one layer to dry slightly before adding the next. A damp surface does not react with the paint as dramatically as a really wet one. Mix your colors with lots of paint to water, or they will look watery and weak when dry.

Different Wet-into-Wet Effects

The effects you achieve with the wet-into-wet technique depends on how wet the paint and the paper are. If the two elements are completely awash with water, then the effect will be loose and random. The drier the paper and the more pigmented the paint mix, the more control you will have and the more definite the marks you create will be.

Applied to very wet paper, the paint bleeds and feathers.

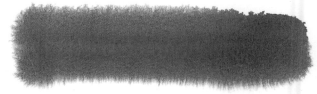

When the paper is damp, the paint blurs at the edges but remains controlled.

With only slightly damp paper, the effect is confined and controlled.

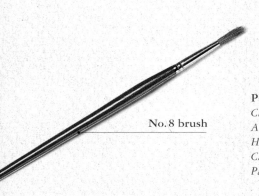

No. 8 brush

Paints
Cadmium red
Alizarin crimson
Hooker's green light
Cadmium yellow
Payne's gray

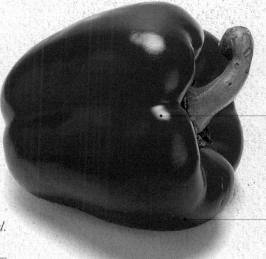

The glossy surface and highlights can be enhanced by semi-random wet-into-wet applications of paint.

The contrast between the very deep and the medium red areas can be heightened by applying wet-into-wet washes.

Red Pepper
The surface of this red pepper is glossy and undulated, so it needs to be unevenly painted. Areas of deep red contrast with sharply defined highlights, which emphasize the form and three-dimensional nature of the subject.

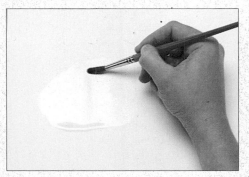

1 Using a no. 8 brush loaded with clean water, brush in the shape of the pepper on your paper. Leave two spots free of water for the highlights on its surface and the area for the stem.

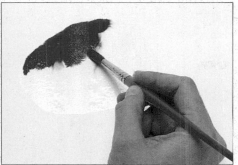

2 Load the brush with thick cadmium red paint and touch it onto the damp paper. Allow the paint to spread and blend randomly. It should not spread beyond the dampened area of paper.

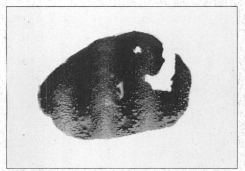

3 Any variation in the paint color will add depth to the surface, so do not worry if the finish is uneven. Try not to let the paint spread into the areas you have left empty for the highlights.

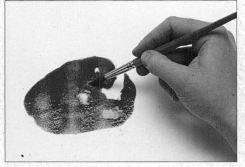

4 Leave the paint until it is almost but not quite dry. Now dip the brush into some alizarin crimson and gently touch it into areas of the pepper that appear paler in color than others. The paint should blend and bleed slightly.

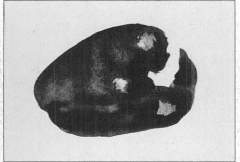

5 By now, you should have created a variation of shades across the surface of the pepper. Alizarin crimson is a cooler, more recessive hue than cadmium red. Allow the red to dry.

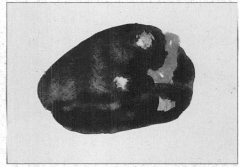

6 Wet the stem of the pepper with clean water. Drop in some Hooker's green light and allow the paint to drift and fill the wet paper.

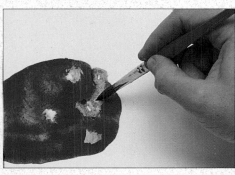

7 Touch some cadmium yellow into the damp green stem, and allow it to blend and merge into it to create contrast and depth.

The Result

The cadmium red and alizarin crimson have merged and blended slightly on the paper, creating a three-dimensional effect that suggests how the light hits some facets of the pepper while leaving others in shade. The pepper appears glossy and the white highlight areas give an illusion of depth. A shadow of Payne's gray around the bottom edge of the pepper enhances the three-dimensional effect.

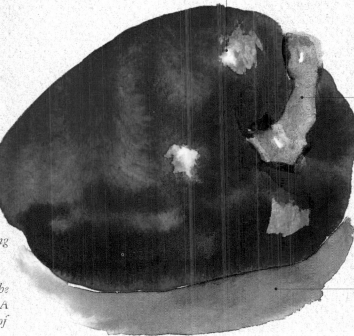

The areas left white create sparkling highlights, enhancing the waxy surface of the pepper.

Hooker's green light and cadmium yellow blend wet into wet on the paper.

A light wash of Payne's gray paint around the bottom edge of the pepper creates depth and contrast.

Practice your Technique

Combining Mixing and Overlaying Colors, Washes, and Wet into Wet

Now that you have learned a variety of techniques, you can integrate them into a more elaborate painting. Few watercolor techniques are as effective when used in isolation as they are when combined. Washes, overlays, and wet-into-wet techniques work particularly well together. Always think about the relationships between shape and color to make sure you achieve a balanced composition.

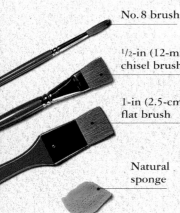

No. 8 brush

¹/₂-in (12-mm) chisel brush

1-in (2.5-cm) flat brush

Natural sponge

Paints
Cadmium yellow
Viridian
Cerulean blue
Burnt sienna
Cobalt blue
Alizarin crimson
Vermilion

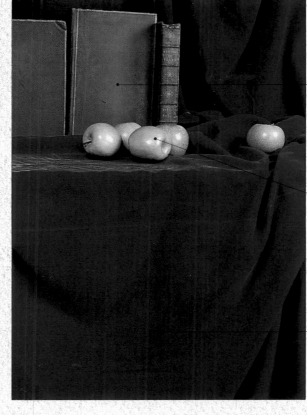

Leather-bound books have flat but unevenly colored surfaces, which are easy to suggest with variegated washes.

The apples' glossy, rounded forms can be conveyed by overlaying colors to build up the right shade.

The fabric's rich color, thick texture, and heavy folds call for a semi-random technique, such as wet-into-wet painting.

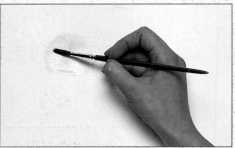

1 *Dampen the areas of the paper where the apples will appear with a no. 8 brush dipped in water. Leave highlight areas untouched so that the paint does not flood into them when you apply it wet into wet.*

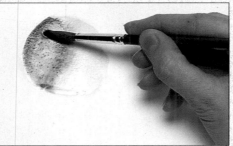

2 *Mix cadmium yellow with viridian to make the basic green tone of the apples. Using the no. 8 brush, touch wet paint onto the area reserved for the first apple. Let the paint flow and spread in a variegated wash.*

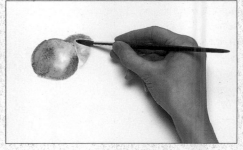

3 *Allow the first apple shape to start drying, then dampen the neighboring one, again leaving highlight areas untouched. Touch paint into the second shape, allowing it to blend slightly into the first apple.*

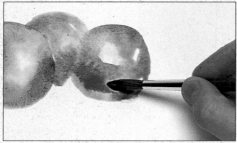

4 *Repeat the exercise for the third apple. Mix together some cerulean blue and viridian. Touch a little paint into the damp surfaces of all three apples to create darker tones and emphasize the round forms.*

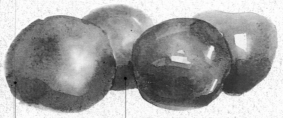

The second color, touched onto drier paper, spreads only slightly, retaining greater definition.

The paint flows and bleeds in areas where the paper is wettest.

Progress Report

The semirandom nature of variegated washes is a perfect way to convey the tonal variation on the surface of the apples. Overlaying the darker viridian and cadmium yellow mix creates the illusion of depth.

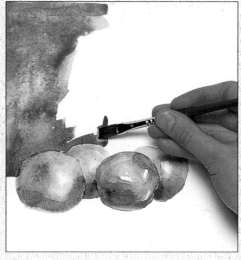

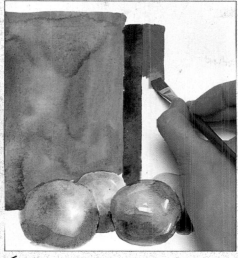

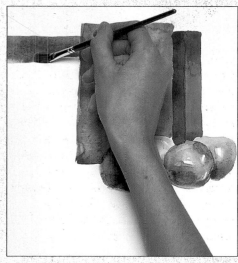

5 Using a 1½-in (12-mm) chisel brush, paint in the shape of the first book in burnt sienna, working with wet paint onto the dry paper. Allow the paint to spread and dry.

6 Mix cobalt blue into the burnt sienna, and paint the spine of the adjoining book. Add a stroke of burnt sienna alongside it, allowing the paint to blend into the previous wash.

7 Add a touch of cadmium yellow to your mix of burnt sienna and cobalt blue. Paint a flat wash to the left of the books to give the impression of a third book. The third book appears to recede, but this will be corrected by overlaying color on the first two books in the final stage of the painting.

Progress Report

The books are now complete. Allow the paint to dry: it will lighten as it dries, enhancing the impression of worn leather. The tonal variation among the three books prevents the composition from appearing too flat. The differences in texture produced by varying how the paint is applied also help to keep the image looking fresh and lively.

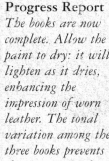

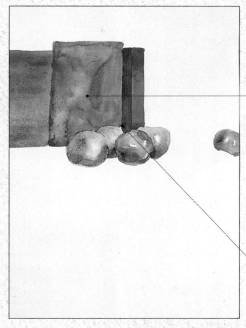

The variegated wash dries in patches, producing a leathery effect that contrasts with the flat washes to its left and right.

The darker-toned shadow enhances the illusion of depth.

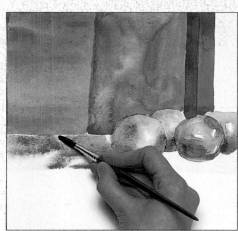

8 Add a touch of alizarin crimson to a large quantity of cobalt blue. Dampen the paper directly below the apples and books with a sponge and drop in wet paint with a no. 8 brush in the dampened area, making sure it does not spread upward.

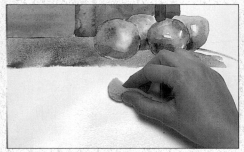

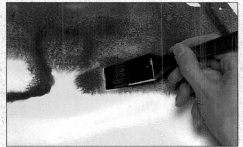

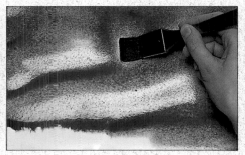

9 Using the sponge, dampen the paper below this newly laid blue wash. Although the paper needs to be really wet for the next step, mop up any puddles so that the surface is evenly dampened.

10 Load a 1-in (2.5-cm) flat brush with the same blue mix and drop large amounts of paint onto the wet paper. Let it stream and collect in the wettest areas to create the impression of folds of fabric.

11 Drop cobalt blue paint into the runs of paint, using the brush to redirect the flow and accentuate the folds in the fabric. Tilt the watercolor board to encourage the paint to spread across the paper.

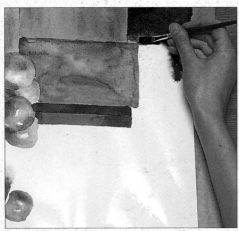

Progress Report
Even though the paper is now covered with watercolor, the image lacks depth. The newly applied blue washes do not yet emphasize the rich quality of the fabric, even though they contrast with the paler blue paint directly underneath the books.

By overlaying cobalt blue on top of wet blue mixes, the fabric color becomes more intense.

See how your preliminary blue washes are much paler in tone when dry than they were when wet.

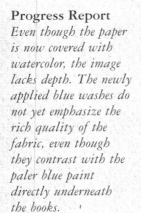

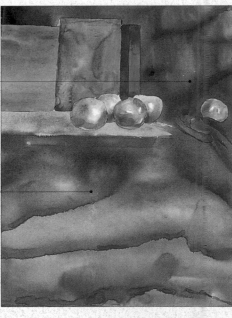

12 *Now turn the watercolor board sideways and paint a thick, flat wash of cobalt blue above the books with the large chisel brush. The books should be dry, so the wash will not bleed into their shapes.*

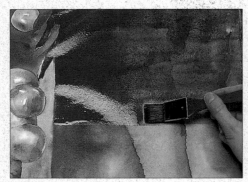

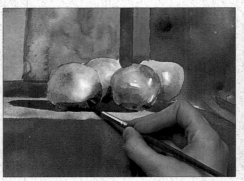

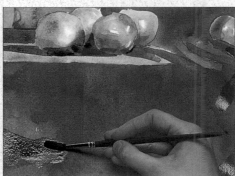

13 *Allow the blue washes to dry completely. Load the 1-in (2.5-cm) flat brush with a cobalt blue and vermilion mix. Turn the board sideways again and overlay new washes to intensify the underpainting. Leave some folds paler than others.*

14 *Using the no. 8 brush, paint more cobalt blue around the apples to make them stand out from the background. Work carefully, making sure that you do not disturb the blue paint.*

15 *Dip the no. 8 brush in cobalt blue and overlay more paint in the folds of the fabric to enhance the color and the thickness of the material. Allow the paint to run across the paper and pool naturally.*

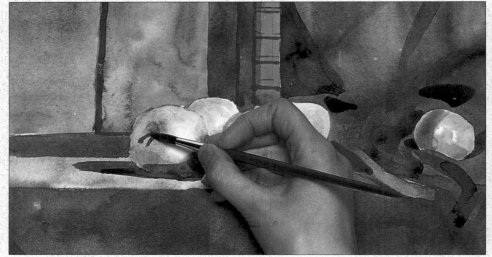

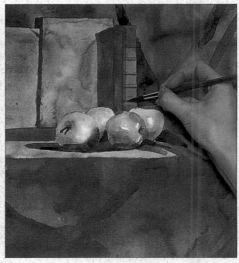

16 *Now define the details in the fruit and books. Dip the no. 8 brush in some burnt sienna and touch in the recesses around the stems of the apples.*

17 *Using the no. 8 brush and burnt sienna, paint lines across the spine of the book on the right to depict a traditional binding. Drop a little cobalt blue into the book on the left to add depth.*

The Finished Painting

The painting is now complete. The blue fabric unifies the image, linking the various shapes together. It is a recessive color and so does not dominate. The leatherbound books, painted using a combination of flat and variegated washes, contain depth and texture. The apples provide a sharp focus, their cooler temperature and sharper highlights adding a crucial contrast to the warm, soft tones of the leather and fabric.

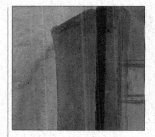

Shadow and depth are conveyed by means of the tonal variation between each book. In each case the paint was applied while the adjoining washes were still damp, so there is some bleeding.

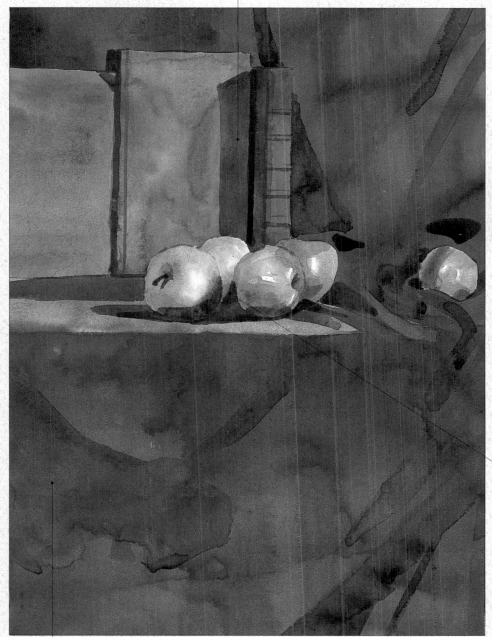

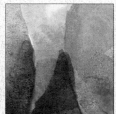

The apples received a variety of treatments. They were painted wet into wet, then wet into damp. Finally details were marked in wet over dry paint. The variegated blue wash around the apples helps to define their shapes, enabling them to stand out from the background.

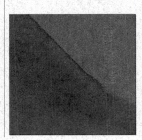

The fabric is made up of a combination of variegated washes and overlays of paint. Make sure, however, that you do not overlay so much color that you lose the fresh, light feeling.

Sponging

APPLYING PAINT with a sponge rather than with a brush is an excellent and very simple method of creating texture and tone. Two types of sponges are readily available: natural and synthetic. Each produces a slightly different effect. A natural sponge is more randomly textured than its synthetic equivalent and creates a more varied finish. A synthetic sponge produces softer results and is better suited to suggesting atmosphere, perhaps in clouds or mist over a landscape.

The size of the sponge also makes a difference. It is best to start with a piece of sponge that fits comfortably into the palm of your hand as this makes it easier to control where you place your sponging marks. Cut the sponge down to size if necessary. If you want to sponge a large area, use a bigger sponge for broader strokes, although you will probably find that the resulting texture is less even than with a small sponge.

Sponging may be done on wet or dry paper and over wet washes or ones that have dried. On damp paper the marks will merge together. On dry paper the marks are more sharply defined. If the paper is too wet, however, the sponge will not create a texture. Dampen a sponge in clean water, squeeze it almost dry and dip it into your chosen mix of paint and then gently press it over the area of the paper that you want to texture. Lift the sponge off the paper cleanly, unless you intend to create a smudged effect. Always wash out your sponges with warm, soapy water before they dry. Rinse them thoroughly and make sure that no traces of paint remain inside the sponge.

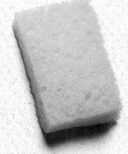
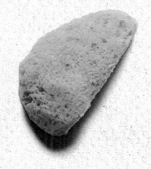

Natural Sponge
A natural sponge is hard to the touch when dry. It becomes softer when wet and is more absorbent than a synthetic sponge.

Synthetic Sponge
A synthetic sponge has a regular pattern. It creates a more sharply defined texture than a natural sponge, especially over a dry wash.

Synthetic Sponge on Dry Paper
Dip a synthetic sponge into diluted French ultramarine blue paint. Gently blot it onto dry paper. The result is textured but soft. Some areas of the paint dry to a crisp edge, while others blend into one another.

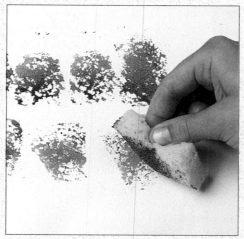

Natural Sponge on Dry Paper
Dip a natural sponge into diluted Hooker's green paint and gently blot it onto dry paper. The result is coarsely textured, with the paint sticking like granules to the surface of the paper.

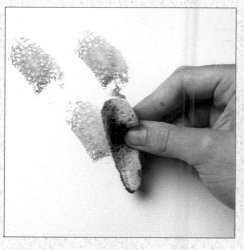

Synthetic Sponge on Wet Paper
Paint a dilute yellow ochre wash over the paper. While it is still damp, blot diluted French ultramarine blue paint onto the paper as before. The paint blurs and mingles with the underlying wash to produce a softer effect than on dry paper.

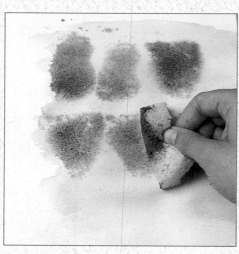

Natural Sponge on Wet Paper
Paint a dilute yellow wash over the paper. While it is still damp, blot diluted Hooker's green onto it with your natural sponge. The result is softer than that of sponging over dry paper but crisper than that of using a synthetic sponge on damp paper.

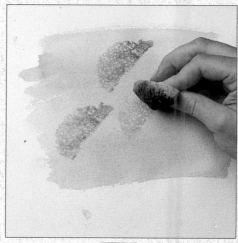

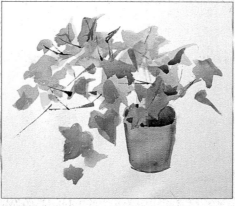

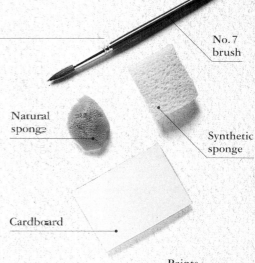

No. 7
brush

Natural
sponge

Synthetic
sponge

Cardboard

The Plant
Because the leaves of this ivy plant are variegated in color, sponging is a perfect way to create texture and overlay additional hues.

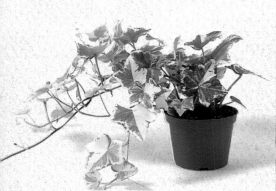

1 *With a no. 7 brush, paint the leaves (Hooker's green, viridian and lemon yellow) and pot (burnt umber and burnt sienna). Dip the edge of a piece of cardboard in viridian and press on the paper for stems.*

Paints
Hooker's green
Viridian
Lemon yellow
Burnt umber
Burnt sienna

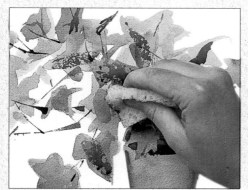

2 *While your underpainting is still damp, dip a synthetic sponge into a dilute mix of Hooker's green and sponge over some of the leaves. The sponge will absorb a lot of paint, so be sure to prepare enough.*

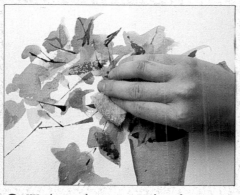

3 *Wash out the sponge. When the painting has dried, reload the sponge with lemon yellow paint. Use a lot of pigment so that it retains its color intensity when dry. Repeat the sponging exercise, concentrating on areas you want to highlight.*

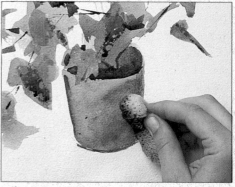

4 *Combine burnt umber and burnt sienna to make a more pigmented mix of the color used for the pot. Sponge over the pot with a natural sponge to create a shadow area down its right edge.*

The Finished Painting
This painting demonstrates the versatility of the sponging technique. Where the pot was still damp when paint was applied with a piece of natural sponge, the paint has blurred, giving a softly shadowed effect. The texture is more varied than you could have achieved with a synthetic sponge. In contrast, where the lemon yellow paint was applied to dry paper with a synthetic sponge, the effect is more grainy.

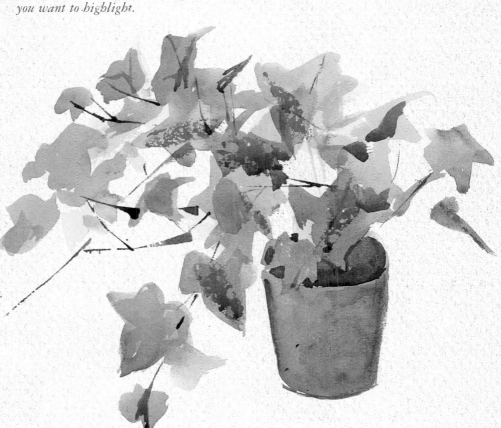

Spattering

B Y SPATTERING PAINT across an image you can create a variety of textures and tones, which is especially useful when you want to suggest depth or highlights. Spattering is done by loading a toothbrush with paint and pulling a plastic palette knife or your thumb toward you over the bristles so that they flick, or spatter, paint onto the painting in a random spray. The further away from the paper you hold the toothbrush, the wider the area you will cover with spatter marks. The amount of water in your paint mix affects the size of the spatter marks, too, with larger marks resulting from a very wet mix. You will also find that you make larger marks when you spatter onto damp paper, as the paint specks spread. Test the technique first on a piece of scrap paper to see how much pressure you need to apply to the bristles and how far away from the paper you should hold the toothbrush to get the effect you want. A light, even spray from a toothbrush held high above the paper is perfect for depicting sandy beaches, while a heavier spatter from a more heavily-loaded brush is good for pebbly or rocky terrains. You may wish to apply a second color on top of the first. To avoid coloring areas of the paper you want to keep clean, mask them off before you begin (see pp. 62–65). For very precise spots of color, use a different method such as stippling (see pp. 54–55).

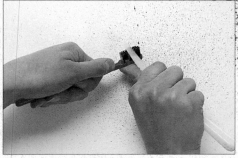

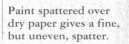

Paint spattered over dry paper gives a fine, but uneven, spatter.

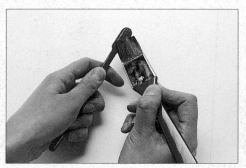

Loading the Toothbrush
Use a broad flat brush to apply paint to the toothbrush bristles before spattering, so that you do not have to keep returning to the palette for extra paint.

Spattering with a Knife
Hold the toothbrush over the paper, pointing toward the area you want to spatter. Pull a plastic palette knife through the bristles to spray the paint.

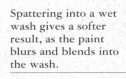

Spattering into a wet wash gives a softer result, as the paint blurs and blends into the wash.

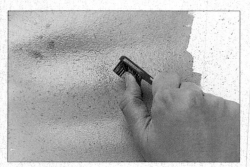

Spatter with your Thumb
For more control over the direction of the spray, pull back the bristles of the toothbrush with your thumb.

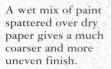

A wet mix of paint spattered over dry paper gives a much coarser and more uneven finish.

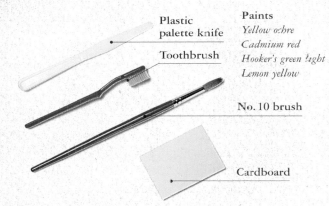

Plastic
palette knife

Toothbrush

No. 10 brush

Cardboard

Paints
Yellow ochre
Cadmium red
Hooker's green light
Lemon yellow

Surface Texture

These oranges have a rough skin, and although they are colored orange all over, there is some gradation in tone. By using various weights of spatter, over both wet and dry paint, you can achieve depth and add interest to the fruit. Each type of spatter produces different results.

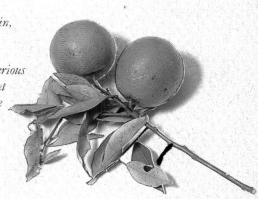

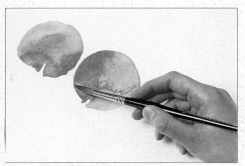

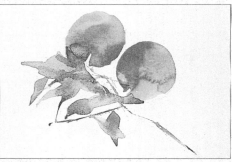

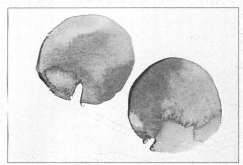

1 *After you have drawn in the shapes of the oranges with a pencil, apply a light, flat orange wash made from yellow ochre and cadmium red with a no. 10 brush.*

2 *Paint the leaves with a mix of Hooker's green light and lemon yellow. For the stems, dip the edge of a piece of cardboard in the paint and press it onto the paper.*

3 *Cut out a mask from a piece of water-color paper, and use it to cover everything but the oranges. The mask protects the areas in which you do not want spatter to appear.*

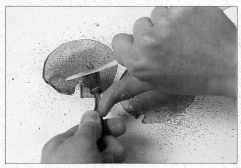

4 *Load cadmium red and Hooker's green light onto the toothbrush with a paint-brush. Drag a plastic palette knife across the bristles to spatter paint over the oranges.*

The paint blurs when spatter is applied to a damp surface.

Spatter applied to dry paper leaves sharply defined paint marks.

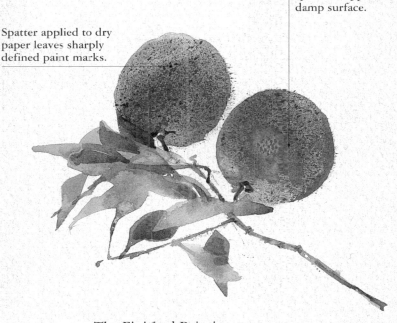

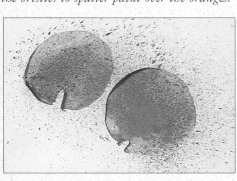

5 *Leave the paper mask in place until you are sure that the spatter marks have completely dried so that you do not accidentally smudge the paint.*

The Finished Painting

The pitted texture of the orange is revealed. Random spattering produced a lively quality that might not be achieved by a more precise and careful rendering.

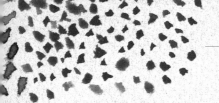

Stippling

STIPPLING IS A TECHNIQUE in which dots of color are applied to the paper with the tip of a brush. You can use a stipple brush to create large areas of dots as you do in stencilling. Alternatively, as in this demonstration, you can use any watercolor brush with a fine point to place individual dots exactly where you want them. As more dots are stippled onto the paper, textures and tones are built up. The technique is slower but easier to control than spattering, and you can create very elaborate patterns and effects this way. You can use just one paint color to produce subtle gradations of tone, simply by altering the size and weight of each dot that you make, or you can combine differently colored dots in patterns. You can stipple directly onto white paper or over a wet or dry wash. The less space you leave between the dots, the denser the color will appear; the more space you leave, the

more light will reflect through. The technique is particularly effective for painting small textured objects such as pebbles and stones.

Stippling was popular with the French Pointillist School, led by Georges Seurat (1859–91). Their technique focused on the relationships between neighboring colors and the light that reflects off them. The Pointillists discovered that the way colors merge in the viewer's eye depends on where the colors are positioned in relation to each other. When complementary colors (see pp. 32–33) are placed next to one another – orange and blue, for example – the two colors appear to vibrate. The Pointillists also discovered that the farther away from a stippled image the viewer stands, the more the dots seem to merge, creating additional hues. This effect is known as optical mixing.

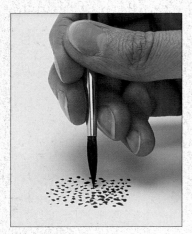

Even Stippling
To produce even stippling, dip an almost dry brush into a thick mix of watercolor paint, making sure that you keep the bristles in a point. Hold the brush vertically and dot the surface of the paper, applying very little pressure.

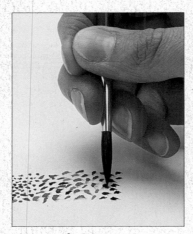

Less Definition
Repeat the exercise using a wetter mix of paint. The dots are not as sharply defined, and the tone varies from one to another. There is also more variation in the size of the dots.

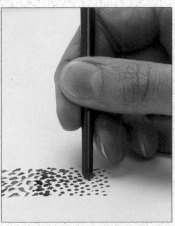

Flatter Results
To produce flatter, more rounded and even results, turn the brush upside down and dip the end of the handle into a thick mix of paint. Quickly but firmly dot the handle down onto the paper.

Stipple Effects
By using brushes of different sizes, working with the handle of the brush instead of the tip, and varying the distance between the dots and the amount of pressure you apply, you can build a wide range of stipple effects. Experiment with the effect of juxtaposing different colors. Try stippling one color on top of or next to another while the paint is still wet: the colors will merge together and create a very different effect from stippling on top of dry paint.

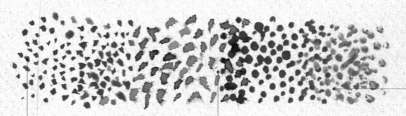

This section was stippled using the end of the brush handle. The paint is quite tacky. The dots become more uneven as the paint gives out.

By loading different amounts of paint onto the brush and varying the amount of pressure you apply to it, you can create dots that vary in weight.

Blending more than one color together produces depth and texture. Where two dots of different colors merge, a third color may be produced.

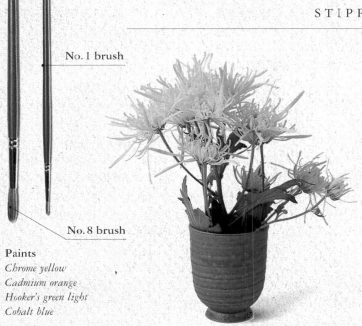

No. 1 brush

No. 8 brush

Paints
Chrome yellow
Cadmium orange
Hooker's green light
Cobalt blue

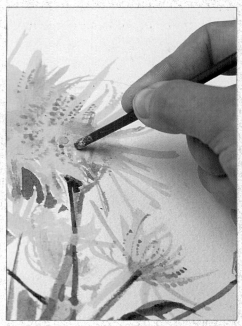

Localized Stippling
These chrysanthemums make a good subject for localized areas of stippling. Start by making a simple watercolor sketch using a no. 8 brush. Paint the flower heads in chrome yellow, with a touch of cadmium orange added to the spiky petals. For the stalks, use a light and a dark mix of Hooker's green light and chrome yellow. Paint the vase with a mix of Hooker's green light and cobalt blue.

1 *Using a no. 1 brush, stipple in the stamens in the center of each flower head, using a thick mix of cadmium orange and chrome yellow paint.*

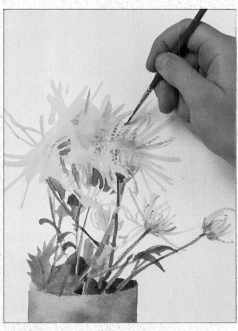

2 *Take the end of the brush handle and dip it into the same mix of paint. Carefully apply much finer dots around the same areas of the flower heads to suggest particles of pollen.*

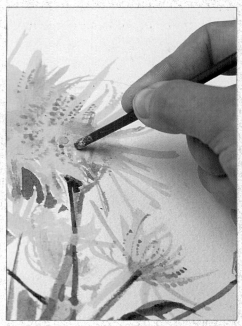

3 *Take the mix of Hooker's green light and cobalt blue that you used for the vase, and add more blue paint to it, until it becomes a much deeper shade of green. Now use this color to stipple marks over the surface of the vase. The texture of the vase is uneven, so make sure you vary the size and weight of the dots.*

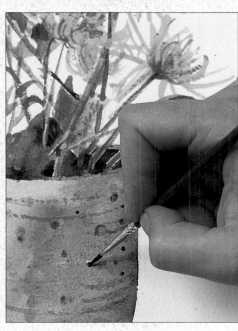

The Finished Painting
Different results were produced in each area of stippling. The light and delicate appearance of the flower heads is achieved by using the tip of the brush and the end of the brush handle. On the vase, irregular stippling with the tip of the brush created form and texture on top of a heavy and solid surface.

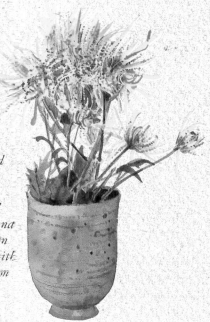

Drybrush

THE DRYBRUSH TECHNIQUE is more akin to drawing than to painting. It can be used to achieve crisply defined masses of lines. The term *drybrush* is a misnomer, because the paint is wet – a brush can never be completely dry in watercolor painting. But by starting out with a brush that is completely dry and then not putting too much paint on it, you can create a very different effect from that produced by flooding paint across the paper. If you splay the bristles of the brush between your thumb and forefinger and drag it across the paper, you can create a delicate feathering effect.

The less paint you apply to the brush, the crisper the effect on the paper. If you are working on dry, rough watercolor paper, the drybrush technique will create a textured effect, with the paint marking only the bumps in the paper, leaving the pits free of paint. On a non-textured piece of paper you will achieve a smoother look, but particles from the underlying paper are still likely to show through. The paint does not saturate the paper in the same way as it does with a wet wash. Drybrush is particularly useful for creating such features as tree bark and fences, but you will quickly discover other uses.

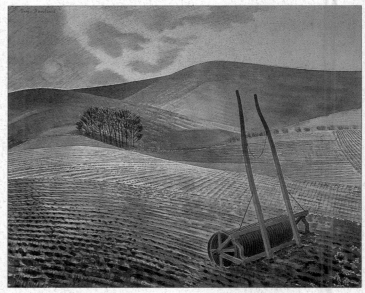

Downs in Winter, Eric Ravilious, 1903–1942
Eric Ravilious used drybrush to achieve a textured, grainy finish to the tilled land in the foreground of this painting, providing an effective contrast to the wet watercolor washes in the sky.

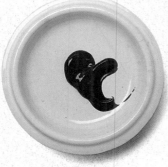

1 *Squeeze paint directly from the tube onto a palette. Do not add water, allowing the paint to retain its viscosity.*

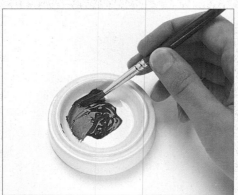

2 *Take a completely dry brush and dip it into the paint. Because the paint has not been mixed with water, the pigment is thick and will coat only the outer hairs, without penetrating deep into the brush.*

From Wet to Dry
You can also achieve a drybrush effect with a brush that has previously been used wet. Instead of reloading the brush, work across the paper until the brush runs out of paint.

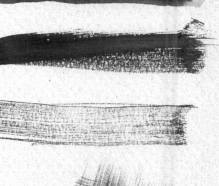

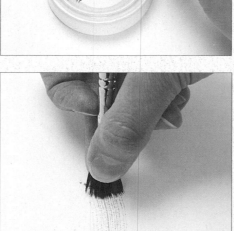

3 *Splay the bristles of the brush with your thumb, then drag the brush over rough watercolor paper. The paint will stick mostly consistently to the raised areas, leaving other parts white.*

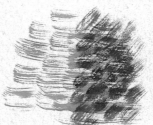

Two-color Texture
Apply a second color, with the brushstrokes running in a different direction, to create texture.

Closely Woven Texture
Crosshatching – making a second series of marks at 90 degrees to the first – creates a closely woven texture.

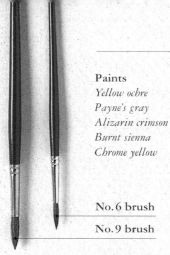

Paints
Yellow ochre
Payne's gray
Alizarin crimson
Burnt sienna
Chrome yellow

No. 6 brush

No. 9 brush

Winter Landscape

This scene allows you to experiment with drybrush on both wet and dry areas. Applied to dried washes, drybrush marks appear spiky. In contrast, when applied over damp washes, they blur and provide a softer effect, which is perfect for painting the reflections shown here.

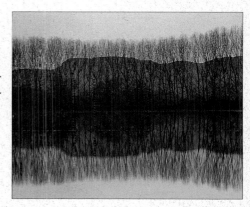

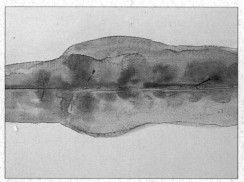

1 *Lay a diluted yellow ochre wash across the top third of the paper, then let it dry. Lay a mix of Payne's gray and alizarin crimson across the middle third for the hill and its reflection. Allow to dry.*

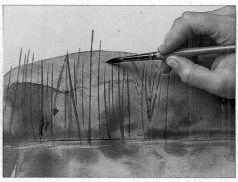

2 *Dip a no. 6 brush in Payne's gray, and squeeze it almost dry. To represent the tree trunks on the shoreline, paint fine vertical lines.*

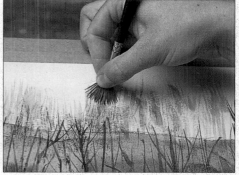

3 *Dip a no. 9 brush in diluted burnt sienna and squeeze it almost dry. Splay the bristles of the brush between your thumb and forefinger, and make feathered strokes over the yellow wash just above the hill.*

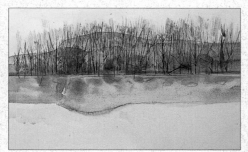

4 *Apply a wet chrome yellow wash over the bottom third of the paper. Tip the board to allow the paint to flow freely across the surface.*

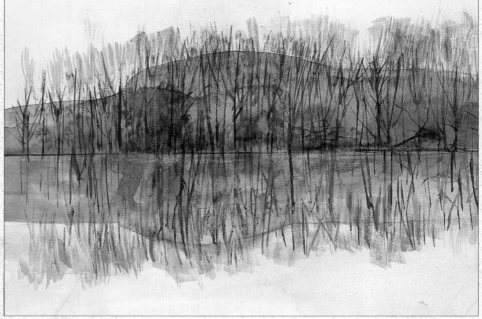

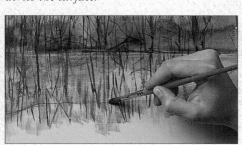

5 *While the bottom third is still slightly damp, paint the reflections using feathered and fine vertical strokes as before. Note how the effect is far softer on the damp chrome yellow wash.*

The Finished Painting

Using the drybrush technique on top of flat, dry washes gives a spiky, yet delicate quality to the silhouetted trunks and branches of the trees on the shoreline. On the damp wash at the bottom of the paper the effect is muted, almost blurred – perfect for these subtle, gently rippling reflections.

Practice your Technique

Texturing Effects

Now you are ready to combine fundamental wash techniques with the more unusual effects you have been practicing. Sponging, spattering, stippling, and drybrush are all excellent texturing methods, and they can be used to enhance the coarse, uneven surfaces of the gravel and sea creatures shown here. They can be used both in specific areas and to create an overall mood.

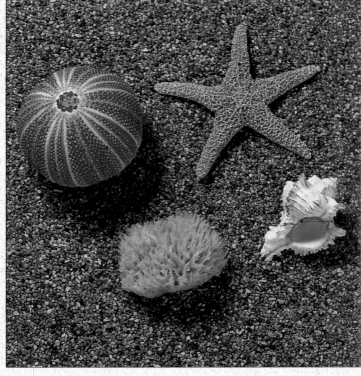

The starfish has an uneven surface, which can be emphasized by sponging techniques.

The fine spots that cover the surface of the sea urchin are best shown by stippling.

Employ drybrush to emphasize the dry, bonelike quality of the shell.

No. 6 brush

Toothbrush

Natural sponge

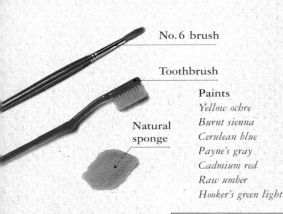

Paints
Yellow ochre
Burnt sienna
Cerulean blue
Payne's gray
Cadmium red
Raw umber
Hooker's green light

1 *Mark in the four shapes of the sea creatures. An outline is sufficient: your drawing does not need to be very detailed. Inset: Using a damp sponge, wet the shapes of the sea urchin, starfish, and sponge.*

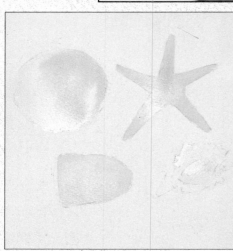

2 *Make up a wet wash of yellow ochre and burnt sienna, and lightly touch this color into the areas occupied by the sea urchin, starfish, and sponge with a no. 6 brush. Allow the paint to spread and bleed into the damp surfaces, wet into wet. Do not make the washes too flat.*

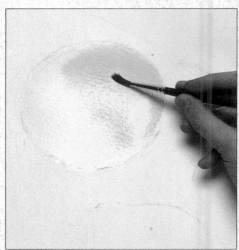

3 *The three shapes should be lightly tinted by the washes. Do not make the color too strong, as you will paint over the shapes later. The yellow ochre and burnt sienna create a warm tone on these three objects, in contrast to the cooler tone of the shell.*

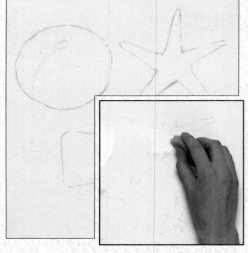

4 *Touch a light wash of cerulean blue and Payne's gray, wet into damp, onto the underside of the sea urchin, natural sponge, and starfish to create shading. The paint should bleed into the underlying washes.*

5 Mix up a wash of cerulean blue and, using the no. 6 brush, touch the paint, wet onto dry, over the raised areas of the shell to further develop the impression of form. As some areas of the shell are white, leave them free of paint. The paper will act as a color in its own right.

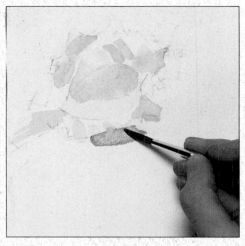

6 Allow the paint to dry. You can see that the sea urchin and the sponge are the least well defined, as the paint has bled extensively across their surfaces. By contrast, the starfish is already gaining a three-dimensional quality. The seashell still appears as an abstract form.

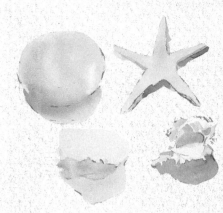

7 Using the no. 6 brush and a mix of burnt sienna and cadmium red, paint each segment of the sea urchin as a curved band. Do not overload your brush or the paint will spread and definition will be lost. Paint a dot to denote the hole at the top.

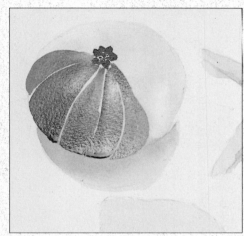

8 Make a mix of burnt sienna and raw umber and, using the brush touch dry, begin building up the form and tones of the starfish. Add a touch of Hooker's green light to the areas that are darkest in tone. Do not let the paint spread.

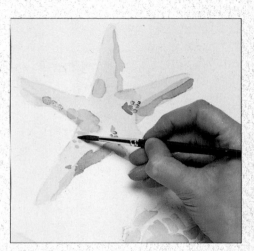

Progress Report

Continue to build up the forms of all four objects, using a mix of yellow ochre and cerulean blue to define the forms of the sponge and the seashell. The surfaces should be well defined by this stage. You are now ready to begin texturing, using stippling, spattering, and sponging techniques. Allow the paint to dry completely before continuing with the project.

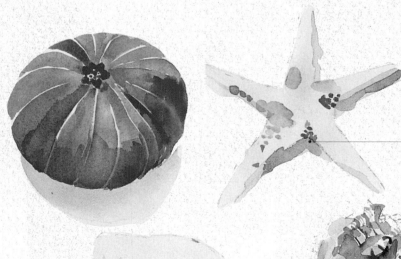

The starfish is flatter than the other objects so its shadow is not as deep. Although the shading is strong in tone, it is limited to a fine line around the tentacles.

Although the sponge is porous, it is a solid object, so you should make its shadow deep to emphasize its form. Add overlays of a light cerulean blue wash to create further depth if necessary.

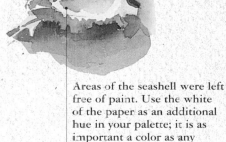

Areas of the seashell were left free of paint. Use the white of the paper as an additional hue in your palette; it is as important a color as any you can mix.

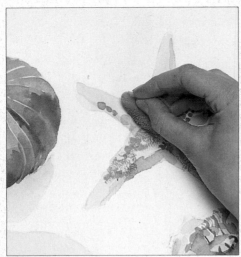

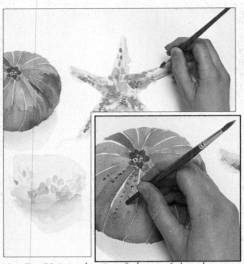

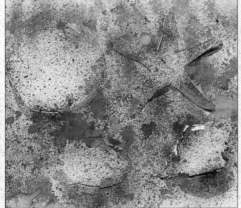

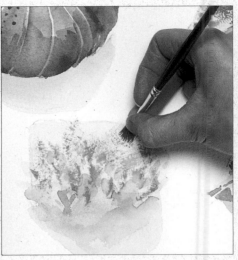

9 *Dip a natural sponge in a thick mix of burnt sienna and raw umber, and blot it over the surface of the starfish to create a mottled texture.*

10 *Using the tip of the no. 6 brush, stipple the individual spines that run down the starfish tentacles with yellow ochre. Inset: Use the handle of the brush to stipple a mix of cadmium red and raw umber down the segments of the sea urchin.*

11 *Dip the no. 6 brush into the yellow ochre. Spread out the bristles between your thumb and forefinger and feather the paint over the surface of the sponge. The brush should produce dry marks, creating texture and developing form.*

12 *Let the painting dry. Lay a thin piece of paper over the top of the image, then lightly trace the four objects. Cut out the paper shapes and place them over each form.*

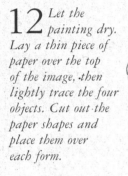

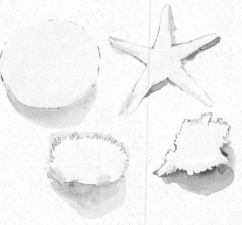

13 *Run your thumb along the bristles of a toothbrush and spatter very diluted yellow ochre across the background surface of the paper. Don't worry if the paint seeps underneath the paper shapes, as the gravel should overlap the sea creatures and integrate into the painting.*

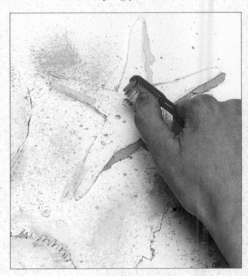

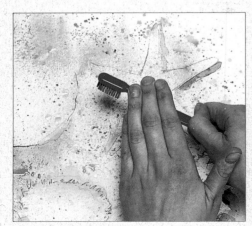

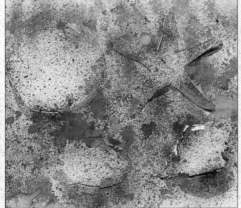

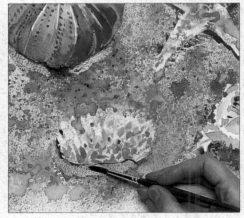

14 *Load the toothbrush with a thicker solution of raw umber and, turning it over, tap large spatters of paint over the yellow ochre. The two colors will merge slightly, but as the second color is thicker, it should retain some definition.*

15 *Make up a thick solution of Payne's gray, and spatter it over the previous colors while they are still damp. Use the two toothbrush methods shown in steps 13 and 14, taking care not to obscure the white of the paper completely.*

16 *When the paint is dry, remove the paper shapes. Define any areas that lack depth or color intensity. The sponge has merged into the background spatter, so add a little Payne's gray around the bottom edge to create a shadow and enhance its form.*

The Finished Painting

Although you overlaid a variety of colors onto the paper, the image remains fresh. The combination of washes and texturing techniques does not block the white of the paper; in fact, it sparkles through the paint. The random background spatter provokes a different mood from the more controlled stippling over the surface of the starfish and sea urchin. Sponging produces a far softer texture.

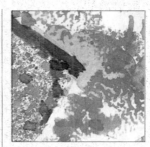

A combination of soft sponging and precise stippling on the starfish gives a three-dimensional feeling as well as conveying the coarse texture.

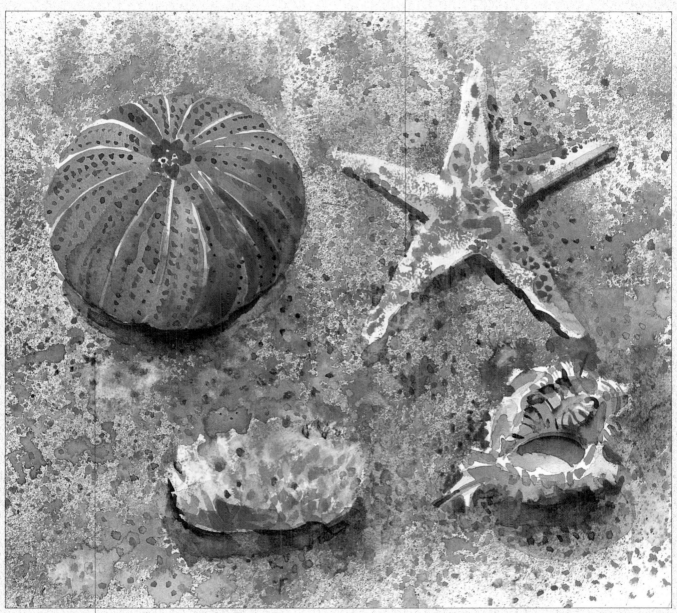

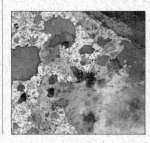

Although spattering is considered a random watercolor technique, you have a certain amount of control over it. By varying the density and color of the paint and the height at which you held the toothbrush away from the paper, you can achieve a variety of effects.

Masking

THE TERM MASK describes any substance that you place on your paper to prevent paint from touching specific areas. There are a number of reasons for using a mask. The first is to add highlights to your work. In pure watercolor painting, where you work from light to dark, you cannot apply white watercolor paint on top of a darker color. In order to include white in your painting, therefore, you have to make use of the whiteness of the paper. One way to do this is to cover up, or mask, specific areas so that the paint cannot touch them. You can also use a mask to block out a large area that you want to remain white, such as a white T-shirt.

Another use of masks is to protect an area on which paint has already been laid down so that another color does not seep into that area and muddy its luminosity. Masks are invaluable in achieving a clean separation between neighbouring color washes – for example, in separating the sky from fields in a landscape.

There are a number of masking media and techniques. Some methods give crisp, sharp lines, while others produce softer, less sharply defined edges. One of the most commonly used masking media is masking fluid. It comes in a bottle and you apply it to the watercolor paper with a brush. You can buy either clear or slightly toned masking fluid. The benefit of the latter is that you can see it even when you have painted over it. Masking fluid is brushed onto the paper in the same way as paint, although it is a thicker substance and, as a result, flows more slowly. It is a perfect way to create white details and highlights in a painting. But always remember to wash out your brush with warm, soapy water as soon as you have finished applying the fluid – otherwise the fluid will harden on the brush and could easily ruin it. When you have finished painting and the paint is completely dry, gently rub off the masking fluid with your fingertips to reveal the white paper beneath.

Masking tape is good for covering larger areas and for situations in which you want a less precise rendering of highlights and whites on the paper. Buy low-tack masking tape instead of the heavily gummed tape used for office applications: it will not damage the surface of the paper when applied. For hard edges or wide strips of white, cut masking tape from the roll. For less crisp and more feathered lines and areas of white, tear it from the roll. When your painting is dry, gently peel off the masking tape. If the tape is firmly stuck down, you may find it helpful to lift up one edge of the masking tape with the tip of a craft knife blade.

Cut Masking Tape

Sharp Edges and Smooth Lines
By cutting masking tape into sections, you can create sharply defined shapes and areas. You may wish to cut into the tape in order to achieve a bend or a curve. If you are careful, you can create smooth lines with this method.

Masking tape

Craft knife

1 *Cut masking tape to the length and angles you require, and place it down firmly on the paper.* Inset: *Cut out shapes with a craft knife and place them on the paper. Make sure that the edges are firmly attached so that paint will not seep under them.*

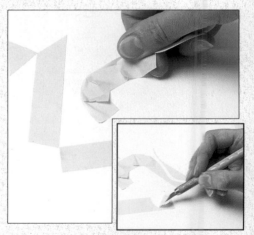

2 *Apply a wash over the tape. (You may wish to experiment with more than one color.) When the wash is completely dry, carefully peel off the masking tape.*

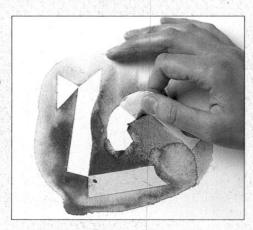

The Finished Result
Masking tape gives extremely crisp results. Make sure that the paint is completely dry before you remove the tape, otherwise it may smudge and ruin the sharp edges you set out to create.

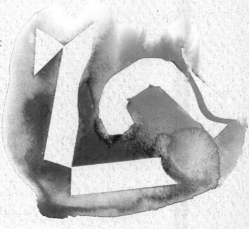

Torn Masking Tape

Soft, Feathered Edges

By tearing the masking tape, rather than cutting it with a knife, you can create softer edges, as the watercolor paint will move more freely within the tear lines and a little paint may even seep under the tape. You may have less control over the direction in which your paint flows, but this random quality can be useful for atmospheric subjects, such as blustery winter skies.

Masking tape

1 *Lay torn masking tape over the areas you want to cover. You may wish to crisscross strips over one another. Try varying the width of the tape pieces.*

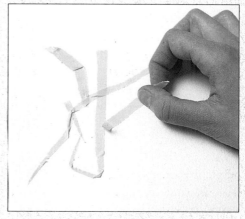

2 *As in the previous example, apply a wash of paint over the torn masking tape and leave it to dry. Then carefully remove the masking tape. You may find it easier to lift up the edge of the tape with the tip of a craft knife blade.*

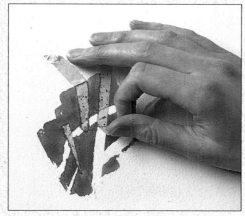

The Finished Result

The torn tape leaves lines that vary in thickness and shape. Torn tape produces softer edges than cut tape.

Masking Fluid

Total Freedom and Control

Masking fluid is by far the most versatile of the masking media. Apply it with an old brush in exactly the same way you brush on paint; you will find that you can create any thickness or shape of line you want. Masking fluid must be allowed to dry completely before you paint over it or the effect will be ruined. Remember, too, that the fluid can ruin your brushes. Always wash them out in warm, soapy water immediately after use.

Brush for masking

Masking fluid

1 *Brush masking fluid onto the paper as if it were paint. You can use masking fluid for both broad lines and very fine details, but be careful not to overload your brush or you will lose control over the fluid.*

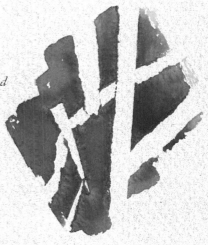

2 *Allow the masking fluid to dry, then apply a wash over it. When the paint is completely dry, gently rub off the masking fluid with your fingers.*

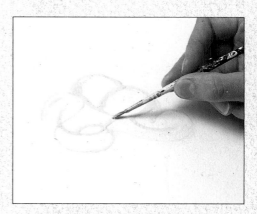

The Finished Result

With masking fluid you can achieve far more varied and subtle effects than with either cut or torn masking tape, from the finest lines and most intricate marks to broad areas.

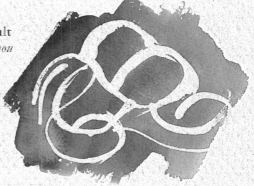

THERE ARE A NUMBER of other masking media that you can use in your work. Wax is an obvious mask for use with watercolor paints: because it is waterproof, any waterbased paint will be unable to penetrate it. Candles and wax crayons work equally well; you can use either white or colored ones to achieve the effect you want. There is one crucial difference between wax and masking tape or fluid: wax is a permanent resist and it cannot be removed at a later stage to show off the whiteness of the paper. Another important difference is that wax can be used to create texture: wax is often used in watercolor painting to give texture to areas of foliage.

The final method of masking is to trace the area you want to cover and place a cut-out paper stencil of the same shape over the paper. With this type of mask, however, there is a risk of paint seeping under the mask and onto the area that you want to protect. If you want to make sure that areas remain covered, it is best to choose another masking medium. If you simply want to cover up one area for a short period of time, using a paper cut-out is a good option.

A word of warning: don't be too quick to remove masking fluid or tape once you have finished your work. Allow your painting to dry completely before you unmask it so that there is no risk of you accidentally smudging the paint. This way you will achieve the crispest lines, the brightest highlights, and the most sparkling results.

Masking for Light Areas

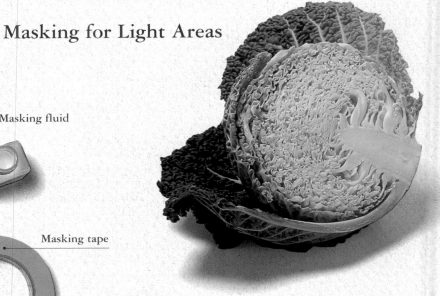

Paints
Viridian
Cadmium yellow
Hooker's green light

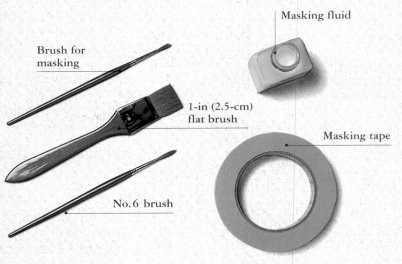

Brush for masking

Masking fluid

1-in (2.5-cm) flat brush

Masking tape

No. 6 brush

Texture and Light
The cabbage's surface is full of tiny crevices and variations in texture and tone. There is also a range of lights and darks. All these elements will benefit from masking techniques.

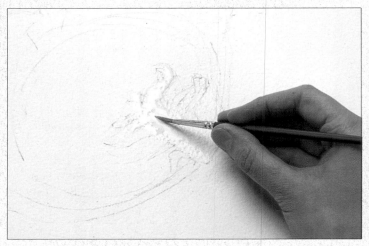

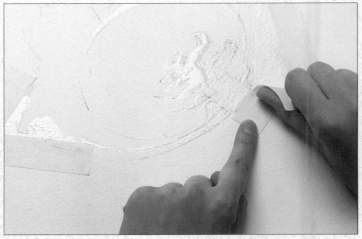

1 *Make a pencil sketch of the cabbage, paying attention to where the light and dark tones and changes in texture occur. Paint the pale base of the cabbage with masking fluid, and allow it to dry. When you paint over the masking fluid, you will still be able to see where it lies underneath.*

2 *Paint the veins on the dark outer leaves in masking fluid. Cut a curve of masking tape, and place it on the paper between the inner and outer sections of the cabbage. It does not matter if the masking tape is slightly torn, as an irregular edge will enhance the textural variation between the leaves.*

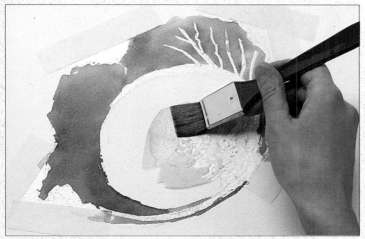

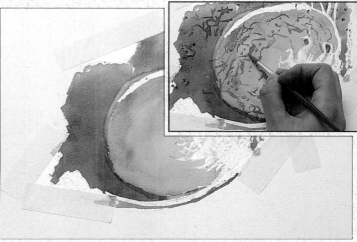

3 Make up a wet wash of each of the three colors in your palette. Using the flat brush, paint viridian on the outer leaves and overlay this with cadmium yellow. Toward the center, paint on a very pale mix of Hooker's green light and cadmium yellow.

4 Continue to overlay paint to build up the colors, retaining a pale center and darker outer leaves. Allow the paint to drift at the edges to create an uneven curve. Inset: Once the paint is dry, use a no. 6 brush to add details in viridian paint.

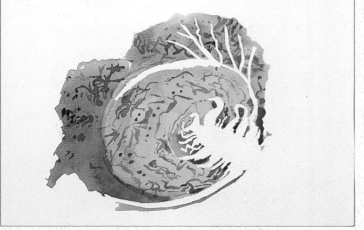

5 Allow the image to dry completely. Remove the masks by carefully rubbing off the fluid and peeling back the tape to reveal the white paper underneath.

Masking tape, cut to the appropriate shape, is used to define the outer rim of the middle section of the cabbage. By separating the outer and inner sections in this way, you create a sense of depth.

The use of masking fluid allows delicate areas, such as the veins on the outer leaves, to be protected from paint until the final stages of the painting.

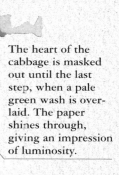

The Finished Painting
Masking fluid and tape have allowed some areas to be left free of paint, thus increasing the tonal contrasts within the painting. These contrasts help to make the cabbage appear three-dimensional.

The heart of the cabbage is masked out until the last step, when a pale green wash is over-laid. The paper shines through, giving an impression of luminosity.

Opaque Effects

WATERCOLOR PAINT is a transparent or semi-transparent medium. Its translucency is one of its greatest attributes, as it allows the white of the underlying paper to show through. However, there may be occasions when you want to apply a light color over a dark one, or produce highlights over an area that has already been painted with a dark wash of color. The solution is to use a type of paint known as gouache: this enables you to obtain results that would be impossible with pure watercolor paint. Gouache, like watercolor paint, is water based. Unlike watercolor paint, however, it is opaque and therefore any underlying color will not show through. The opacity of gouache offers a dramatic contrast to the translucency of pure watercolor paint, bringing an extra dimension to your work. You can buy it ready mixed in a wide range of colors.

The gouache most commonly used in conjunction with watercolor paint is Chinese white. Mix it on your palette with a conventional watercolor paint and you will obtain an opaque, milky alternative to the transparent hue. Alternatively, you can use Chinese white as a color in its own right, to block in highlights or to paint in a white subject on top of a dark underlying color.

Gouache can be used thick (straight from the tube) or thinned with water. The amount of water you use affects how opaque the gouache is. Certain colors are more opaque than others, and some become semiopaque when mixed with large quantities of water. Although it is not a pure watercolor medium, gouache was popular with such watercolor masters as J.M.W. Turner, Edgar Degas, and Henri Matisse. Use gouache sparingly, however: if you overuse it, it will mask the translucency of the paper and make your work look heavy and lifeless.

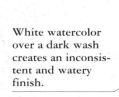

1-in (2.5-cm)
flat brush

No. 7 brush

No. 1 brush

Chinese white gouache

Cardboard

Black
India
ink

Paints
Hooker's green light
French ultramarine blue
Chrome yellow

Light on Dark

Because of the translucency of the paint, in conventional watercolor painting it is impossible to apply a light color on top of a dark one without the underlying color showing through. Gouache, however, is opaque and dense and will completely cover any underlying color, enabling you to create highlights and light areas with ease.

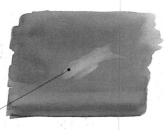

White watercolor over a dark wash creates an inconsistent and watery finish.

By using Chinese white gouache instead, a strong block of opaque paint renders the area bright white.

Swan
Using traditional watercolor techniques, you would need to mask out the swan before painting the dark blue watercolor washes. By using Chinese white gouache straight from the tube, you can paint a light area on top.

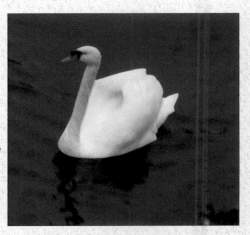

1 *Apply a variegated wash of Hooker's green light and French ultramarine blue with a 1-in (2.5-cm) flat brush. Inset: Dip the edge of a piece of cardboard into the paint and make horizontal marks to suggest ripples on the water. Allow to dry.*

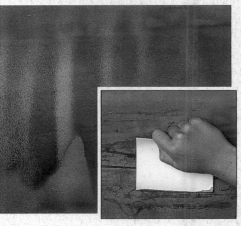

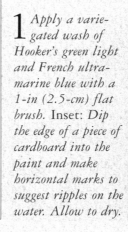

2 Load a no. 7 brush with undiluted Chinese white gouache straight from the tube, and mark in the general shape of the swan. Because the paint is so thick, it will block out the color of the wash beneath it and dry to an opaque finish. Allow the Chinese white gouache to dry.

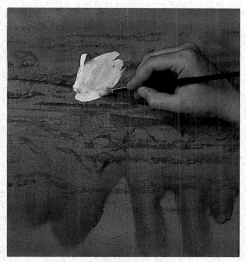

3 Mix a touch of French ultramarine blue into some Chinese white gouache on your palette to produce an off-white hue, and use it to add detailing to the swan's body and wings. Use pure Chinese white gouache for the highlight areas such as the tip of the tail feathers.

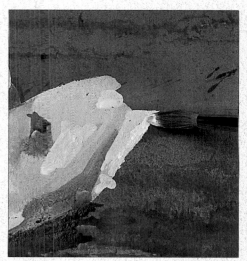

4 Use a no. 1 brush to paint in the swan's beak with Chinese white gouache. When it has completely dried, paint over the beak with a thin wash of chrome yellow. Then clean the brush, dip it in black India ink, and fill in the details of the bird's eye and beak.

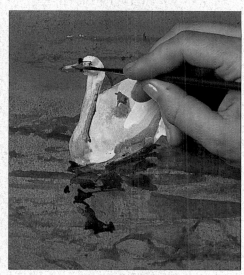

5 Using the no. 1 brush dipped once again in black India ink, draw a line down the length of the swan's neck to make it appear more three-dimensional. Use the same technique around the bird's tail feathers so that they seem to be layered on top of one another.

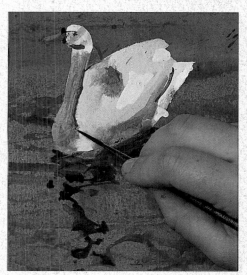

The Finished Painting
The painting is now complete. The white swan contrasts well with the translucent quality of the blue water and the deep shadow painted around it. The combination emphasizes both the fluidity of the water and the solidity of the swan.

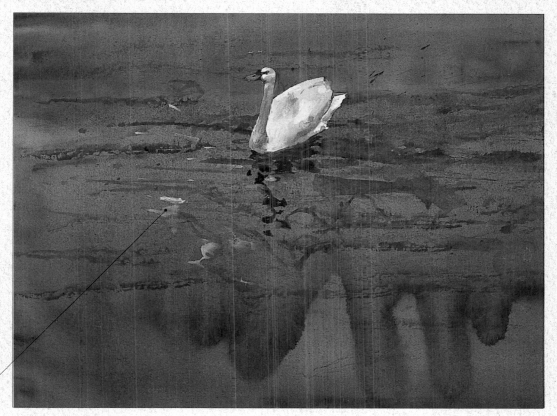

Broken marks of Chinese white gouache on top of the blue wash create the impression of movement in the water's surface.

Additives

YOU CAN CHANGE the properties of watercolor paint by mixing it with other substances. The range of possible additives – things that you add to the paint – is very wide. Some additives slow down the paint's drying time, while others speed it up. The amount by which you accelerate or decelerate the paint's drying time depends on how much of the substance you add. Other substances change the character of the paint, making it more glossy and viscous, or more opaque.

Additives that slow down the drying time of paint are called retarders. Different retarders affect the look of the paint in different ways, but they all enable you to spend more time exploiting the qualities of wet paint without worrying that it will dry before you have finished. The most common retarder is glycerin. By adding only a very small quantity – a few drops – to the water you are going to use with your paint, you will notice a great difference. Glycerin makes the paint more gluelike and malleable, so you can control it better on the paper. Gum arabic is another popular retarding medium. It can be mixed in varying quantities with watercolor paint to create some interesting effects. It also makes the paint appear more gelatinous and transparent. In fact, when gum arabic is used, the paint looks more like an oil glaze than a layer of conventional watercolor.

Honey that is mixed with water before being mixed into paint creates a similar effect to gum arabic. Again, it retards the drying time of the paint, enabling you to spend more time working wet into wet. When dry, the paint looks more intense in color and more luminous.

To speed up the drying time of watercolor paint, add either oxgall or rubbing alcohol to the paint. These are handy alternatives to the common practice of using a hair dryer. Of course, for outdoor painting, one of these additives is also more practical.

To alter the texture of your watercolor painting, try adding salt to a wet wash. Allow it to dry and then brush it away. It will lift out areas of the paint and is a useful way of creating highlights. The resulting texture can be utilized to suggest clouds in the sky or waves in the sea. Sand is a good substitute, but you may not be able to remove every last particle from the paint once it has dried.

Gum Arabic for Shiny Finish

Adding gum arabic to your watercolor paint has two effects: it slows down the drying time of the paint, giving you longer to work on creating your image, and it turns your translucent watercolor paint into a glutinous, shiny mixture that is perfect for recreating surfaces such as varnished wood. In this example, a 50:50 mix of gum arabic and watercolor paint was painted over the surface of the wooden board upon which the flowers are positioned. Inset: To create texture in this slow-drying paint, scrape your fingernails through it while it is still damp. You can move the paint around to create an interesting pattern of whorls in the wood. You might prefer to experiment with other implements such as a comb to produce finer lines or the end of your brush to produce more even lines.

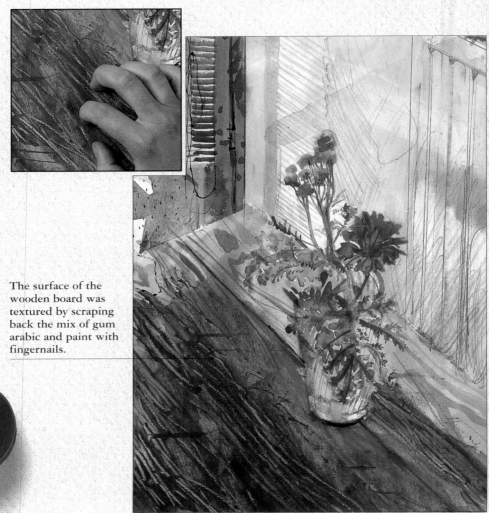

The surface of the wooden board was textured by scraping back the mix of gum arabic and paint with fingernails.

Gum arabic

Salt for Granular Texture

You can use fine grains of salt or salt crystals as additives. The effect varies depending on which one you choose. A layer of fine salt takes out tiny particles of paint, producing an even but grainy surface. Large salt crystals lift out areas of paint more unevenly.

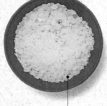

Salt

1 *Paint a flat wash using the color of your choice, making sure that you make the paper fairly wet with the paint.*

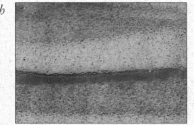

2 *While the paint is still wet, shake some salt crystals over the top of it in a random arrangement. Leave it to dry.*

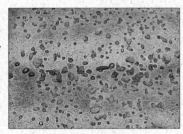

3 *When dry, gently brush or shake off the salt. The salt lifts out the color, leaving an unevenly textured surface.*

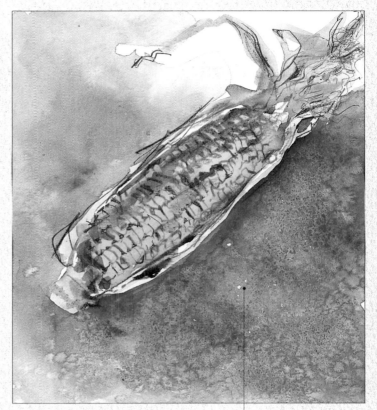

Textured Background

Large salt crystals were sprinkled over the blue background while it was still wet. Once the painting was dry the salt was removed, taking with it relatively large areas of paint and leaving behind a textured surface.

The granular surface of the blue background contrasts with the flatter finish of the areas to which water-color was applied conventionally.

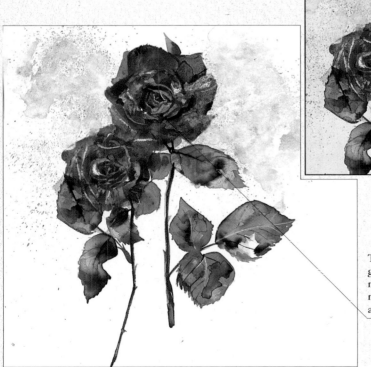

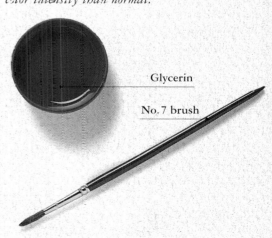

Glycerin to Retard Drying

A drop of glycerin mixed with your initial background watercolor wash slows down its drying time. Inset: In this example, while the initial wash was still damp, a rose was painted on top of it in pure watercolor paint and water. Normally, this paint would quickly be absorbed into the underlying wash, but adding glycerin gives you more time to manipulate your image. You will also find that the paint dries with a greater color intensity than normal.

The addition of glycerin to the petals makes them appear more intensely colored and slightly glossy.

Glycerin

No. 7 brush

Practice your Technique

Selecting a Technique

Now that you have mastered several techniques, your challenge is to decide which ones are most appropriate to your subject. This exercise gives you ample opportunity to practice color mixing, wet into wet, opaque effects, additives, or drybrush and other texturing techniques. The crisp outlines required around the head, legs, and tail feathers are a perfect chance to practice masking. Live animals move quickly, so painting from a photograph is your best option.

To enhance the sharp, spiky outline of the tail feathers and prevent the paint from spreading too far, use masking fluid.

The feathers are glossy. Add gum arabic to the paint to impart this quality to the finished work.

Brush for masking

Natural sponge

Gum arabic

No. 6 brush

Masking tape

Plastic palette knife

Masking fluid

Paints
*Cadmium yellow
Cadmium red
Burnt sienna
Payne's gray
Viridian
Burnt umber
Cerulean blue
Chinese white gouache
Rose madder*

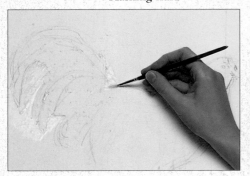

1 *First draw the rooster with an HB pencil, concentrating on the main shapes of the body, head, tail, legs, and feet. Then, using an old brush and masking fluid, outline the spiky tail feathers.*

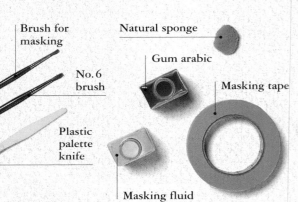

2 *Mask the outline of the breast feathers and the bird's underbelly with curves of cut masking tape. Fold and overlap the tape as in the earlier practice exercises (see pp. 62–63) to produce an even line.*

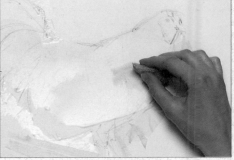

3 *Wet the surface of the bird's body with a natural sponge dipped in water. Then dip the sponge in cadmium yellow paint and press it onto the wet paper, allowing the color to spread randomly.*

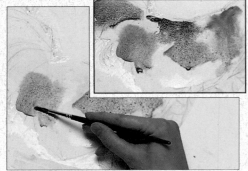

4 *Touch cadmium red and burnt sienna onto the body with a no. 6 brush. Inset: Add more wet-into-wet washes of Payne's gray, viridian, burnt umber, cerulean blue, and cadmium yellow.*

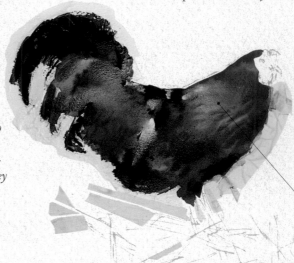

Progress Report

Colors are allowed to run and blend wet into wet over the surface of the paper. They underpin the main body colors and form of the bird. Details will be incorporated at a later stage.

The colors blend as they spread into one another, creating additional hues.

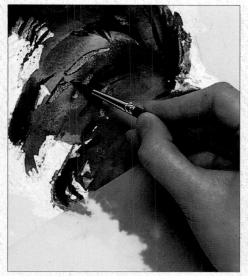

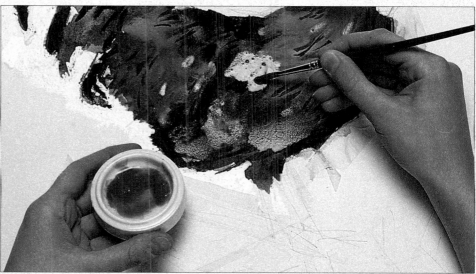

5 Allow the paint to dry, preferably for 24 hours. Now you can begin to add details by overlaying the same and other colors. You may find it helpful to place a piece of tracing paper under your hand to protect the image as you work.

6 The feathers on the bird's back gleam like oil where the light reflects off them. To enhance the glossiness, mix some gum arabic with burnt sienna and cadmium red and overlay it on these feathers.

The gum arabic retains its shine and brilliance when dry.

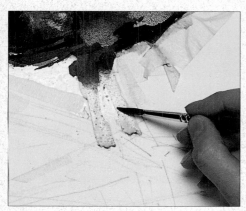

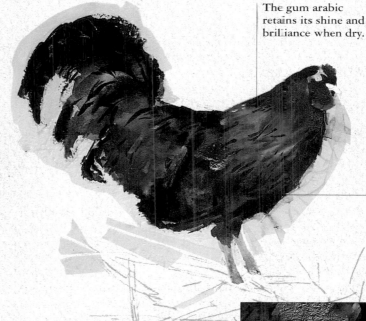

The feathers around the curve of the bird's breast, underbelly, and tail are darker than those on the more colorful body.

7 Paint in the bird's legs with a very pale wash of Payne's gray. (The feet are hidden by the straw, so you do not need to paint them.)

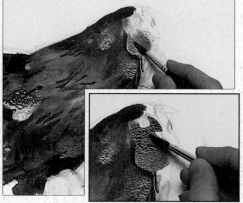

Progress Report
Bring out the highlights in the feathers by applying light streaks of Chinese white gouache, cadmium yellow, and viridian on top of dry underlying washes. Curve your brushstrokes to emphasize the rounded form of the bird's body.

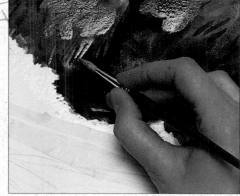

8 Paint the rooster's comb wet into wet, with a cadmium yellow and cadmium red mix. Inset: Mix Chinese white gouache with the same colors, and paint the area around the comb to develop contrast.

9 Load a dry no. 6 brush with a thick solution of cadmium yellow. Lay further highlights on the bird's body, especially over the rich oranges and blues, to emphasize the glossiness of the feathers and their bulk.

Progress Report

The success of this image depends entirely on patient overpainting. Allow the paint to dry now, and assess how far the picture has developed. You may need to build the feathers further. If you have made some areas too dense or dark, block them out with Chinese white gouache and then paint additional washes of pure watercolor on top to rebuild them in lighter hues.

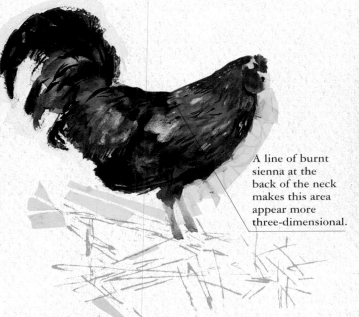

A line of burnt sienna at the back of the neck makes this area appear more three-dimensional.

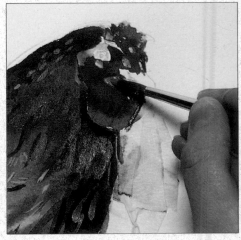

10 *Mix up a watery pool of rose madder, and lightly touch it into the head area around the comb with the no. 6 brush. Paint touches of Chinese white gouache over it to add further highlights and form.*

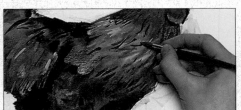
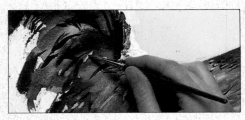

11 *Use a combination of colors to build up the feathers further – cadmium red mixed with cerulean blue for the deeper purple feathers (top) and cadmium red mixed with cadmium yellow for the fine feathers on the breast (bottom).*

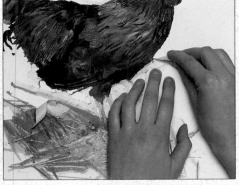

12 *Mix a wash of cadmium yellow and, using the no. 6 brush, drop the paint wet into wet over the surface of the straw. Allow the paint to spread across the paper, but do not worry if some areas are left untouched.*

13 *Mix cadmium yellow with viridian to a straw color and add a drop of gum arabic. Using the no. 6 brush, paint lines across the paper, crisscrossing backward and forward. Inset: Drag a plastic palette knife through the straw area.*

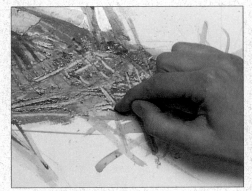

14 *Wash the no. 6 brush with warm, soapy water. Use your fingernails or a comb to score through the paint, creating the impression of pieces of tangled dry straw sticking out in all directions.*

15 *When the painting is completely dry, remove the masking tape very carefully, making sure that you do not tear the surface of the paper as you work. Then rub off the masking fluid with your fingers.*

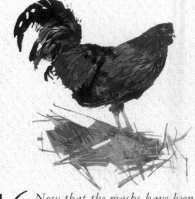

16 *Now that the masks have been removed, you can see how spiky the tail feathers look. Overlay more dark and light tones across the body of the bird wherever you feel it is necessary.*

The Finished Painting

*The gradual buildup of colors paid off.
The colors are rich and vital, the dark
viridian and blue tones contrasting beautifully
with the brighter cadmium yellow, cadmium
red, and touches of Chinese white gouache.
The addition of gum arabic produced
an effective gloss over the surface of the bird,
much like an oil paint glaze. The dry,
straight pieces of straw contrast with the
softness of the feathers and add an extra
dimension to the composition.*

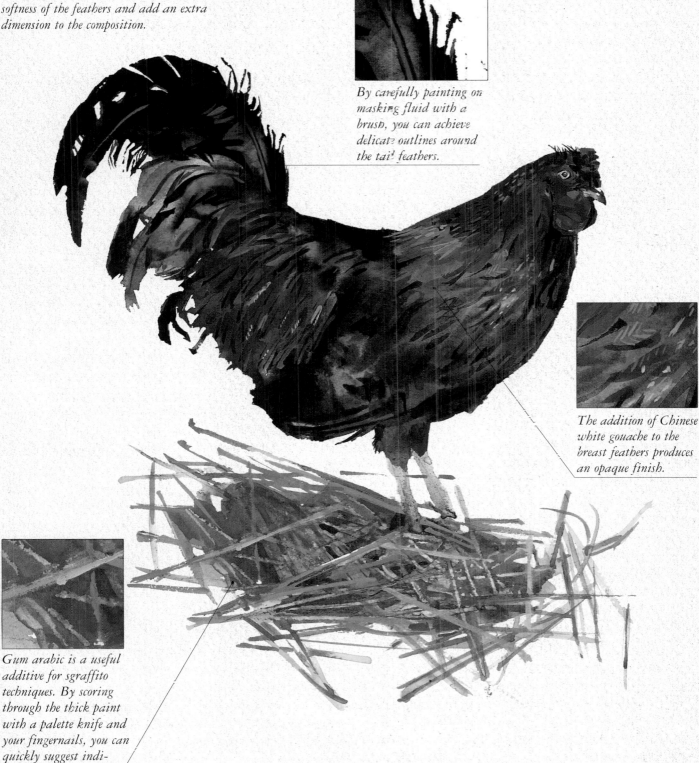

*By carefully painting on
masking fluid with a
brush, you can achieve
delicate outlines around
the tail feathers.*

*The addition of Chinese
white gouache to the
breast feathers produces
an opaque finish.*

*Gum arabic is a useful
additive for sgraffito
techniques. By scoring
through the thick paint
with a palette knife and
your fingernails, you can
quickly suggest indi-
vidual pieces of straw.*

Under- and Overdrawing

PEN, INDIA INK, and watercolor paint make excellent companions. India ink is permanent when dry, but when wet it can be blurred and manipulated to flow with watercolor paint and create a range of subtle effects. It is used in two ways: to draw an image before watercolor paint is applied over it (underdrawing) and to add structure and detailing to loose washes by applying it on top of watercolor paint (overdrawing). With both these methods, the pen-and-ink marks will become an integral aspect of your painting, so use the technique only if you want the ink lines to remain visible.

It is worth investing in a good-quality nib that will not blot ink on your paper. However good your nib is, do not have too much ink on your pen. This lessens the chances of making unwanted blots on the paper.

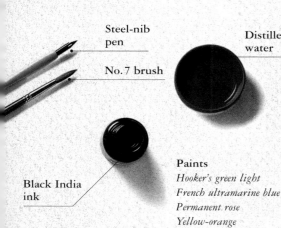

Steel-nib pen

No. 7 brush

Distilled water

Black India ink

Paints
Hooker's green light
French ultramarine blue
Permanent rose
Yellow-orange
Viridian

Underdrawing

Underdrawing – drawing your subject in pen and ink before applying watercolor – enables you to combine the precise detailing of pen-and-ink work with the intense colors of watercolor paints. This technique is popular with botanical illustrators. Always allow the ink to dry completely before you add the watercolor, unless you want the two media to merge into one another and create soft effects.

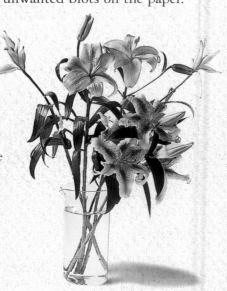

1 *Load the nib with black India ink, and mark in the main forms. Lightly dilute the ink with distilled water in some areas, and vary your pressure on the pen to achieve different weights of line. Inset: Continue until you have a fairly elaborate drawing.*

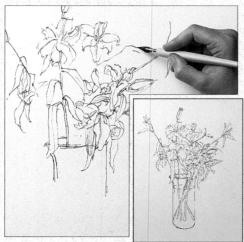

2 *Once the ink has dried, begin to block in areas of color using a no. 7 brush. Use a mix of Hooker's green light for the leaves and stalks, combining it with a very light wash of French ultramarine blue for the water and the ends of the leaves.*

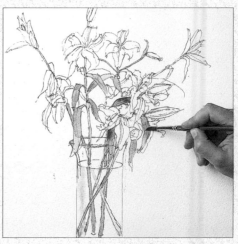

3 *Using various strengths of permanent rose, paint in the pink details of the flowers. Dampen the paper in some flower head areas, then drop in color, allowing it to spread slightly. In other areas, apply paint directly to the dry surface.*

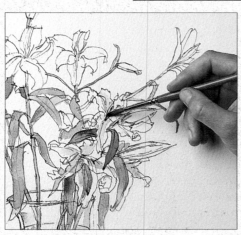

The Finished Painting
A yellow-orange mix makes some petals stand out, while a combination of viridian and orange is used for the recessive buds. A strong mix of permanent rose, applied after the flowers have dried, defines the spots on the petals. The pen-and-ink underdrawing has allowed this delicate detailing in the flowers.

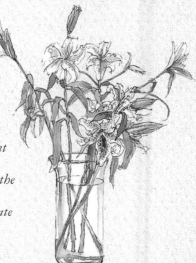

YOU CAN CREATE a surprisingly wide range of marks using a pen and ink. You can make fine lines by holding the pen in the same way as you would if you were writing. For wider marks, turn the pen over and draw using the reverse side of the nib. If you want to vary the weight of the marks you make, vary the amount of pressure you apply to the nib.

For softer effects, dilute the ink with distilled water. Do not use tap water, as it will separate from the pigment rather than dilute it. If you allow the ink to dry completely before adding watercolor, then there is no risk of it smudging. However, if the ink is still damp, it might "muddy" any paint laid over it.

Overdrawing

Applying ink over watercolor paint that has already been laid down gives much freer, looser results. If you apply ink over damp watercolor, you can achieve soft effects – a useful method of creating shading over areas of your work. Alternatively, pen and ink may be used once the watercolor is completely dry in order to add crisp, sharp details to your painting.

Paints
Permanent rose
Yellow ochre
Cobalt blue
Hooker's green light
Lemon yellow
French ultramarine blue

1 *After lightly sketching the flowers with an HB pencil, use a no. 7 brush to apply loose strokes of permanent rose, in varying degrees of intensity, over the petals. Add yellow ochre and cobalt blue for the closed buds.*

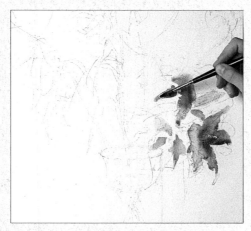

2 *While the paint is still damp, start to overdraw with pen and ink, allowing the ink to mix with the watercolor to create soft lines. For fine details, allow the paint to dry before you start to use the pen and ink.*

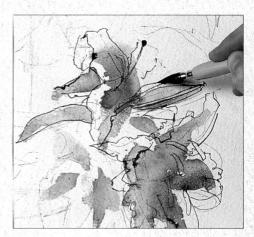

3 *Paint in the leaves with a combination of green tones, derived from Hooker's green light and a mix of lemon yellow and French ultramarine blue. Draw over them with the back of the nib to create thicker and darker lines.*

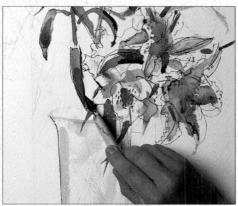

4 *The pen-and-ink work adds structure to the areas of color and gives a different textural quality to the painting. You can use watercolor pencils of the same colors to define areas that appear too pale.*

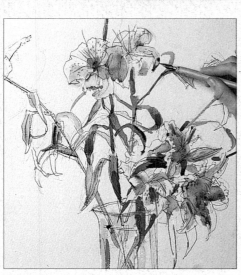

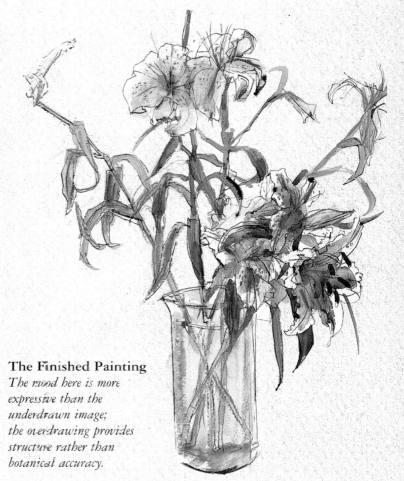

The Finished Painting
The mood here is more expressive than the underdrawn image; the overdrawing provides structure rather than botanical accuracy.

Sgraffito

SGRAFFITO IS A TECHNIQUE of scraping through a top layer of paint to reveal the underlying paper. You can use the technique on its own, but it is more often combined with other methods and media to create surface texture or highlights.

A craft knife blade is one of the most popular sgraffito tools, as the point can be used to scratch out minute details and fine lines. It is perfect for creating such subjects as long grasses or highlights. On some occasions, however, you may want to achieve texture across a wider surface area. In such instances, instead of using the point, you can drag the edge of the blade across a broad area, dislodging the paint and the surface of the paper as you go.

By rubbing a rough grade of sandpaper hard across a surface of dried paint, you can create some interesting marks. Even the end of a sharpened brush handle or fingernail make useful sgraffito tools.

Scratching into paper can easily damage its surface. This is nothing to worry about unless you think that you might want to overlay further details or build up paint after sgraffito has been applied. Obviously, a heavy paper – say 300 lb (see pp. 18–19) – is preferable to thin paper, which tears more easily. You can practice sgraffito over damp areas of paper and create soft effects, but for the most dramatic results you will find that it is best applied over dry areas of color.

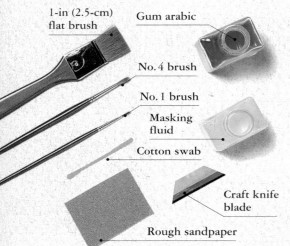

1-in (2.5-cm) flat brush

Gum arabic

No. 4 brush

No. 1 brush

Masking fluid

Cotton swab

Craft knife blade

Rough sandpaper

Paints
Burnt umber
Hooker's green light
French ultramarine blue
Cobalt blue
Cadmium orange
Payne's gray

Deer in a Lake
This natural outdoor scene, with its dappled light, dark vegetation, rippling water, and grasses and reeds, offers plenty of opportunity for you to practice sgraffito. These features can all be emphasized using this technique.

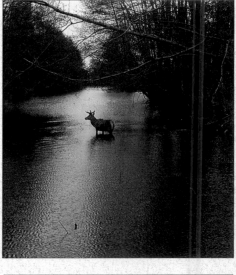

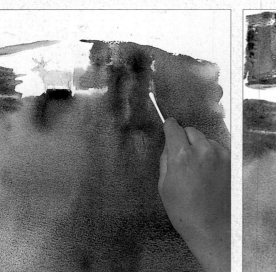

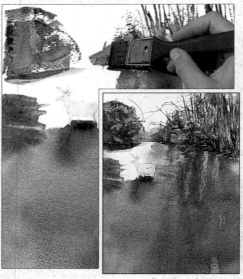

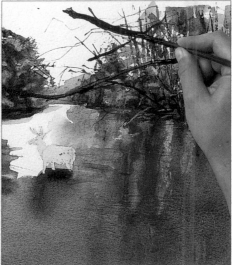

1 *Draw the shape of the deer and mask it out. Flood the paper with a mix of burnt umber and Hooker's green light in the tree area and French ultramarine and cobalt blue for water. While the blue paint is still wet, score through it with a cotton swab to create a shimmering effect.*

2 *Using a 1-in (2.5-cm) flat brush dry to the touch, paint in the vegetation with mixes of Hooker's green light and burnt umber. Inset: Make a wetter mix of burnt umber and cadmium orange, add a drop of gum arabic, and continue to build up the foliage using the no. 4 brush.*

3 *Drag the end of the brush handle through the damp foliage to scratch off some of the damp paint. The gum arabic added in step 2 thickens the paint and slows down its drying time, so you have time to create textural contrasts.*

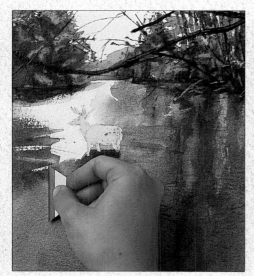

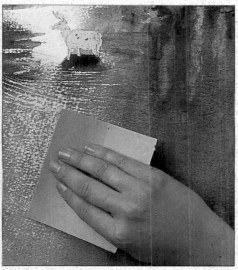

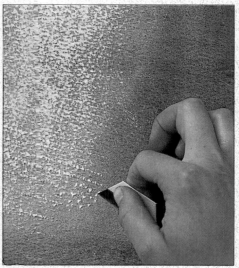

4 Once the wash in the lake area is dry, scratch the surface with the edge of the craft knife blade, creating a rippled texture. Keep the blade edge flat and apply pressure evenly as you drag it across the paper.

5 Create further texture in the water by rubbing across it with rough sandpaper. The rough watercolor paper responds well to this treatment and the results suggest the shimmering surface of the water.

6 Pick off pinpoints of paint with the point of the craft knife blade, lifting the paint clean off the paper to reveal the sparkling white of the paper beneath.

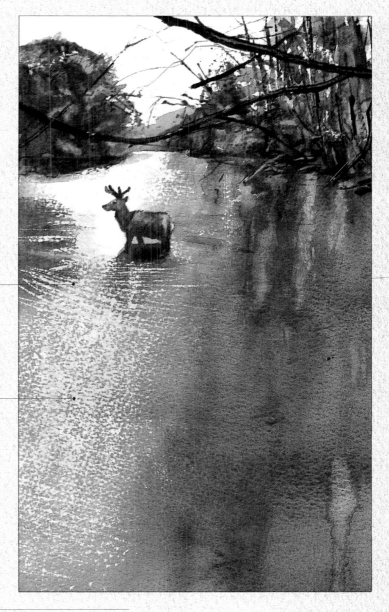

Linear marks over the water, curving across the paper, make interesting ripples and suggest movement and depth.

Rough sandpaper rubbed over the surface of the water creates light, shimmering effects, which enhance the atmosphere.

The Finished Painting

Once you have finished, rub off the masking fluid and paint in the detail of the deer with the no. 1 brush. Emphasize the features in Payne's gray. Compared with the textured surface of the foliage and water, the deer is clearly defined and painted with rich pigments. It is the central focus of the painting, and the sgraffito marks on the surface of the water help draw the viewer's attention upward toward the animal.

Paint Resist

THE PAINT RESIST method is an unusual way of producing sharply contrasting areas of light and dark in your painting. The first step is to paint an underlying picture using pure watercolor and marking in any highlight areas with Chinese white gouache. Let this dry completely, then paint a layer of black India ink over the top of it, completely blocking out the image. After about ten minutes, when the ink is dry to the touch, wash it away with warm water. (It is important not to let the ink dry completely, otherwise it will permanently obliterate the underlying paint.) The ink will fall away from any areas that have been treated with the paint, revealing the original color. This is because, provided the watercolor and gouache were completely dry before you applied the ink, they act as a resist, preventing the ink from reaching the paper underneath. Any area that has not been treated with watercolor or Chinese white gouache, however, will be stained black.

This method is the reverse of normal watercolor techniques: instead of using the white of your paper as an extra color, you need to paint in any highlights or areas of white with Chinese white gouache or protect them with masking fluid. In planning the picture, you must also leave any areas that you want to appear black in the final picture free of paint, including not only the background, but also spaces between colors on the image itself. Paint resist is a semirandom technique, but it is worth spending time and patience perfecting this method for the effects you can attain.

Black water-soluble pencil

1-in (2.5-cm) flat brush

No. 7 brush

No. 3 brush

Chinese white gouache

Black India ink

Rag

Paints
Lemon yellow
Cerulean blue
Payne's gray
Spectrum red
Chrome yellow
Hooker's green light

Sponge

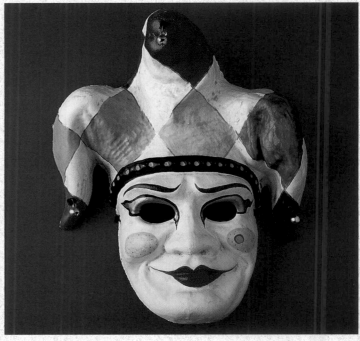

Developing a Mask
This mask makes a good subject for the paint resist technique. The image is bold yet complex, and the paint is applied like patchwork to build up the different sections. Bright colors are counterbalanced by large areas of white.

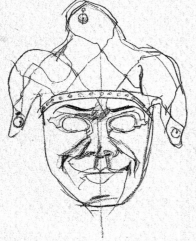

1 *Make a black watersoluble pencil sketch of the mask. Make sure the features are balanced and the proportions accurate. Lightly crosshatch the darker areas.*

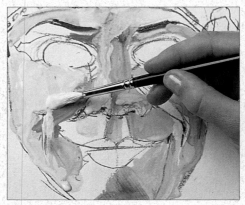

2 *Mix Chinese white gouache with touches of lemon yellow, cerulean blue, and Payne's gray. Following your sketch, paint on these colors with a no. 7 brush.*

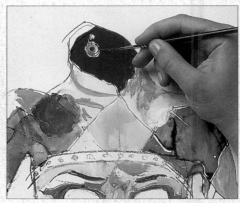

3 *Using the no. 3 brush, add strongly pigmented spectrum red to the lips, cheeks, and (shown here) hat. Leave spaces of clean paper between each area of color.*

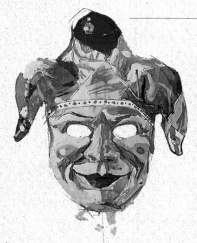

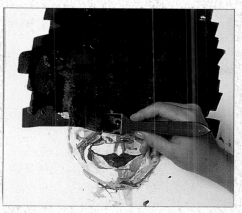

4 Build up colors and details, using chrome yellow for the central diamond on the hat, Hooker's green light to the right of it, and a mix of Chinese white gouache and spectrum red to the left. Allow the painting to dry completely.

5 Load a generous amount of black India ink onto a 1-in (2.5-cm) flat brush, and paint broad sweeps across the image from top to bottom until you have completely covered the paper.

6 Once the image is blocked out by the ink, allow it to dry for at least 10 minutes. Test that it is touch dry with the back of your hand.

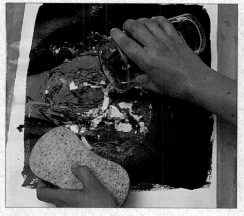

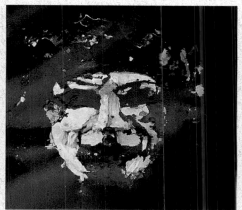

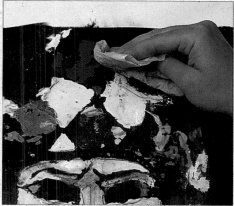

7 Place the paper over the edge of the sink, and pour warm water over the painting, blotting away any loose ink with a sponge. Work quickly but gently: you do not want to dislodge the watercolor paint.

8 The image will gradually reappear, emerging first in areas where the Chinese white gouache is thicker than the watercolor paint.

9 Ink now stains those areas of paper that were left free of watercolor. Blot off any loose ink with a rag or a piece of tissue paper, dabbing at the surface rather than using a sweeping action.

The Finished Painting

The image has now reemerged, and the black outline creates a theatrical effect. The paint that had dried into the watercolor paper before the ink was applied shines through to the surface once more, while all areas that were left unpainted, such as the eyes, now appear completely blackened. Care in the initial planning stages is essential.

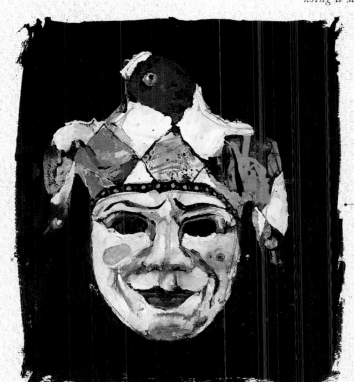

The ink creates a dramatic backdrop, allowing the colors of the mask to stand out vividly.

Bleach into Ink

WATERCOLOR PAINTING generally relies on subtle gradations in tone, colors merging together, and, above all, the translucency of the paint allowing the white of the paper to show through. There may be occasions, however, when you want solid areas of black to block out any hint of the underlying paper. The bleach-into-ink technique is one way of achieving this.

Start by covering your paper with a wash of water-soluble ink. When it is dry, paint bleach on top of it in whatever shape you choose, blotting off the bleach with an absorbent paper towel as you work. (If you leave the bleach on for too long it will eat into the paper and destroy it.) The bleach will dissolve the ink, leaving a slightly discolored space on the paper. Allow the bleach to dry completely, then paint the space with your chosen watercolor paint. Areas not touched by the bleach will, of course, remain covered in ink.

The only special equipment you need is a bottle of ordinary household bleach. Remember, however, that bleach is highly corrosive. Always keep the bottle out of the reach of children and replace the lid immediately after use. Never let bleach come into contact with bare skin; if you do accidentally splash it onto your skin, rinse it off immediately. Finally, always rinse your brushes in warm water as soon as you have finished working.

This technique works only with water-soluble ink: bleach does not remove permanent ink or watercolor paint. You should also use heavy paper, as the paper must be strong enough to withstand the corrosive properties of the bleach. It is difficult to bleach out precise shapes or fine lines, as the bleach tends to spread outward, so choose subjects with simple shapes. The contrast between the translucent watercolor and the dense ink surrounding it, however, is very effective.

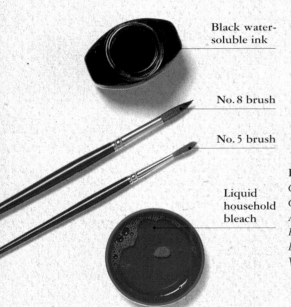

Black water-soluble ink

No. 8 brush

No. 5 brush

Liquid household bleach

Paints
Cadmium red
Cadmium yellow
Alizarin crimson
Hooker's green light
Lemon yellow
Viridian

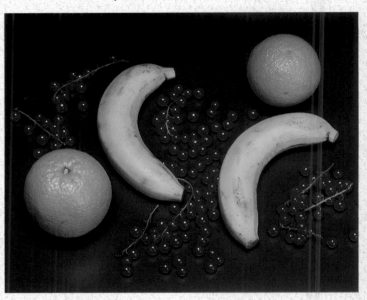

Color on Black
This composition demands a technique that allows the vibrant colors of the fruits to stand out from the background. Bleach into ink is a perfect choice.

1 *Paint a wash of water-soluble black ink over your paper with a no. 8 brush, then let it dry. It will dry lighter than it appears when first put down.*

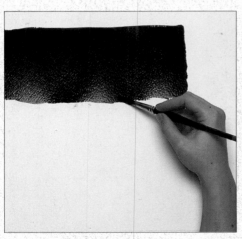

2 *Dip a no. 5 brush into the undiluted bleach and paint in the shape of the orange. Inset: Blot off any excess bleach with a paper towel. The bleach will lift out the ink.*

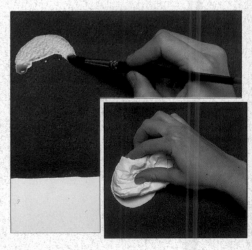

3 Continue to bleach out the shapes of the other fruits, blotting off any excess bleach as you work. The paper will appear slightly discolored where the bleach has touched it. You can use this tonal variation to your advantage.

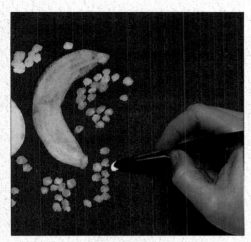

4 When you have bleached out all the fruit shapes, blot the surface of the paper to remove any excess bleach. While you wait for the bleach to dry, rinse out your brush with warm, soapy water.

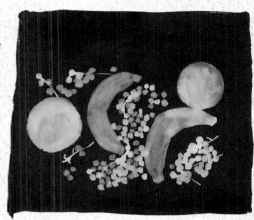

5 Paint the oranges using the no. 5 brush dipped in a mix of cadmium red and cadmium yellow. Inset: Use a cadmium red and alizarin crimson mixture for the berries and Hooker's green light mixed with lemon yellow for the underside of the bananas.

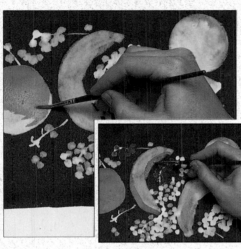

6 Leave some areas free of paint, allowing the paper color to show through. Complete the image by painting in the berry stalks with a mix of cadmium yellow and viridian.

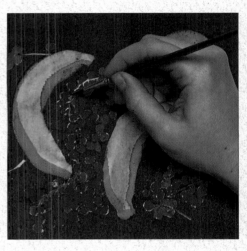

The Finished Painting

The dot on the orange was painted in with the green mixture. Paint was also added to the bananas to give them more substance. The shapes stand out against the flat, dark background, and the variation in tone on the fruits gives them a three-dimensional quality.

The rough texture of the paper enhances the pitted skin of the oranges.

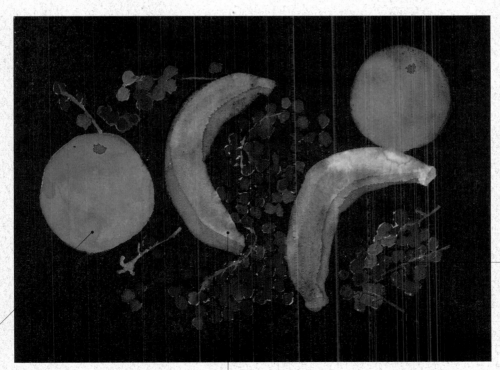

The redcurrants stand out like jewels against the dark background. The translucency of the paint also helps in this respect, as does leaving some areas free of paint to imply glossy highlights.

The discolored paper left by the bleach has become an integral part of the image.

Altering Paper Surfaces

ALTHOUGH ALL GOOD-QUALITY watercolor papers are manufactured specifically to suit the watercolorist's needs, you may at times find that you need a different kind of surface. You may, for example, want to change the speed at which the paint dries or to give your work a distinct texture. To do this, you can explore ways of altering the paper's surface to suit your purpose.

There are various possibilities. Using such tools as a craft knife, razor blades, or sandpaper, you can bruise or score the surface of the paper to break down the sizing. This technique changes the texture of the paper, letting the paint sink into the cracks and cuts; it also enables the paint to be absorbed into the paper more quickly. If you score into the paper, take care not to tear it or make a hole. One way to minimize the risk of tearing is to choose a heavyweight paper, which is less susceptible to damage. You can build up the surface of the paper by coating it with a water-based medium such as gesso or acrylic paint. This makes the surface of the paper less absorbent, retarding the drying time of the paint and giving you longer to manipulate it. You can change the entire surface of the paper for a unified look or select specific areas for more localized effects. This technique also allows you to repaint areas that you are not satisfied with (see p. 148).

Sandpaper

Using sandpaper, you can break down the surface sizing of paper and make it more absorbent. Simply rub the sandpaper over the paper in a gentle circular motion. Rubbing with sandpaper also affects the texture of the paper, making it scratchier and rougher to the touch. When paint is applied, it is absorbed unevenly, leaving a textured finish.

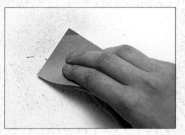

Coarse sandpaper

1 *Use a coarse grade of sand-paper and a heavyweight watercolor paper. Rub the sand-paper over the surface of the paper in a circular motion to break down the sizing.*

2 *The texture of the paper is noticeably different in areas that have been rubbed with sandpaper. In addition, any paint applied here is absorbed more quickly than usual.*

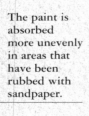

The paint is absorbed more unevenly in areas that have been rubbed with sandpaper.

Craft Knife Blade

A craft knife blade is another useful tool for breaking the surface sizing of the paper. Drag the edge of the blade across the paper to rub away the top layer or score into the paper, producing very precise lines. A razor blade would have the same effect; in either case, wrap the edge of the blade in masking tape to protect your fingers.

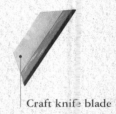

Craft knife blade

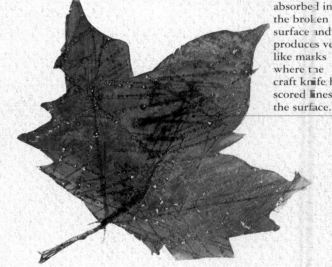

Paint is absorbed into the broken surface and produces vein-like marks where the craft knife has scored lines in the surface.

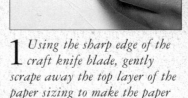

1 *Using the sharp edge of the craft knife blade, gently scrape away the top layer of the paper sizing to make the paper more absorbent.*

2 *Using the point of the craft blade knife, score into the paper. The incisions hold more paint than the unscored areas, and this creates a textured pattern within your painting.*

Gesso

Although gesso is traditionally associated with oil and acrylic painting, it may also be used to alter the surface of watercolor paper. If you paint it across your paper, it will form a skin. Unable to penetrate the gesso, the paint dries slowly through its contact with the air rather than being absorbed into the paper, thus giving you longer to work with it. The more humid the atmosphere, the slower the drying time.

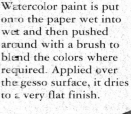

No. 4 brush

Gesso

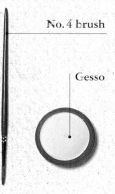

Watercolor paint is put onto the paper wet into wet and then pushed around with a brush to blend the colors where required. Applied over the gesso surface, it dries to a very flat finish.

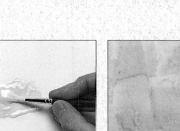

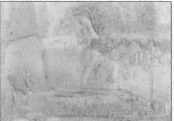

1 *With a no. 4 brush, apply the gesso either flat and smooth or in a more uneven manner, as here, to create an interesting surface texture.*

2 *When the gesso is dry (it will take three to four hours), wash watercolor paint over it. The paint will dry more slowly than usual, allowing you to work with it longer.*

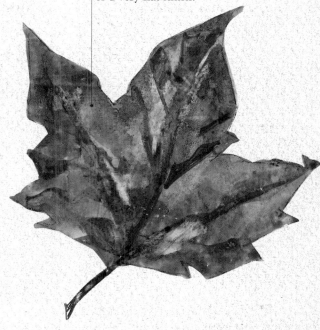

White acrylic paint

Acrylic Paint

Acrylic paint is a thick water-based paint. It is more viscous and less translucent than watercolor paint and often has a glossy appearance. It is also less absorbent than watercolor paint, so watercolor paint applied on top of dry acrylic paint sits on the surface rather than being absorbed into the paper, giving you more time to work with it.

Plastic palette knife

Comb

1 *Using a plastic palette knife, spread undiluted white acrylic paint over the surface of your watercolor paper. It has a thick, buttery consistency.*

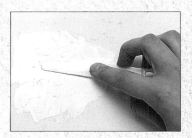

The watercolor paint dries unevenly on the surface of the acrylic, giving the work a textured appearance.

2 *Before it dries, use a comb or any other suitable tool, such as your fingernails or the edge of a piece of cardboard, to score lines into the paint.*

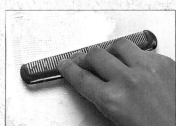

3 *Score crosshatched or random lines into the acrylic paint. Let the acrylic dry before applying watercolor over the top.*

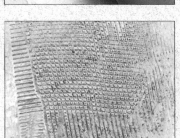

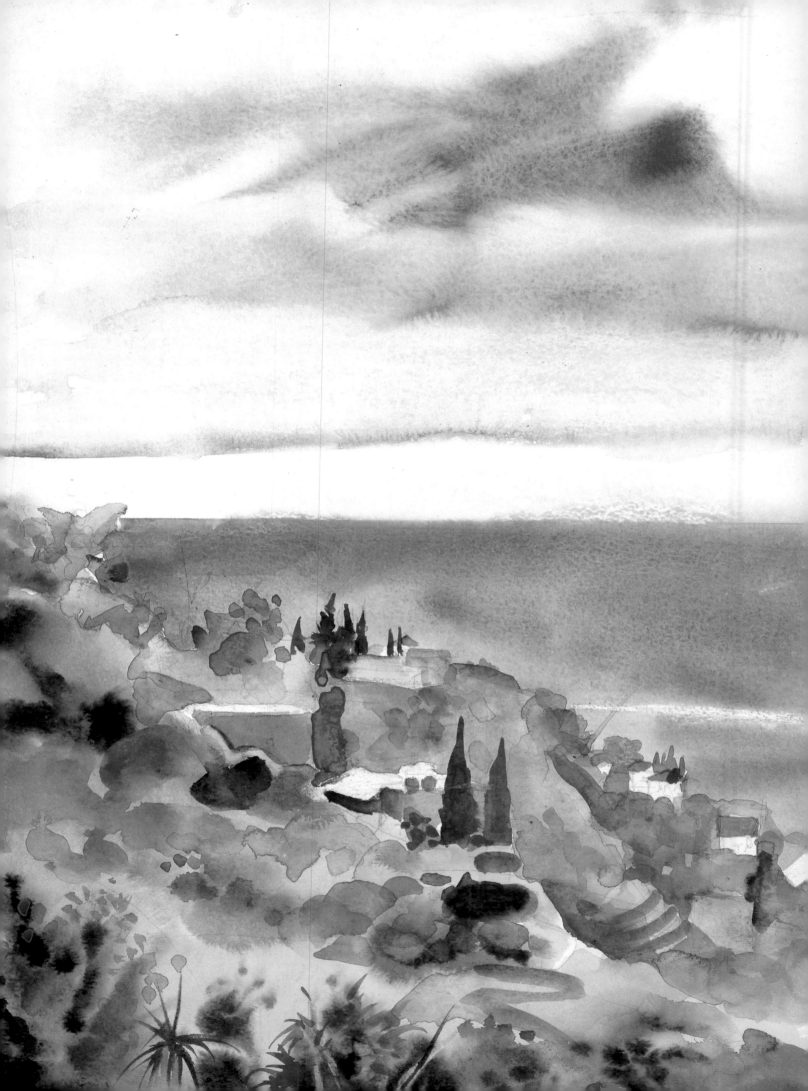

The Projects

LIGHT:
Direction and Quality

LIGHT IS INTANGIBLE. To convey it successfully in a painting you need to look at how it affects the objects on which it falls. Your first step is to determine where the light is coming from. Once you know this, you can analyze exactly how it affects your subject. If the light source is a window, for example, a shaft of light entering through it may bathe one element in bright light but leave the rest of the image in subdued shadow. If light is flooding the subject from above, then the illumination may be flat and uniform.

Light affects the color of objects too. Strong, direct light, for example, can bleach out color from the objects that it hits. Areas cast in deep shadow can be conveyed by washing a neutral tone, such as Payne's gray, across them. For subjects that lie in between these two extremes (and this is likely to apply to most of your work), use a wider range of colors – but remember that the tone may vary from light to dark within a small area, particularly if the object in question has a multifaceted or uneven surface. Look carefully to see exactly where the tones need to change. The tones within the shadow areas will shift too.

The quality of light and the moods it can create in a painting vary enormously. A subject illuminated by an artificial light source, whether it be electric light or a candle flame, has a different quality and mood from one lit by daylight. In scenes lit by natural light the time of day, weather conditions, and season are all important – and constantly changing – factors that will dictate both your approach and the colors you use.

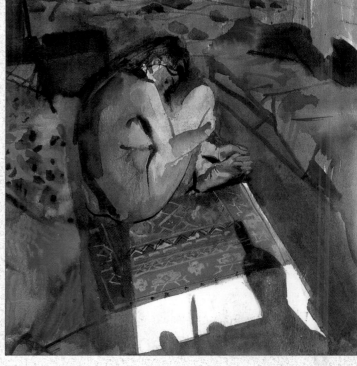
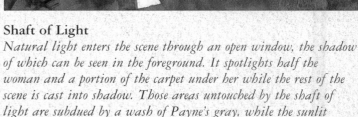

Shaft of Light
Natural light enters the scene through an open window, the shadow of which can be seen in the foreground. It spotlights half the woman and a portion of the carpet under her while the rest of the scene is cast into shadow. Those areas untouched by the shaft of light are subdued by a wash of Payne's gray, while the sunlit areas are portrayed with clean, pure colors.

Bright Light and Long Shadows
The positions and shapes of shadows tell us a lot about the time of day in outdoor paintings. Here, the sun casts a bright light across the left side of the standing stones, but long shadows have fallen to the right. Long, oblique shadows such as these are cast in early morning or late afternoon, when the sun is low in the sky. At noon, with the sun directly overhead, the shadows would be far shorter. Note how the shadows are painted in a shade of green that is darker in tone than the rest of the grassland.

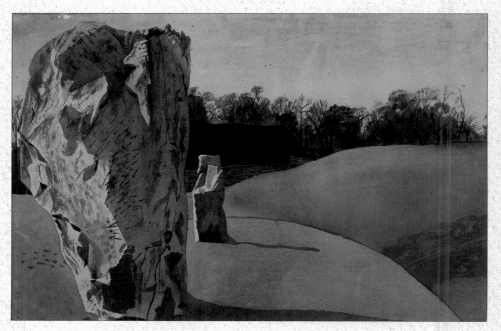

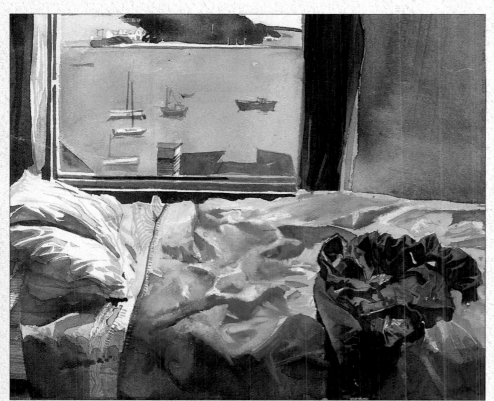

Direct Light Through a Window

Although the sun itself is not visible in the picture, light enters the scene through the window, so it is obvious where the light is coming from. The sun is high in the sky: it floods across the sheets, highlighting the folds in the fabric, which are picked out by the application of thick Chinese white, in contrast to the flat gray areas of shadow. The denim jacket also picks up the strong sunlight, with some areas highlighted by dashes of cerulean blue and the shadow areas painted in a darker Prussian blue. The view of the harbor scene outside creates a picture within a picture. The light on the interior is far brighter than on the external scene, a useful device for making it the picture's center of interest.

Backlighting

In this painting, natural light enters the room through the floor-to-ceiling French windows. The light source is behind the subject and, as a result, less detail is evident in the figure than in the area behind her. Stronger backlighting would produce a silhouette, in which no detail would be visible. The woman's dress is painted in grays, with the folds highlighted in white, to emphasize the fact that she is standing in shadow. The mood outside the windows is brighter and flatter than in the tonally subdued interior, and this contrast increases the feeling of solitude and loneliness. You can always use light to underscore the mood you wish to convey.

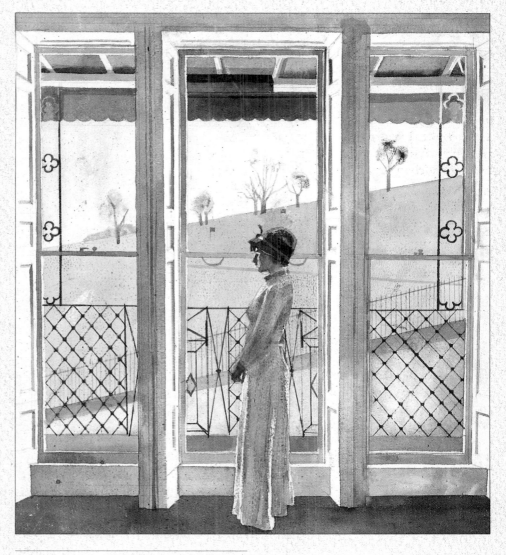

LIGHT:
Throughout the Day

PAINTING THE SAME subject at different times of day is a useful exercise, as it will help you to analyze the effect of light and respond to it in your work. You will find that objects appear to change color, with both the intensity and the tonal values of colors varying as the hours go by. Shadows, too, change dramatically, lengthening and shortening as the sun arcs through the sky. They also shift in color and position, so you need to look carefully at their angle and hue.

Light is an important factor in creating atmosphere in a painting, and you will find that the atmosphere alters significantly as the day progresses, from the gentle light of morning through the bright light at noon to the lengthening shadows that denote the arrival of evening. Watching the way light changes on a simple subject, such as this dish and orange, is the best way to develop an appreciation of its moods and effects on your painting. Divide the daylight hours into four periods – morning, noon, afternoon, and evening – and try to analyze the lighting characteristics of each.

Morning

Early morning light is delicate and subtle, with more diffuse shadows than at any other time of day. Here light enters the picture from the left, casting a long shadow across and under the plate to the right of the orange. The orange reflects color into its shadow, so the main shadow color of cerulean blue is overlaid with a warm mix of cadmium yellow and red, then given a touch of cooler alizarin crimson. The right half of the orange is in shadow. The flat Payne's gray shadow cast by the plate has a second, or echoing, shadow on its outer edge.

Cadmium red and cadmium yellow are overlaid with burnt umber to develop form and shadow.

The soft light creates a double shadow around the plate, painted with overlays of Payne's gray.

The neutral gray shadow helps to define the edge of the plate. Detail is clearly apparent.

Noon

By noon the sun is high in the sky, producing short, sharp shadows. The sun's rays bleach out the detail on the plate. With the contrasting rich tones of orange and green on the fruit and the white light on the china, the image is more dramatic than the early morning painting. The shadows have moved toward the front of the plate and are angled slightly left of center. The shadow under the orange is intense crimson and the one around the plate a dark gray.

The alizarin crimson shadow contrasts with the colors used on the fruit.

The flat gray shadow throws the edge of the plate into bright highlight, sharply defining its shape.

The shadow around the plate is starker than in the image painted in early morning.

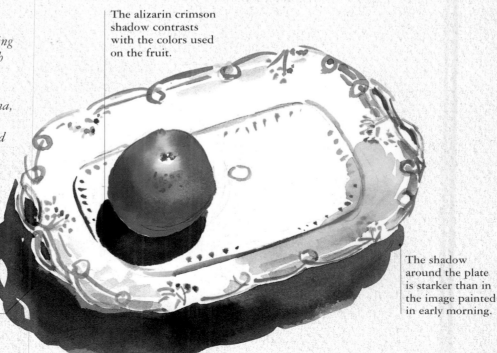

Midafternoon

By midafternoon the shadows have begun to lengthen as the sun travels across the sky. The light is lower but stronger than in early morning. Light enters the scene from the top right. The sun is still high in the sky, and details begin to sharpen as the light falls at a more oblique angle than before. The front of the orange is in shadow, so the tones are darker and longer than at noon; they fall to the left of the orange. The area to the right of the orange is still bleached out by bright sunlight.

The orange lies partially in shadow. Its surface appears more textured than at noon.

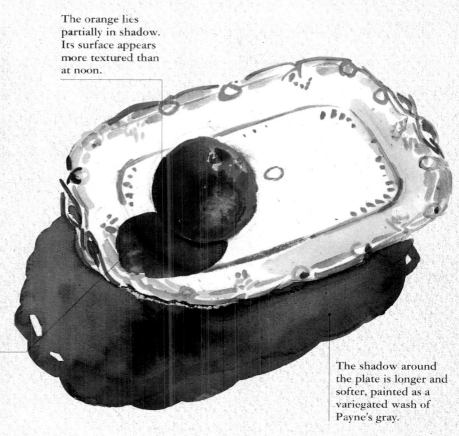

The shadow of the orange is painted with a mix of cerulean blue, cadmium yellow, and cadmium red paint. It is closer in tone to the color of the orange itself.

The shadow around the plate is longer and softer, painted as a variegated wash of Payne's gray.

Evening

By dusk the sun is lower in the sky and produces longer shadows, far deeper in tone than at any other time during the day. Highlights are subdued, and there are few areas of white left in the image. The orange is more sculptural in form and texture. The colors are much richer, and the long shadows are tinged with a filter of green and pink light from the setting sun. There is a definite echo of shading around the main shadow, which spreads away from the plate.

Warm and cool tones mingle in the surface of the orange, as the low light creates high contrast and sharper definition.

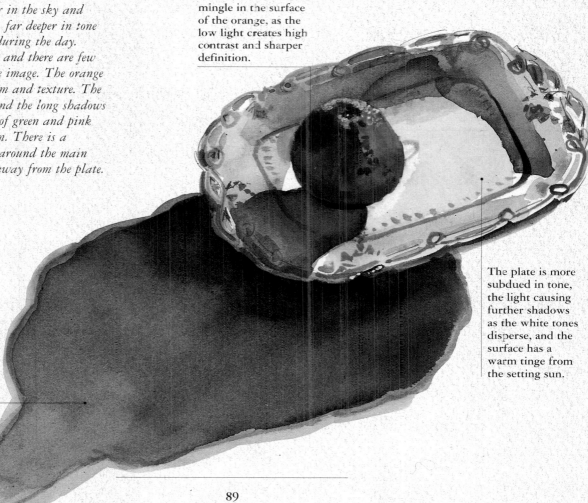

The shadow is longer than at any other time of day and is painted with overlaid mixes of Payne's gray, alizarin crimson, and a touch of cerulean blue.

The plate is more subdued in tone, the light causing further shadows as the white tones disperse, and the surface has a warm tinge from the setting sun.

LIGHT:
Outside the Picture

IN ORDER TO PRODUCE a representational painting, you need to paint authentic-looking lighting even when the actual light source is not shown in the picture. Your viewers should be able to tell immediately whether, for example, an interior scene is lit by natural daylight or by artificial light, such as an electric lamp. They should get some indication of the time of day and, particularly in

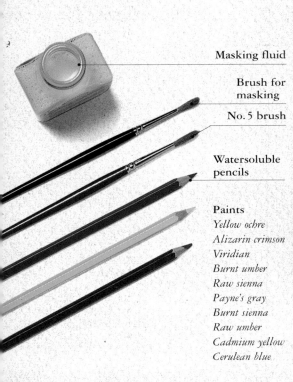

Nassau, Winslow Homer (1836–1910)
The light source in this painting is overhead, bathing the image in a bright stark light. The foreground sand is bleached out by the sun, and contrasts with the dark line of land on the horizon.

outdoor scenes, of the prevailing weather conditions. The only way you can achieve this is by paying close attention to the direction and quality of the light (see pp. 86–87).

There are several ways to provide the necessary clues to the light source. The length of shadows, for example, can help indicate the time of day. The time of day in turn affects the quality of natural light: the higher the sun is in the sky, the brighter the light. At dawn, therefore, the light is softer than at midday. Of course, sunlight is not always direct. Often it is obscured by a layer of clouds, which refract its rays and produce a more even, diffuse light. Natural light also changes from season to season. At the height of summer the light may appear warm and yellow – especially on a hazy hot day, when it appears almost as a film of shimmering color. In winter the light is far cooler, sometimes appearing blue in tone.

If you are working from a real-life scene, remember that the light will change while you paint. There is no point in concentrating on the direction the light is coming from, only to realize halfway through your work that it has shifted. One way of avoiding this is to sketch an arrow lightly in the margin of your work, pointing out the direction and angle from which light is entering the scene. You will then be able to keep the direction and angle of light consistent, even if you are working on your painting over a long period of time.

Masking fluid

Brush for masking

No. 5 brush

Watersoluble pencils

Paints
Yellow ochre
Alizarin crimson
Viridian
Burnt umber
Raw sienna
Payne's gray
Burnt sienna
Raw umber
Cadmium yellow
Cerulean blue

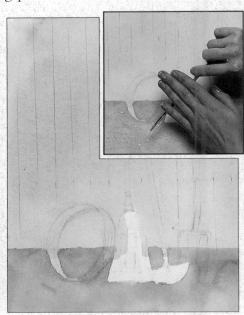

Summer Sunlight
Midafternoon summer sunlight enters the picture from the left side. The light at this time of year and day is soft and warm, producing long, dark shadows.

1 *After sketching the tools in pencil, yellow ochre and alizarin crimson were washed over the fence and viridian over the ground, leaving the brightest areas white. Inset: Spatter masking fluid over the ground area.*

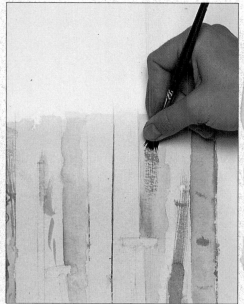

2 Splay out the bristles of a no. 5 brush, and dip them in a mix of burnt umber and raw sienna. Use the drybrush technique to create the impression of wood grain on the fence posts. Vary the intensity of the color to create interest.

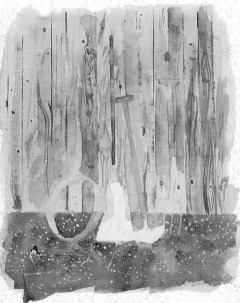

3 Using the no. 5 brush, drop a variegated wash of Payne's gray and burnt umber over the ground to add texture to the gravel. The tone should be much warmer than in the fence posts.

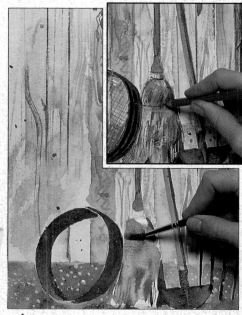

4 Paint the tools, using mixes of burnt sienna, raw umber, and yellow ochre for the wooden handles; cadmium yellow for the brush, and cerulean blue for the hoe. Inset: Define details on the brush with red, blue, and yellow watersoluble pencils.

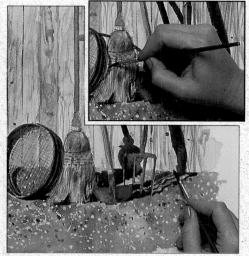

5 Remove the masking fluid from the ground. With a mix of viridian and Payne's gray, paint in the shadows at exactly the same angle to one another, making them solid but wavering at the edges to suggest movement. Inset: Vary the color with burnt sienna around the sieve.

The Finished Painting
The shadows lack the detail of the tools yet they are just as solid in form because they are painted in such dark colors. The contrast between the detailed rendition of the tools and the flat tones used for their shadows helps to evoke a feeling of summer light.

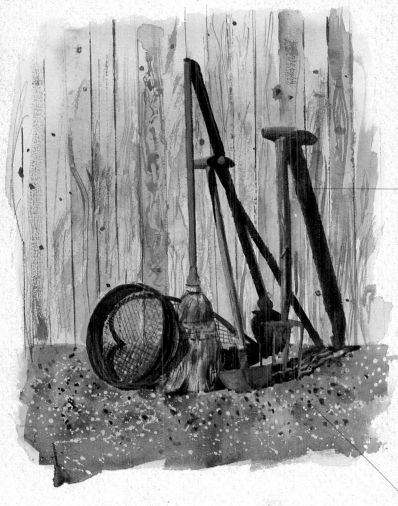

The contrast between the shadows on the handles and the pale fence posts emphasizes the dramatic midafternoon lighting.

When the masking fluid is removed, the white areas enhance the texture in the foreground.

LIGHT:
Within the Picture

A LIGHT SOURCE THAT IS visible within the picture area, as in this painting project, brings a whole new set of challenges. The previous six pages demonstrated how light affects the appearance of the objects on which it falls. The same is true here, but you must also determine how best to paint the light source without allowing it to dominate your composition.

To make the experiment even more challenging, in this project you are going to paint the candle and flowers by the light of the candle alone. The candle will illuminate your palette and brush as well as the still-life setup. You will choose different colors in this light than you would in a well-lit studio and in this way discover new tonal relationships between colors on your palette. Don't be afraid to use new color combinations.

Candlelight, along with the highlights and shadows it produces, oscillates constantly; as the flame flickers, there are minute changes in the direction of the light and the shadows merge and separate dramatically. To convey this constantly changing light in your painting, you must resist the temptation to paint sharply defined areas of highlight and shadow. You do not want to "freeze" the action as in a photograph. Instead, place light and dark tones close to one another throughout the painting.

Flowers by Candlelight
The only light source, both within the picture and in the studio, is the candle. It helps to know where colors are located on your palette, as they will appear subdued in the candlelight.

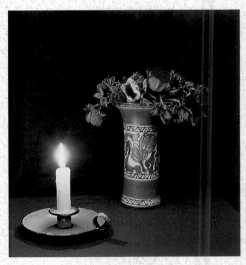

No. 4 brush

No. 8 brush

1-in (2.5-cm) flat brush

Paints
Payne's gray
Hooker's green light
Yellow ochre
Viridian
Cobalt blue
Cadmium red
Alizarin crimson
Cadmium yellow
Scarlet
Raw sienna
Lemon yellow

1 *Make a preliminary sketch; then, working by candlelight, paint the main colors on the candlestick and vase with a no. 4 brush. Use Payne's gray, Hooker's green light, yellow ochre, and viridian, dropping the colors wet into wet onto dry paper.*

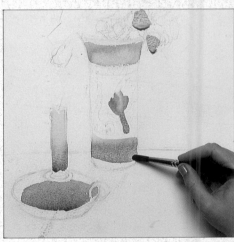

2 *With a 1-in (2.5-cm) flat brush, wash in the background fabric and tabletop wet into wet, using Payne's gray, cobalt blue, and Hooker's green light. Inset: Cadmium red, and alizarin crimson with a touch of yellow ochre can now be washed wet into wet into the tabletop.*

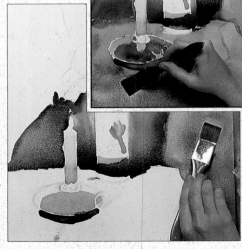

3 *Using the flat brush, mark in the flower petals with alizarin crimson. Continue to build the background washes, overlaying colors and turning the board so that the paint can spread across the painting.*

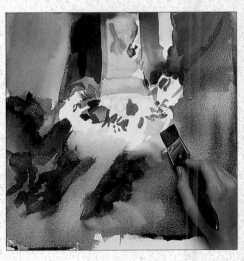

4 With a no. 8 brush, touch in the yellow glow on the candle with cadmium yellow. Begin to build details, blending bright, light colors such as cadmium yellow, cadmium red, and viridian into the flowers to enhance their richness.

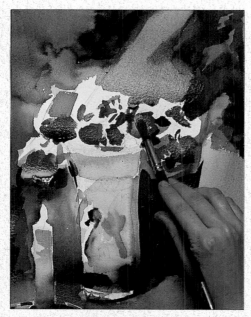

5 The shadows on the background fabric and candle encourage the eye to dwell on the flowers and the flickering light source, both of which appear brighter than the surrounding shades. Enhance this contrast by overlaying Payne's gray on the shadows where necessary.

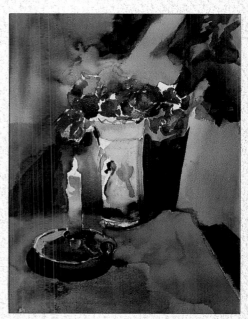

6 Add more detail to the flowers with the no. 4 brush. Use the blue-red of alizarin crimson for the center of the flowers and the yellow-red of scarlet for the petals, since cool colors recede while warm colors advance. Leave areas white to emphasize the flickering light. Inset: *Paint the pattern on the vase using raw sienna.*

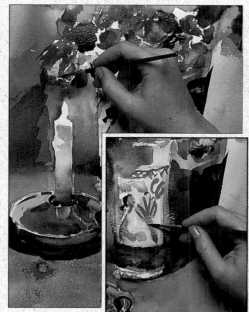

7 Now paint in the candle flame, using the no. 4 brush. It appears far brighter and clearer in color than the richer tones of the fabric and flowers. Use cool lemon yellow in the center of the candle and the warm tone of cadmium red around its circumference.

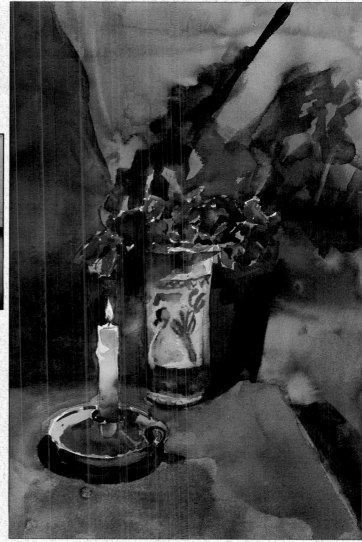

The Finished Painting

The flickering candlelight appears warm and strong compared with the dark tonal quality of the surrounding fabric, which it casts into shadow. In contrast to these deep tones, the flowers are highlighted by the flame, and glow out from the heart of the image.

THE NATURAL WORLD:
Seasonal Landscapes

EACH SEASON BRINGS with it new challenges for the landscape painter. For a start, the tonal qualities of the landscape change dramatically depending on the time of year, so you will need to alter your palette accordingly. The overall mood of a summer landscape, for example, is different from that of a winter one. To convey this shift in atmosphere, you need to pay attention to warm and cool colors, letting the temperature of your palette (see pp. 32–33) echo that of the season you are painting. If you overemphasize cool green hues in a summer scene, for example, you risk the result appearing too springlike, while if you let cool blues predominate, the result could look wintry. Here and on the next three pages is a series of landscape scenes painted at different times of the year which demonstrate ways in which you can adjust the temperature of your palette to suit the season.

Spring

In temperate climates, spring bridges the period between the ice-cold temperatures of winter and the heat of summer. The mixture of cool and warm temperatures that you encounter in the colors of a springtime landscape suggests this link. In this painting, wet-into-wet washes of cool blue-greens on the distant hills and cerulean blue in the sky contrast with the warmer cadmium yellow and viridian in the foreground. The overall impression is one of freshness and new growth.

The sky is painted in a gradated wash of cool cerulean blue.

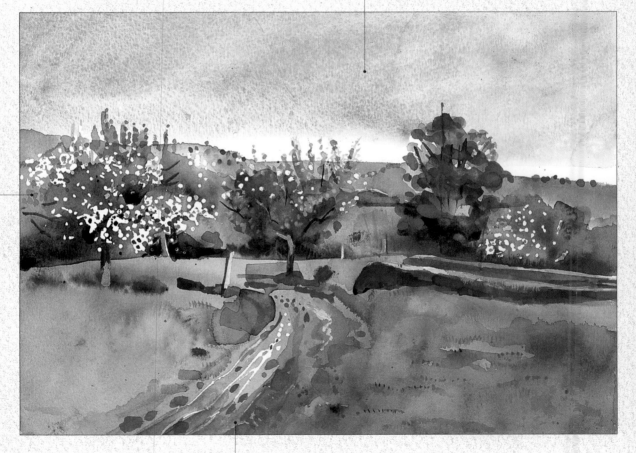

The wet-into-wet wash of cadmium yellow and viridian hints at freshness and new growth.

The mix of blue-greens with a touch of cadmium orange and yellow suggests the rejuvenation of the land.

ONE WAY TO CREATE an overall atmosphere in a seasonal painting is to use a colored paper. You can color your own paper by painting a very dilute wash – a warm ochre for summer, for example, or a cool cerulean blue for winter – over your watercolor paper and allowing it to dry before you begin your painting. Always remember that the white of the paper is your greatest ally in watercolor painting. Make the background color so dilute as to be almost imperceptible; otherwise you run the risk of deadening the scene and destroying the translucent quality for which watercolor painting is renowned. Alternatively, you can buy tinted papers in pale hues of blue, oatmeal, green, and cream. The main problem with using these papers is that they block the translucent quality of standard watercolor paper. Don't rely exclusively on the paper to provide the overall temperature of the scene, however: you must still use the colors in your palette to capture the warm and cool qualities you see before you. The paper is only the background: it is up to you to bring the scene to life.

In the summer you might like to paint a landscape outdoors. A word of advice: never paint in direct sunlight because the paint will dry much too quickly, making it difficult to work effectively. Moreover, bright sunshine will affect your tonal judgment, and when you get back to your studio, you are likely to be disappointed in what you see. Instead, find a painting spot in the shade where you are not dazzled by the brightness of the light.

Summer

Before beginning to paint, the artist washed a very dilute yellow ochre over the paper, making the overall temperature of the scene warmer than in the springtime example. Washes of cadmium yellow punctuate the image, the warm tones suggesting overhead sunlight. The dark tree trunk and shadows provide tonal contrast. Bright colors are stippled and spattered in the foreground to suggest summer blooms. No extra color is added to the sky, as the focus of the image is the warmth of the sun permeating through to the land below.

The cool green wet-into-wet washes in the background create the impression of distance.

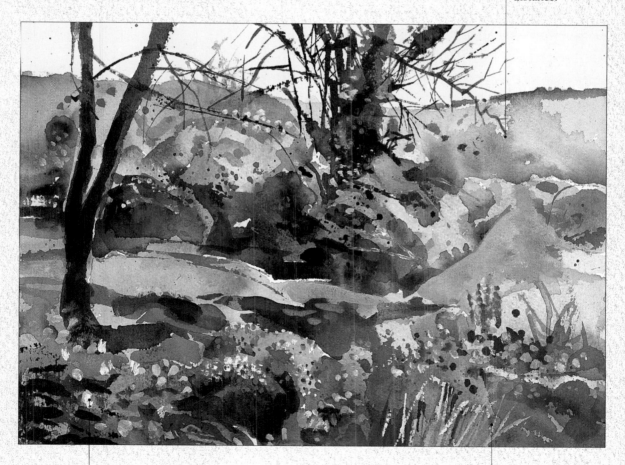

Touches of Chinese white gouache are spattered over the foreground to create highlights in the flowers and foliage.

Wet-into-wet washes and overlays of stippling combine with sgraffito to create a rich and textured foreground scene.

WHATEVER SEASON YOU ARE PAINTING, if you are to achieve a successful landscape you must imbue your work with a sense of light. Look at the quality and direction of the light in the scene in front of you (see pp. 86–93). Notice how the light affects the objects that it touches. Does it, for example, graze the surface at an oblique angle to reveal form or bleach out color in a strong burst of overhead sunlight? Think about the colors and techniques you need to use to portray this.

Harmony and discord both play important roles in landscape scenes. Although a harmoniously composed landscape of analogous colors is restful on the eye, it is sometimes a good idea to include a surprise element. You might, for example, add a different tone or a hue of a contrasting temperature simply to change the pace of the painting, or arrange the scene to provide an unexpected center of interest.

A straightforward representation of the scene is not the only approach you can take. You can often capture the essence of a landscape by allowing watercolor paint to flow randomly, wet into wet. Spend some time looking at the colors in the landscape, then use your palette to work variegated washes together to produce an abstract tonal response. Finally, add touches of detail, in watercolor or pen and ink, to unify the scene and allow the viewer to interpret and share your experience.

The trees are suggested by a wet-into-wet mix of cadmium red and cadmium yellow, creating an area of intense color on the horizon.

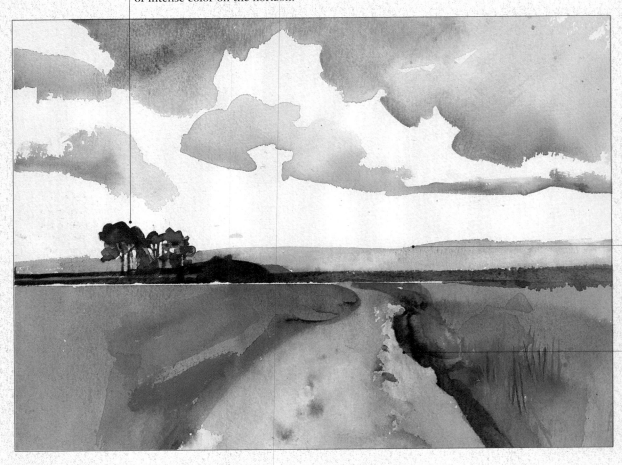

The pale pink wash of the distant hills echoes the warm tones in the foreground, enhancing the richness and warmth of the fields and the path.

Damp brushstrokes laid over the wet-into-wet washes define the edge of the path.

Fall

The colors of fall are deliberately exaggerated to create an intense impression of the season. The painting is separated into three horizontal parts, with the horizon line in the middle of the picture and a faint wash of distant hills in the background beneath an open sky. Wet-into-wet streaks of cobalt blue and Payne's gray, combined with a touch of yellow ochre, create a high but warm sky. In contrast to this subtle approach, a grove of vivid cadmium red trees on the horizon ensures that there can be no mistake about the season. The fields and the path in the foreground are painted in soft variegated washes of warm hues – cadmium orange, yellow, and a touch of burnt sienna – to reinforce the autumnal mood.

Winter

To capture the cool atmosphere of a winter season, you need to use a palette of cool colors. Here, cobalt blue, cerulean blue, Payne's gray, and viridian are the dominant colors. In this picture, the first step is to paint a very dilute, almost imperceptible wash of cerulean blue over the paper to reinforce the sense of general coolness. Much of the paper is otherwise left free of paint, with simple touches of color creating the impression of uneven snow lying on the ground. The horizon line is high. We cannot see the tops of the trees: the composition is cropped so that we feel close to the snow-covered earth. The horizon line is painted with a streak of cobalt blue in order to emphasize the bitter chill of the day.

Drybrush strokes are used in a feathering technique to express the fine lines of the trees.

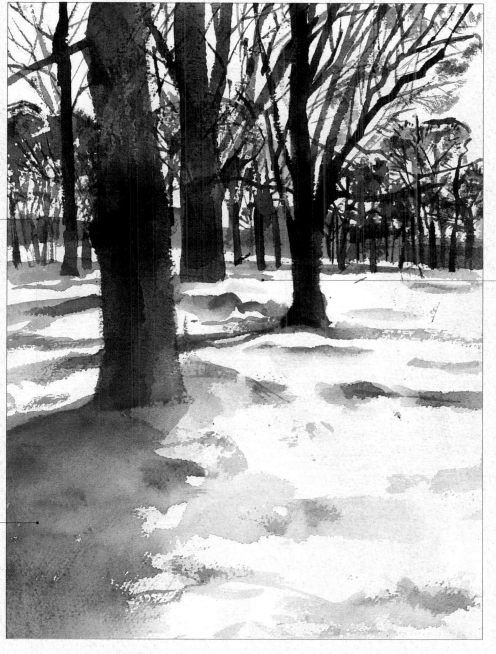

A strip of cobalt blue paint along the horizon line creates the impression of all-pervading iciness.

Lines of cobalt blue mixed with yellow ochre are added to create a contrast in tone and to add a hint of warmth to the scene.

A strong blue shadow falls from the trees, reinforcing the coolness of the light reflected off the snow.

THE NATURAL WORLD:
Distant Landscapes

To GIVE THE IMPRESSION of distance in a landscape, you need to apply some fundamental painting principles. The first thing to remember is a basic law of perspective: the farther objects are from you, the smaller they appear to be. Use this fact to your advantage. Putting small figures or trees on the horizon line with

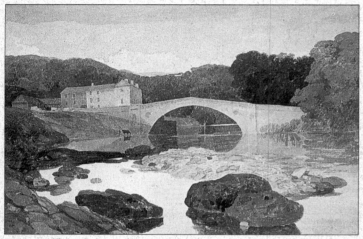

Greta Bridge, J. S. Cotman (1782–1842)
To suggest scale, the foreground rocks are similar in size to the building behind the bridge. The gradually narrowing view of the water from foreground to background also suggests a sense of distance.

larger ones in the foreground, for example, is a sure way to give a feeling of scale and distance. Color, too, can be used to convey a sense of distance. The sky and land are paler as you get closer to the horizon line, while colors progressively darken in tone as you move toward the foreground. One way of achieving this effect is to build up layers of color in the foreground of a scene. To make it easier to ascertain the relevant watercolor tones without being distracted by details, squint your eyes when you look at the scene. Texture is also more evident as you move toward the foreground.

Before you begin painting, decide on your composition. Remember that you do not have to paint exactly what you see. If the scene is complicated, simplify it by removing any elements that do not enhance it. Sometimes you may wish to add an element that is not there in reality. Never be a slave to nature. Instead, try to capture the essence of the scene by concentrating on the dominant colors and shapes. Capturing the essence of a landscape is fundamental to creating a successful work, and like all aspects of painting from life, it depends on accurate observation. Even if you do not have time to paint in the open air, make a few color sketches directly from nature and refer to them once you are back in the studio.

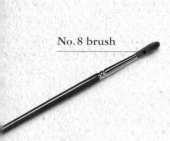

No. 8 brush

Paints
Alizarin crimson
Cerulean blue
Raw umber
Viridian
Cadmium yellow
Hooker's green light
Cobalt blue
Cadmium red

San Miniato, Italy: Daybreak
This composition is divided into three parts: the rich tones of the foreground, followed by paler and cooler midtones, and finally the warm colors of the dawn sky.

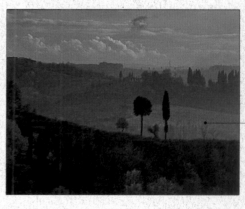

Paler colors in the middle ground emphasize the distance in this landscape.

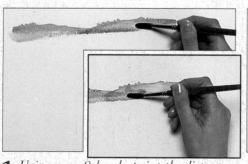

1 *Using a no. 8 brush, paint the distant hills in an alizarin crimson/ cerulean blue mix. Inset: When dry, apply further layers, adding more cerulean blue each time.*

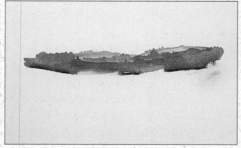

2 *When the paint is dry, paint a line of raw umber over the lower half of the blue. Use less water, allowing the paint colors to become darker.*

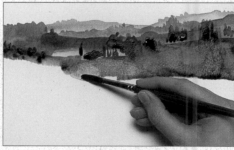

3 *Paint the trees and shrubs in raw umber and the fields with a raw umber and viridian mix. Add a touch of cadmium yellow to the distant fields.*

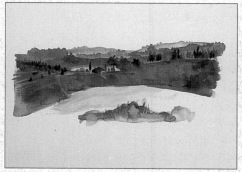

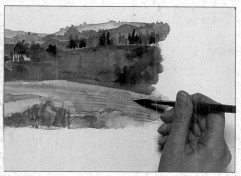

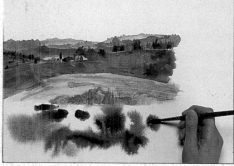

4 Paint a wash of cerulean blue in the middle ground. Allow it to dry, then paint an irregularly shaped block of cadmium yellow and viridian together below it.

5 Use the wet brush to add water over the top of the dried colors, and wash in more viridian and cadmium yellow, wet into wet, softening the overall impression of the middle ground as you work.

6 Still using the no. 8 brush, wet the foreground of the paper. Now, using intensely pigmented viridian, Hooker's green light, and cadmium yellow paint, lay a variegated wash across the foreground. Allow the paint to spread randomly.

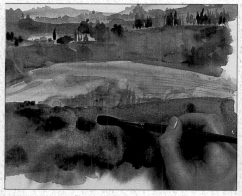

7 Let the paint dry. Add some raw umber and cerulean blue to the foreground to develop rich, intense hues and textural effects. Use lots of water to keep the paint wet as you work.

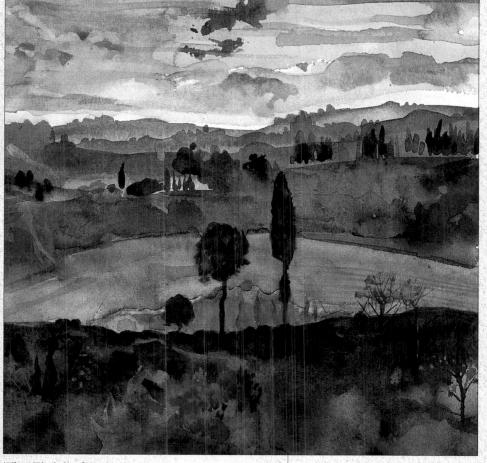

8 Paint the shapes of the trees in the middle ground with a dark mix of viridian and cobalt blue, then drop a variegated wash into the sky, wet on dry, first using very dilute cadmium red, then very dilute cadmium yellow. Inset: Allow the paint to dry, then overlay it with cerulean blue.

The Finished Painting

Three tonal bands help develop a feeling of distance in this composition. The foreground is painted with rich wet-into-wet washes; the middle ground is paler and therefore less significant. The purple-blue of the far hills draws the viewer's eye toward the horizon and the pale but warm oranges and blues in the sky above. The three trees provide a change in scale between the foreground and middle ground, emphasizing the distance between the two.

The silhouetted trees in the middle ground are an effective way of indicating great distance: the trees behind them are both smaller in scale and paler in color.

THE NATURAL WORLD:
Skies

IN GOOD LANDSCAPE PAINTINGS the sky is carefully integrated into the composition, not something to be washed in at the very last stage of a painting once the land has been completed. The fresh, translucent quality of watercolor makes it a natural choice for painting the sky, as it can capture the ever-changing nature of the subject. By combining fresh wet-into-wet painting with damp and dry overlays of color, you can achieve a sensitive and realistic representation.

The appearance of the sky is affected by many factors, including the direction and strength of the wind, the humidity in the air, the position and angle of the sun, the time of day and year, and the type of landmass below. Consider all these things before you begin painting.

No sky is uniform in color. Even the clearest blue sky includes areas of inconsistency, and it almost always appears lighter toward the horizon. As a result, it is often best to use a combination of gradated and variegated washes (see pp. 42–43) when painting a sky. There are exceptions to this rule – for example, areas where the sky meets a large mass of water. In such instances, the sky may appear to darken in tone, absorbing color from the water below. In addition, every sky you paint will differ in tone, depending on the season and climate. At the height of summer a blue sky may be a warm ultramarine blue; in winter it may become a cool, pale cerulean blue.

Clouds have fascinated artists for centuries, and capturing their fleeting effects as they race across the sky is one of the greatest challenges of painting in watercolor. Whether soft and white, like balls of cotton, or stormy and electric blue, clouds are a rich source of inspiration for the artist. Quick studies, such as those by the English artist John Constable (1776–1837), are often the most effective way of capturing their transitory beauty. Although portraying the sky accurately is important, so too is impulse. Let your watercolor make some of the decisions for you and allow accidental runs of paint to become part of your composition.

View from Bussana Vecchia, Italy

The sky in this painting commands our attention, taking up half the picture area. Painted at the height of summer, the sky is composed of white clouds punctuated by areas of rich cobalt blue. Although the sky is overcast, the clouds are light and the day is bright. The blue in the sky is exactly the same color as the sea below, the two elements creating a natural backdrop to the verdant landscape. A variegated wet-into-wet wash of blue across the sky, drifting into areas of the paper that have been left white, gives the impression of cloud formations.

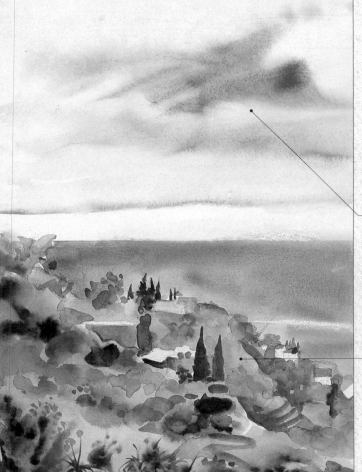

Areas of bright cloud are suggested by leaving areas of the paper free of paint.

The wide range of greens in the landscape provide a dramatic contrast with the color of the sky.

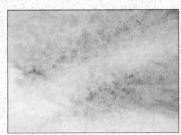

The sky was painted with the wet-into-wet technique (see pp. 44–45). When creating such a subtle effect as this, use plenty of water and only a small amount of paint.

French Landscape

In this breezy springtime scene, large cumulus clouds move swiftly along. In such instances it is important to re-create the drama of the cloud formations and a sense of their ephemeral existence. The rolling forms are repeated in varying colors: some areas are left white, while others are painted wet into wet with a combination of Payne's gray, alizarin crimson, and cadmium yellow. The blue in the sky is dropped onto the wet paper, with variegated washes of cerulean blue.

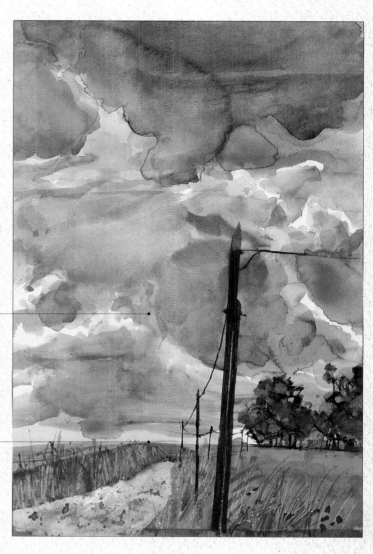

Mixtures of Payne's gray and alizarin crimson in various strengths are dropped wet into wet to form rolling clouds. Once these dry, further layers of paint are dropped into areas of darker tone.

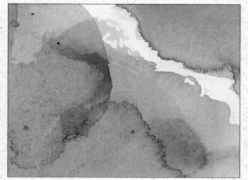

Parts of the paper are left white to create the impression of bright highlights, while adjoining wet-into-wet washes of gray and purple provide rich tonal and textural contrasts.

The sky dominates the composition, with the trees and telephone poles directing our eyes up toward it and the path leading our eye to the horizon line.

Hove, England: Sunset

Watercolor and Chinese white gouache are combined to produce an opaque and textured skyline above an abstract townscape. The setting sun creates bands of rich color across the sky, with the tones becoming warmer as they reach the horizon line. The eye is drawn to the heart of the image — the circle of the setting sun itself, positioned in the center of the horizon.

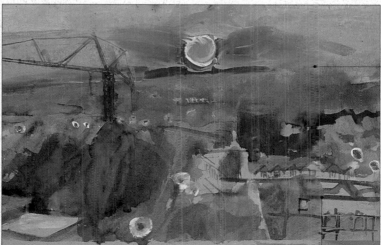

The bands of rich color melt into one another, ensuring that the sky does not appear segmented.

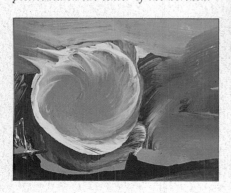

The sun and the patch of sky surrounding it are both painted in a mixture of cadmium red and cadmium yellow. A swirl of Chinese white gouache around the sun allows it to stand out.

The colors in the skyline are repeated in the townscape below, creating a sense of cohesion between the land and the sky.

THE NATURAL WORLD:
Water

WATERCOLOR PAINT is a perfect medium to use for interpreting water: the transparency of the paint and the fluid, liquid quality of wet-into-wet washes are ideally suited to the subject.

One of the most fascinating things about water is its transitoriness. Even an area of water that appears to be completely still is constantly changing as the breeze causes ripples on the surface or the changing light alters colors. Rather than trying to capture a specific moment in time, concentrate on re-creating the atmosphere of the scene, aiming to evoke the mood and spirit rather than render every droplet precisely.

Painting fast-running or turbulent water is an exciting challenge for a watercolorist. If you decide to paint a river flowing at full strength, or a storm-tossed sea with waves crashing furiously, carefully observe the scene before you start to paint. The water may seem to flow randomly, but if you look hard enough you will soon discover patterns and repetitions. Not only do the patterns of water movement repeat themselves, but so do the shapes that appear within them as the water flows around obstacles or cascades over a rocky ledge.

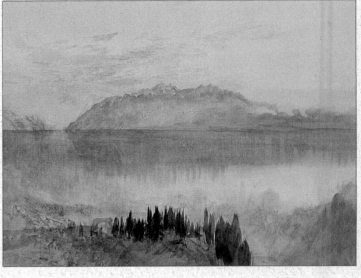

Lake Geneva with Dent d'Oche,
J.M.W. Turner (1775–1851)
Turner used wet-into-wet watercolor washes to achieve this light-infused study of Lake Geneva. In his determination to capture the atmosphere of the scene, Turner sacrificed much of its detail for abstract colors and textures.

Falling Water
This waterfall scene contains contrasting rhythms, with the water frothing at each step before cascading downward. Subtle blue and green overtones help to prevent the scene from appearing entirely monochromatic.

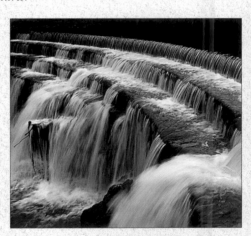

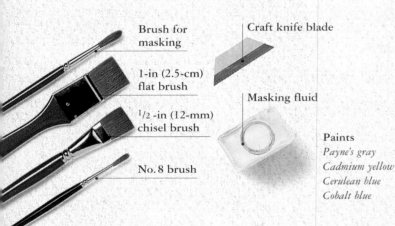

Brush for masking

Craft knife blade

1-in (2.5-cm) flat brush

Masking fluid

1/2-in (12-mm) chisel brush

No. 8 brush

Paints
Payne's gray
Cadmium yellow
Cerulean blue
Cobalt blue

1 *Make a detailed sketch of the scene using an HB pencil, then apply masking fluid with an old brush to mask out the highlights. When the white paper is revealed in the final stages, it will play an important role in the completed picture.*

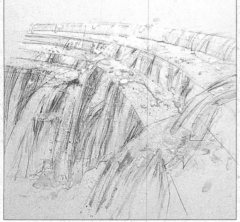

2 *Using a 1-in (2.5-cm) flat brush, wash horizontal sweeps of Payne's gray along each step and vertical sweeps down each fall of water. Inset: Use the edge of a 1/2-in (12-mm) chisel brush to create hard lines.*

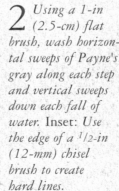

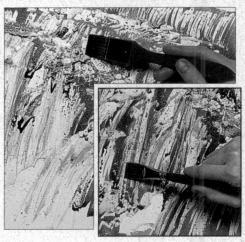

3 While the paint is still damp, overlay cadmium yellow paint on the darkest areas of falling water with a no. 8 brush to darken and enrich the Payne's gray. Now add some cerulean blue and cobalt blue to heighten the tonal variations.

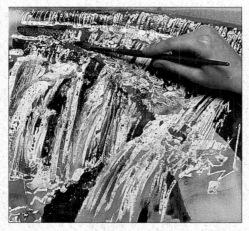

4 Allow the painting to dry, then remove the masking fluid. Large areas of the paper are now completely free of paint. To redress the balance and add greater tonal variation, you now need to texture the white areas of the paper.

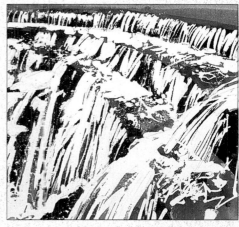

5 Use a damp no. 8 brush to blend areas of cerulean blue to create midtones in the white areas. Vary the cerulean blue tones. Inset: Apply fine vertical marks of cerulean blue to create an impression of falling water.

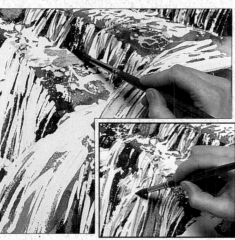

6 Allow the picture to dry. To create an impression of spray, rub the edge of the craft knife blade over areas of the waterfall to lift out paint and leave a rough surface. Use the tip of the blade to pick out tiny specks of paint and create "highlights."

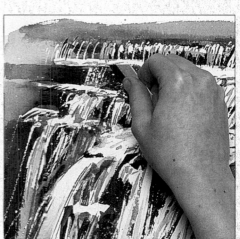

The Finished Picture

The picture is finished when you feel that there is enough variation between the areas of bright white highlight and dark Payne's gray. You do not want the picture to appear too stark and monochromatic, so you must make sure that there are plenty of midtones. The falling water appears icy cold and smooth, while the frothing, bubbling water on the steps creates a change in pace and energizes the overall picture.

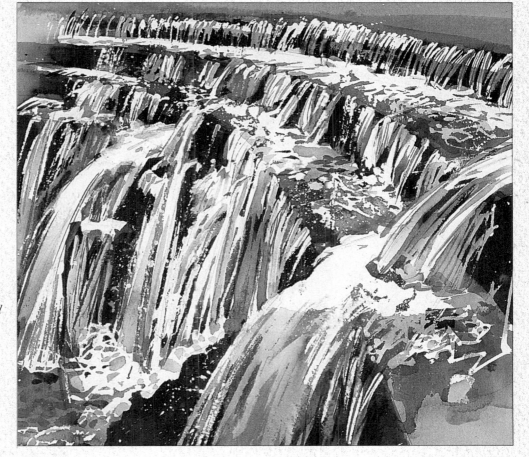

WATER SCENES HAVE many moods, from still ponds to cascades of foaming water, and you need to adapt your technique to suit the mood of the scene. For calm areas such as still lakes or lagoons, use flat, simple washes of color, perhaps interspersed with random spatters of masking fluid to create occasional highlights. Lines of masking fluid, overlaid by flat washes of color and then rubbed away once the paint has dried, give clear and simple impressions of flat water, too. To produce the effect of a broken surface of flat water – perhaps on a horizon line or around the rudder of a boat – try drybrushing color over previously untouched watercolor paper. Often, you will need no more than a simple gradated wash of two blue tones to create the impression of still water running away to the horizon line. For atmospheric, misty waters, soft wet-into-wet effects are often the most effective.

St. Ives, Cornwall, England

Calm, flat water in the distance merges into the sky, leaving only the subtlest hint of a horizon line, where the very pale Payne's gray wash of the sky blends into viridian in the sea. In contrast the foreground water ripples as it approaches the jetty and the rocks. Subtle overlays of yellow ochre and viridian produce an effective impression of movement on the water surface. The overall appeal of the picture stems from the emphasis on the character of the water over elaborate details.

In contrast, if you wish to achieve the impression of fast-running water, whether it be the spray from a waterfall or waves crashing in the sea, a combination of watercolor techniques is best. Drybrush marks are perfect for creating ripples in the surface of the water; making calligraphic-style marks on the surface with a Chinese brush is another useful technique (see pp. 30–31). To create an effective representation of spray, spatter Chinese white gouache over dry watercolor paint, using an old toothbrush. Stippling is another useful technique for splashes of water. You can also use a sponge to produce unusual textures in the surface of the water. This method gives you a degree of control over the marks, while at the same time enabling you to create the impression of randomness. One material that comes into its own when you are painting water is masking fluid. You can use it extensively to block out areas of fast-running water, while you paint local areas where the surface is calmer. You can also spatter masking fluid onto unpainted paper to produce the effect of froth and spray once the masking fluid is rubbed away and the white paper is revealed.

The most common mistake in painting water, as with any other subject, is overworking the paint. Always try to keep your depictions of water uncomplicated and spontaneous: if you overlay too many layers of color, you will lose your greatest asset – the natural freshness and transparency of the paint.

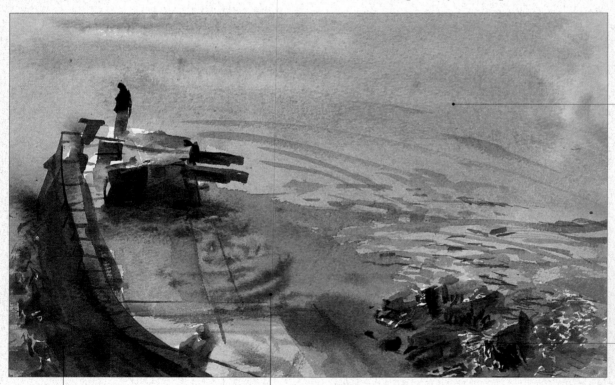

The water in the far distance lies undisturbed and is laid in with a variegated wash of cobalt blue and viridian.

Where the water is disturbed by rocks, Chinese white gouache is added to create touches of spray.

The water has a glassy appearance, which is created through a single thin layer of viridian.

Shadows on the surface of the water are created by subtle overlays of a more intensely pigmented layer of viridian and cobalt blue.

Weir

To capture the force and energy of water bubbling through a weir, you need to use lively techniques. Here, Chinese white gouache, applied over dry watercolor washes, has a tremendous impact. The bright white of the spray and froth is created by stippling and spattering; use the Chinese white straight from the tube to create a change in texture for the froth rising above the water. The waves are painted with Chinese white gouache mixed wet into damp over pale green washes made from a mix of yellow ochre and Hooker's green light.

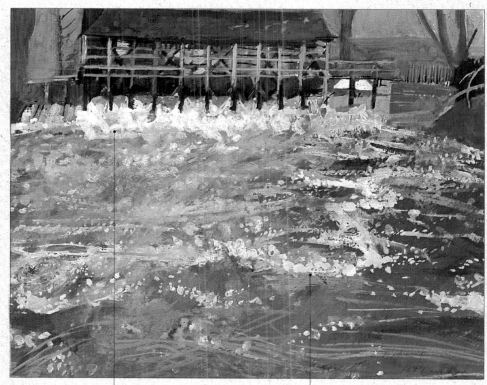

Extensive use of Chinese white gouache under the weir gives a sense of energy to the water.

Paint is spattered and stippled onto the paper to convey the turbulence of the water.

Mooring the Gondola

Although we see only a small area of water in this scene, there are many variations within it. The boat disturbs the water surface, producing both ripples and shadows. The ripples are achieved by using wet-into-wet variegated washes of greens and blues, which are allowed to blend together. The shadows are created by carefully outlining the area in Payne's gray and then dropping a mix of cobalt blue and Payne's gray onto the dampened paper and allowing it to spread randomly. The water behind the boat is a mix of Hooker's green light and cerulean blue, with the addition of a little yellow ochre and Chinese white gouache. This color becomes darker toward the foreground and turns to near-black at the bow of the boat. The change in tone helps to impart a sense of distance.

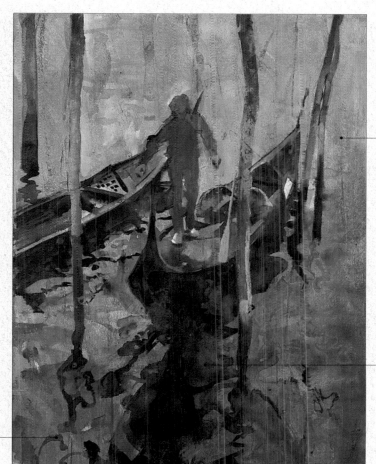

Still water is created by applying a single wash of each color and then letting the colors intermingle on the surface.

There is no distinct line between the boat and the water. The two objects blend together, so the bottom of the boat appears to be submerged under the water's surface.

The reflections in the surface of the water are suggested by a dark wash of cobalt blue and Payne's gray.

THE NATURAL WORLD:
Flowers and Foliage

DETAILED RENDERINGS OF flowers and foliage have been popular among watercolorists for centuries. Some of the most important botanical illustrators worked in the 18th and 19th centuries, developing the first detailed documentation on plants. Pierre Joseph Redouté (1759–1840), a French artist whose work abounds with beautiful transparent washes and remarkable stippled effects, is the most famous. Both he and his followers were committed to painting plant forms with absolute accuracy.

You may wish to delineate the stamens and veins on flowers and leaves with the same precision as these botanical illustrators, or you may prefer a less detailed but more emotive response. Either way, the most important thing is to study your subject with care before you attempt to paint it on paper to ensure that you remain faithful to the forms and colors.

Of course, different plants require different techniques. Some cry out for a delicate, light touch; pure watercolor washes enhance the paper-thin transparency of their petals. Others, more vivid in color and glossy in texture, benefit from the use of additives such as gum arabic to enrich their surfaces (see pp. 68–69). Masking fluid is a must for rendering precise details (see pp. 62–65). Drybrush (see pp. 56–57) is a useful way of creating the delicate veining of petals and leaves.

Often you will need to employ only a limited palette of colors to capture the subtle qualities of flowers and foliage. Many petals and leaves comprise a range of closely related hues, which are best reproduced by the subtle mixing of a few essential colors.

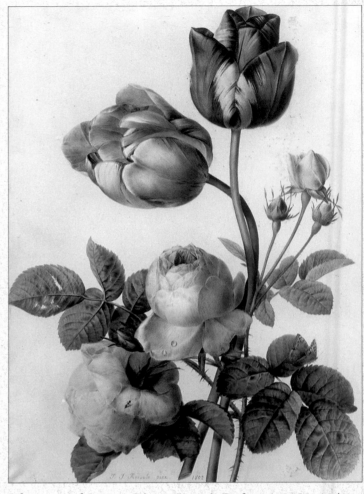

Flowers and Insects, **Pierre Joseph Redouté (1759–1840)**
A careful buildup of color washes conveys the petals' translucency. Highlights are exaggerated to emphasize the flowers' roundness.

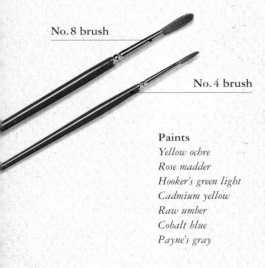

No. 8 brush

No. 4 brush

Paints
Yellow ochre
Rose madder
Hooker's green light
Cadmium yellow
Raw umber
Cobalt blue
Payne's gray

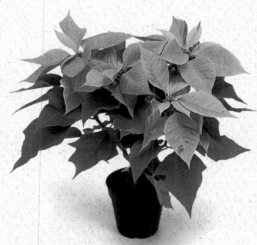

Poinsettia
The leaves of this poinsettia have the delicacy of tissue paper, encouraging deft wet-into-wet work and overlays of color.

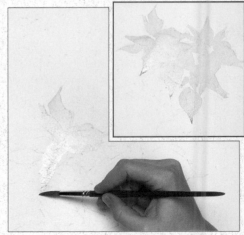

1 *Paint the pink leaf shapes using yellow ochre and a no. 8 brush.* Inset: *When dry, add a second coat. Let the paint run, creating variegated areas within the leaves.*

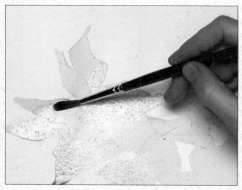

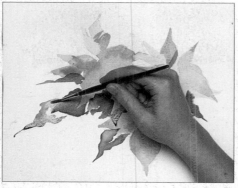

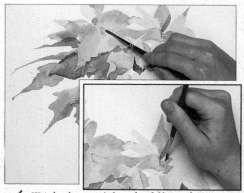

2 Load the no. 8 brush with very dilute rose madder, and start to build up tone on the pink leaves. The paint will flow over the yellow ochre, allowing some of it to show through.

3 Using a no. 4 brush, paint the darker leaves in Hooker's green light. While the leaves are still wet, drop cadmium yellow into the paler areas and let the paint spread and mix on the paper.

4 With the no. 4 brush, fill in the areas between the pink leaves with touches of cadmium yellow. Inset: Use the tip of the brush to paint the tight areas between overlaid leaves.

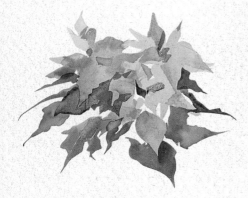

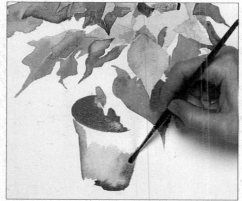

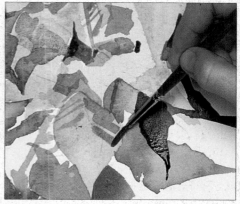

5 The shaded areas of the leaves are painted with a touch of raw umber. The tips of the leaves should diminish into fine points. Paint the shapes precisely and work deftly, with quick strokes.

6 With the no. 4 brush, begin to build up the shape of the pot, using cobalt blue, Payne's gray, and raw umber blended wet into wet on the paper. When dry, overlay a light wash of Payne's gray.

7 Mix cadmium yellow and rose madder on the palette, then paint in the veins and shadows on the leaves.

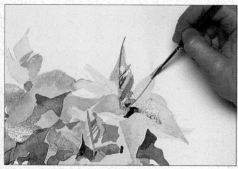

8 Use the tip of the no. 4 brush, shaped to a fine point, to overlay very precise lines of a mix of yellow ochre and rose madder on top of the leaves. These lines emphasize the three-dimensional nature of the leaves and their delicate shapes.

Leaving areas free of paint allows light to shine through from the white paper and enhance the delicacy of the poinsettia.

Payne's gray is blended with raw umber in the soil area to add a sense of space in the center of the painting.

The Finished Painting
Light brushstrokes and allowing the paint colors to mix on the paper give this painting a fresh and immediate feel. The contrast between the pale and the dark leaves adds drama.

THE NATURAL WORLD:
Foliage and Fields

GREEN IS THE MOST common and the most varied color found in nature. To paint natural subjects realistically, therefore, you need to become proficient at mixing green. Muddy greens will do nothing to enhance your landscapes. Look for the many different variations, from deep olive to fluorescent lime.

For yellow-greens, combine Hooker's green light or viridian with varying amounts of yellow ochre, burnt sienna, burnt umber, or cadmium yellow. For blue-greens, mix Hooker's green light or viridian with cobalt blue or cerulean blue. Experiment with overlaying colors directly on the paper rather than mixing them on the palette: you may find that the same combination looks very different when mixed in different ways.

It is not only the range of the greens you use that will make or break your painting, but also the freshness of the shadows you incorporate into the image. Try to use recessive colors, based on blue. Don't be tempted to paint the undersides of leaves with a dark hue, such as undiluted Payne's gray, as this may appear too dominant when placed next to fresh green tones.

The amount of detail you incorporate into a painting of foliage depends on the effect you hope to achieve. Too much detail may bring the background too far forward within the overall composition, whereas too loose an impression in the foreground may lack structure. For large areas, achieving the right balance between bulk and space is crucial. You want to convey an impression of depth as well as light in the foliage, so make sure that there are quiet interludes between areas of rich color.

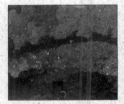

Areas of recessive blue contrast with paler green tones to produce varied cool and warm tones in the background.

Cow Parsley and Fields

This image makes extensive use of the color green to produce a wide range of effects. Dark mixes of viridian and cobalt blue create an impression of foliage in the background trees. Flat washes of yellow-greens in the middle ground contribute to the sense of distance and scale in the picture. Fine drybrush work in the foreground enhances the detailing on the grasses.

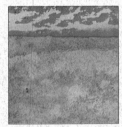

In the middle distance pale green tones, made up of light green and yellow, are washed over the rough paper, suggesting the field's irregular texture.

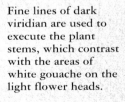

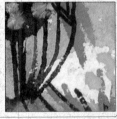

Fine lines of dark viridian are used to execute the plant stems, which contrast with the areas of white gouache on the light flower heads.

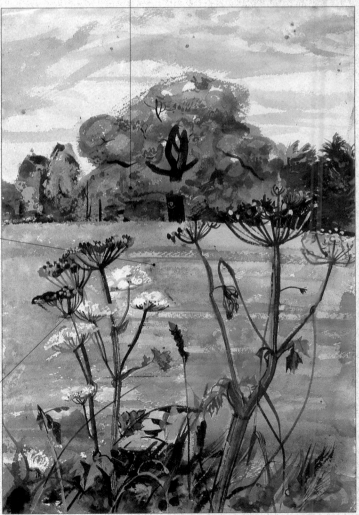

The Red Tree

Foliage is not always green, especially in the fall, when you are likely to see rich displays of red and orange leaves. Here cadmium red and alizarin crimson were drybrushed and blended into the main foliage, with some spaces left between the leaves to give a sense of the luminous sky above. Even though this tree is covered in red leaves, the image is underpinned by a range of wet-into-wet combinations of viridian and Hooker's green light.

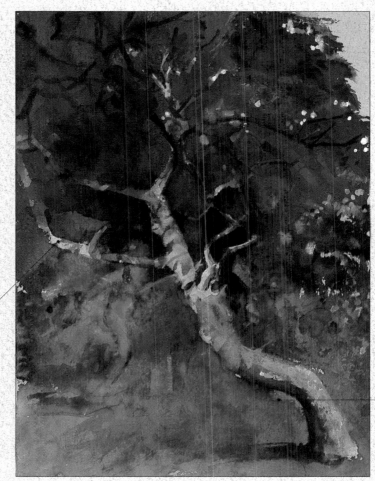

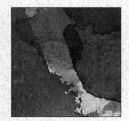

The red leaves are interspersed by spaces left free of paint, and fine branch lines help give the impression of depth.

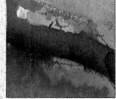

Yellow-green tones are blended wet into wet in the foreground to provide contrast and balance. White gouache brings out the silvery bark of the tree.

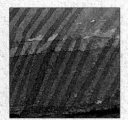

Layers of viridian are overlaid by drybrush marks, which serve the dual purpose of creating texture and leading the eye down toward the center of the painting.

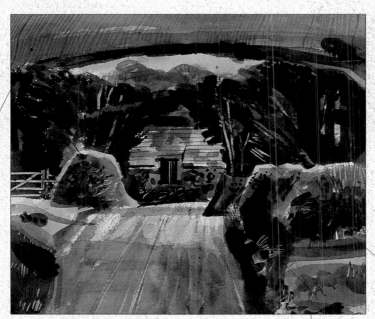

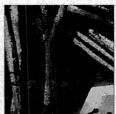

In the middle ground the textures are enriched and extended as the color range becomes wider, drawing the eye into the center of the painting and leading directly toward the cottage.

Farmhouse on a Country Lane

Washes of dark and light greens in the background create a patchwork of fields, rising toward the horizon. They are separated by abstract marks representing hedgerows and woodland. The image is structured around the valley in the center of the painting, where a small cottage dominates the scene. A canopy of foliage leads our eye toward it.

Scratching through the surface with a sharp implement such as a craft knife or razor blade throws the highlights into sharp focus.

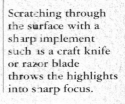

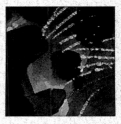

THE NATURAL WORLD:
Living Creatures

UNLIKE MOST PEOPLE, who can maintain a single pose for a whole painting session, animals have great trouble sitting still. For your first attempts choose an animal that you can study and paint regularly – perhaps your own pet or a friend's dog or cat. The key words are observation and patience. You will soon realize that patterns of behavior are often repeated. The way a dog stretches out and crosses its paws to scratch its nose, the way a cat licks itself clean – these are characteristic actions. Once you have fixed them in your mind, you will find it much easier to re-create your subject in paint.

To capture an animal walking, pouncing, or running, you need a basic understanding of the way in which its limbs work. Photographs or a videotape can be useful in showing you the sequence in which an animal moves its legs and body. But don't attempt to copy a photograph or video still of your dog or cat: the frozen frame will distort and flatten the image, rendering your painted copy lifeless and unnatural.

Wildlife offers different opportunities. Many artists go out on location to collect reference material for wildlife painting, often taking photographs and making on-the-spot studies and color notes. If you can't go into the wild, try visiting a zoo or wildlife park. Keep your location sketches simple, concentrating on the main shapes and movements without worrying about the finer details.

Study of Tabby in Repose, I

After the main shape of the cat is dampened in with water, yellow ochre, Payne's gray, and burnt sienna watercolor pigments are blended wet into wet and allowed to spread to imitate the shape of the cat's body. The contrasting light and dark tones give the impression of depth and bulk. Black pen-and-ink lines are then added on top of the damp paint to develop form and fill in details. Because the underlying paint is still damp, the ink lines blur slightly. Around the edges of the animal sharp pen-and-ink lines are drawn in once the paint has dried, creating the impression of spiky individual hairs.

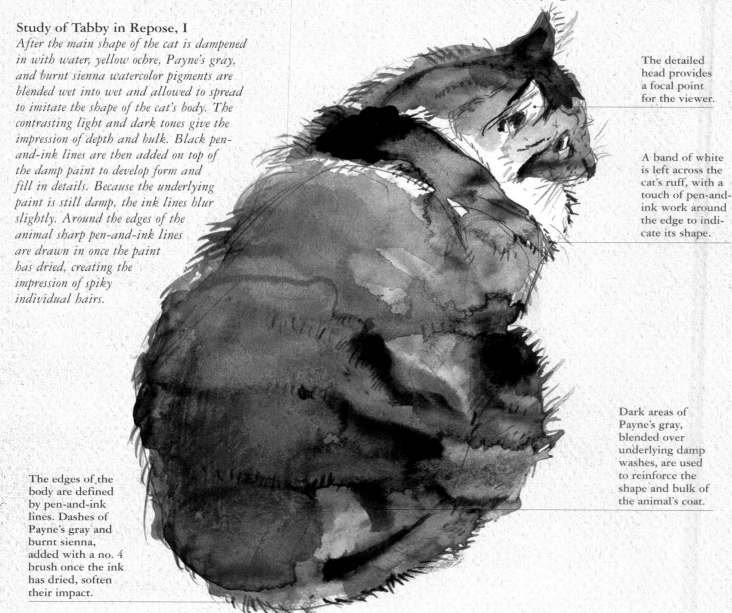

The detailed head provides a focal point for the viewer.

A band of white is left across the cat's ruff, with a touch of pen-and-ink work around the edge to indicate its shape.

Dark areas of Payne's gray, blended over underlying damp washes, are used to reinforce the shape and bulk of the animal's coat.

The edges of the body are defined by pen-and-ink lines. Dashes of Payne's gray and burnt sienna, added with a no. 4 brush once the ink has dried, soften their impact.

Study of Tabby in Repose, II

In this instance the wet-into-wet Payne's gray, burnt sienna, and yellow ochre are allowed to dry, then details are added in dry media – graphite pencil and soft charcoal. Compared with the previous example, this method gives you greater scope for detailing and capturing texture and form. Use both the point and the side of the pencil and charcoal sticks to produce broad strokes and fine lines. The charcoal helps you to create soft, blended marks, while the pencil lends itself to much finer, more linear details. This method is ideal for working quickly, as you can put down the basic shape before the animal moves and then add the details later.

Detailed pencil work on top of the water-color washes indicates fine hairs and soft markings in the fur, giving form.

Charcoal is rubbed into the cat's back with the fingertips to create a darker tone and an impression of soft fur.

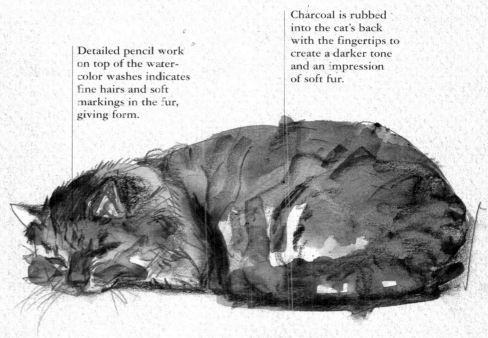

Study of Tabby in Repose, III

This more elaborate study uses gouache as well as wet-into-wet watercolor and pen and ink. This combination of techniques enables you to develop a rich and textured array of fur effects. Chinese white gouache is used for the highlights on the face and ears and is stippled over the body to provide fine markings. Around the ruff and tail, Chinese white is mixed with yellow ochre to produce warm highlights. Smudged pen and ink on the head create tonal contrast and shading.

Precise pen-and-ink work is used for the finest details, such as the whiskers and the shape of the nose.

Pure Chinese white gouache is stippled onto the body to create highlights and reinforce form.

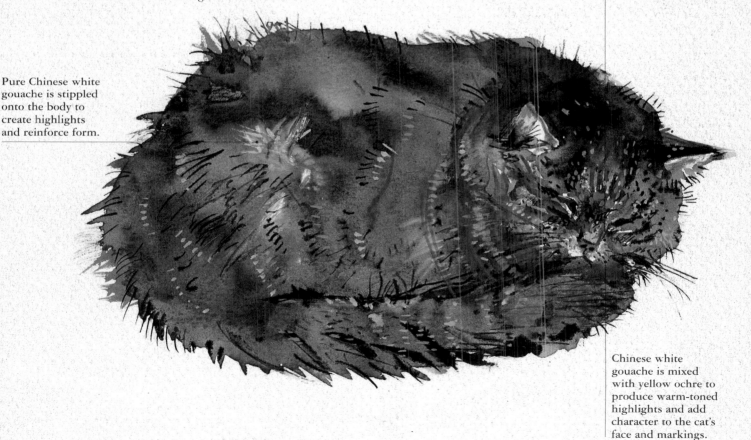

Chinese white gouache is mixed with yellow ochre to produce warm-toned highlights and add character to the cat's face and markings.

WHEN IT COMES to painting details, fur and feathers can seem intimidating to the beginner. When depicting fur, don't try to paint every single hair; you will end up with an over-fussy painting at the expense of capturing the general characteristics of the animal. Instead, exploit the "furring" qualities of watercolor paint to imitate the soft quality of the animal's coat. Allow the paint to blend wet into wet to suggest the bulk of the body, then add sharp lines to give the impression of a few individual hairs around and over it. Dark markings on a tabby cat, for example, are always useful for defining shape, while light areas are generally best left free of paint. Try to capture the main shape of the animal while it is in repose; then you can turn your attention to painting the details after it has wandered off.

Feathers are another interesting challenge. Here, too, it can help if you know a little about the bird's anatomy as different parts of a bird contain different types of feathers. Feathers over the breast area are generally small, soft, and downy; those located on the tail and wings, which are used in flight, are longer, finer, and more precisely shaped. As when painting fur, try to underpin the shape of the main feathers with flat washes of color and then add the details later.

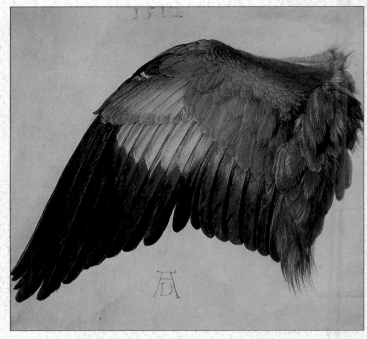

Wing of the Roller, Albrecht Dürer (1471–1528)
Albrecht Dürer was one of the earliest watercolorists. He combined pure watercolor with gouache to create opaque areas within translucent watercolors, achieving fine detail, as displayed in the anatomical rendering of this bird's wing.

Fur

No. 8 brush

No. 3 brush

Natural sponge

Paints
Payne's gray
Cobalt blue
Burnt umber
Chinese white gouache
Alizarin crimson

Creating the Impression of Soft Fur
If you attempt to reproduce each hair, the overall appearance will be far too spiky. Instead, use the blending quality of wet-into-wet work to create a soft base and imply a furry texture by overlaying color wet into damp and wet into dry.

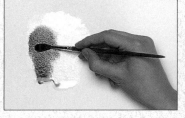

1 *Dampen the paper with a sponge. Using a no. 8 brush, drop a dark mix of Payne's gray, cobalt blue, and burnt umber onto the paper, allowing it to spread into the wet area.*

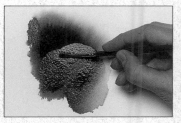

2 *While the paint is still damp, add fine marks of Chinese white gouache with a no. 3 brush. The marks will bleed slightly into the damp paint, creating a soft effect.*

The Finished Painting
The first layer of paint was dropped in wet into wet, with later layers applied to an increasingly dry base. The final details, marked wet on dry, stand out sharply.

Overlays of color give an impression of thick, soft fur.

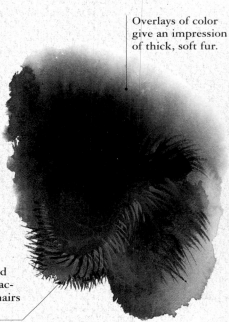

Sharp lines painted wet over dry characterize individual hairs within the mass.

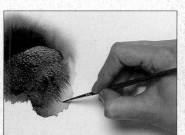

3 *Using the no. 3 brush, apply touches of alizarin crimson over the white markings to add warmth and depth. This step makes the image appear more three-dimensional and gives interesting tonal contrast.*

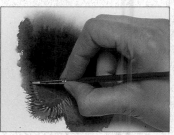

4 *Build up the texture, using the no. 3 brush loaded with the original mix of Payne's gray, burnt umber, and cobalt blue. Add fine hair lines around the bottom outer edge to enhance the suggestion of fur.*

Feathers

No. 1 brush

No. 3 brush

No. 8 brush

Natural sponge

Paints
Yellow ochre
Alizarin crimson
Payne's gray
Burnt umber
Chinese white gouache

Downy Breast Feathers

The majority of feathers on a bird's breast area are small, soft, and downy. As with soft fur, a good way of creating the effect of breast feathers is to use blended wet-into-wet washes, overlaid with a few sensitively placed fine lines to give the impression of individual feathers within the mass.

The Finished Painting

Combining wet-into-wet, wet-into-damp, and wet-into-dry work gives texture and tonal variation. Applying fine details with a no. 1 brush suggests light and dark feathers within the mass.

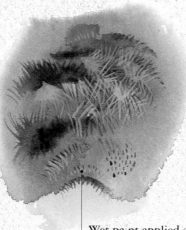

Wet paint applied over a damp surface bleeds and softens as it spreads.

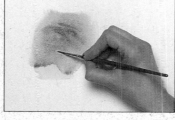

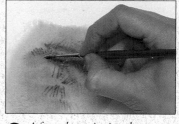

1 *Dampen the paper with a sponge. Using a no. 8 brush, drop yellow ochre onto the paper and alizarin crimson over it. Add fine lines of Payne's gray, alizarin crimson, and burnt umber with a no. 3 brush.*

2 *After the painting has dried, take a no. 1 brush and add further fine lines on top of the softer ones, using the same colors, to develop a rhythm of lines over the feathered area.*

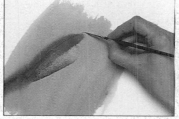

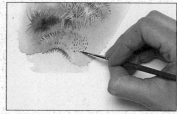

3 *Crosshatch lines of Chinese white over these markings, using the no. 1 brush. The white lines should be spiky to suggest the structure of the feathers.*

4 *Using the no. 1 brush, apply darker dashes of a mixture of Payne's gray and yellow ochre around the bottom edge to suggest ruffled breast feathers.*

Individual Tail Feathers

For large tail feathers, more detail is necessary. Each bird's feathers are marked and shaped differently, so study them well before painting them.

Paints
Yellow ochre
Payne's gray
Chinese white gouache
Burnt umber

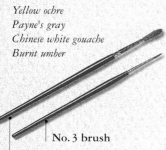

No. 3 brush

No. 8 brush

The underlying color of each feather is suggested by building up wet-into-wet layers of paint.

The Finished Painting

Although the three feathers are loosely painted, each is clearly visible. A combination of wet-into-wet, wet-into-damp, and drybrush techniques has been used to produce the feathered effect.

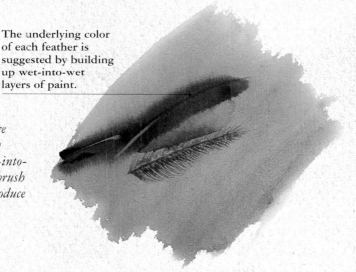

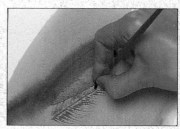

1 *Paint a yellow ochre wash. While damp, paint the first feather's shape in Payne's gray, using a no. 8 brush. Allow this to dry slightly, then add Chinese white gouache over it.*

2 *With a no. 3 brush, paint the shape of a second feather underneath the first, as in the previous step. Then paint the spines of the feathers, using a line of Payne's gray.*

3 *Paint the spine of a third feather with the no. 3 brush. Using a Payne's gray and burnt umber mix, create a feathered effect on each side of the spine with the drybrush technique.*

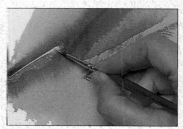

4 *With the no. 3 brush, apply Chinese white gouache over the lower part of the spines of the two larger feathers to create highlights and enhance the shape of each individual feather.*

THE NATURAL WORLD:
Combining Your Skills

San Gimignano, Tuscany

This project gives you the opportunity to combine several of the techniques explored earlier in this section – composition, creating an impression of distance through use of color and varying scale, and different ways of portraying foliage and sky – with some of the fundamental techniques of watercolor painting.

No. 8 brush

No. 6 brush

No. 4 brush

Brush for masking

Tinted masking fluid

White masking fluid

Plastic palette knife

Natural sponge

Gum arabic

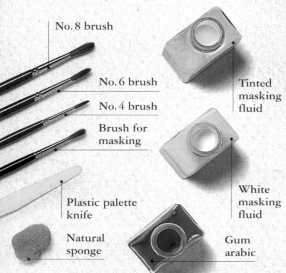

Paints

Cerulean blue	Hooker's green light
Alizarin crimson	Yellow ochre
Raw umber	Burnt umber
Viridian	Raw sienna
Cadmium yellow	Payne's gray
Burnt sienna	Cobalt blue

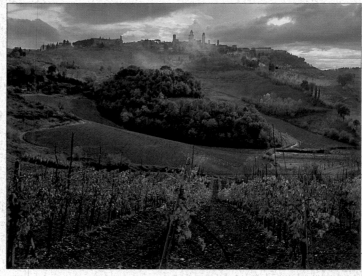

The background hills and sky are paler in tone than the foreground, and this helps to imply distance.

The converging lines of the vineyard lead the eye into the center of the composition.

The richness of the foreground calls for a variety of texturing techniques.

Preparatory Sketch

Make a charcoal sketch to help you to judge the tonal values of the scene. Add a lot of detail to the sketch in order to improve your aesthetic understanding of the overall view.

1 *After lightly sketching the scene in HB pencil, mask out most of the sky with tinted masking fluid and allow it to dry. Taking a no. 8 brush, begin to paint in the silhouette of the distant village with a mix of cerulean blue and alizarin crimson.*

2 *Still using the no. 8 brush, add a little raw umber and viridian in front of the village, working wet into damp. The cool tones of the village imply a sense of distance; the warm tones suggest that this part of the scene is nearer the viewer.*

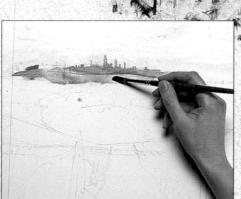

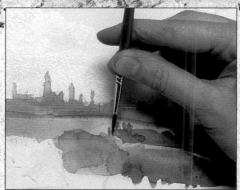

3 *Let everything dry. Wet the middle ground with clean water. Drop spots of cadmium yellow, burnt sienna, and Hooker's green light over the dampened area. Holding the brush vertically, make short marks to describe the village towers.*

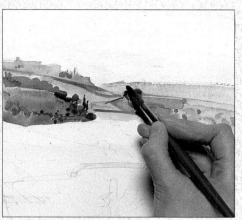

4 Add yellow ochre and burnt umber to your palette as you build the overlapping hues, drawing out the details of fields and the buildings on the horizon line with the no. 8 brush. Add a little cerulean blue to either side of the hilltop to suggest the sky.

Progress Report
The rich tones in the middle ground help to lead the eye toward the village nestled on the horizon line. Now leave the painting to dry and assess your progress.

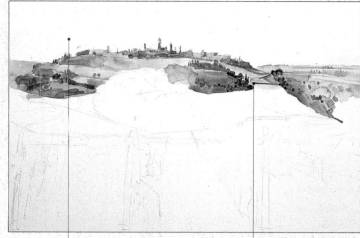

Note how the sky color recedes into the background against the richer hues of the landscape beneath it.

The hues become richer toward the foreground, developing perspective in the painting.

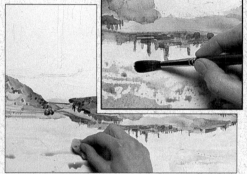

5 Turn the painting upside down. With a natural sponge, wet the sky. Inset: Drop alizarin crimson and yellow ochre over the surface using the no. 8 brush. While it is still damp add cerulean blue, producing a lilac hue.

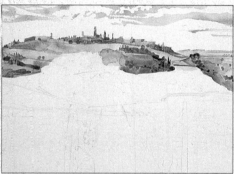

6 As soon as the paint is dry, remove the masking fluid from the sky area. Note how much of the sky is left white. This suggests the high, billowing white clouds above the richly hued landscape. Leave the sky now and move back toward the foreground.

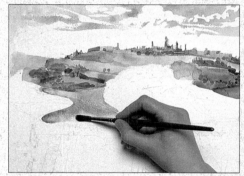

7 Using the no. 8 brush, build up the fields around the central grove with a flat wash of raw sienna and yellow ochre, adding a little burnt umber for warmth. Allow the paint to dry. You may need a second layer to get the right color density.

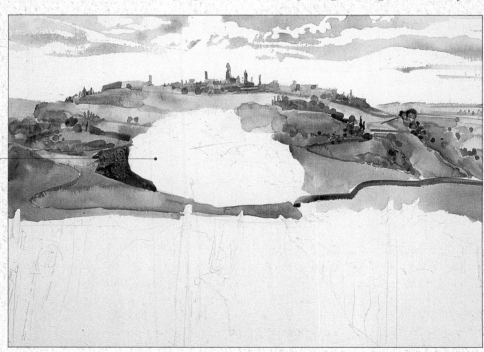

The grove is left free of paint while the surrounding fields and woodland are built up.

Progress Report
Raw sienna, yellow ochre, and burnt umber have been used to build the plowed fields to the right of the grove. Layers of viridian and Hooker's green light are applied to the surrounding landscape, with varying tones to ensure textural interest.

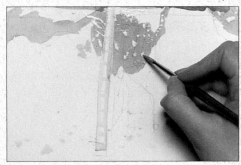

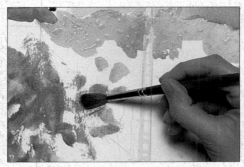

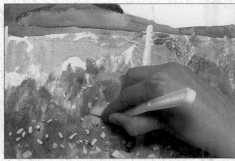

8 *Brush white masking fluid over the vineyard fencing and allow to dry. Lay a variegated cadmium yellow wash over the foreground, varying the strength of the paint to produce texture. When it is dry, dot white masking fluid over the paint.*

9 *Make a thick, dark mix of yellow ochre and burnt sienna, then add a few drops of gum arabic. Using the no. 8 brush, mix the colors together on the paper in the foreground to build up an interesting texture and a range of earthy tones.*

10 *After painting a mix of Hooker's green light and yellow ochre, again mixed with gum arabic, over the earth tones to add contrast, score into the paint with a plastic palette knife to create random textured effects. Allow the paint to dry.*

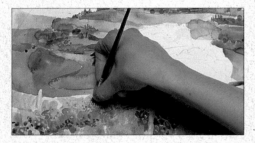

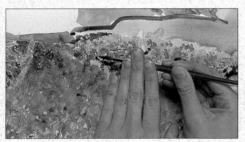

Progress Report
The foreground has now developed into a rich and complex array of colors, tones, and textures. The white masking fluid stands out against the rich colors on the ground, extending the tonal range. The spatters of light and dark tones create tonal contrast and natural highlights.

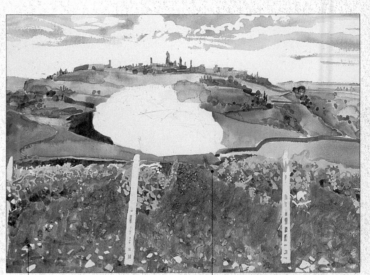

11 Top: *Using a no. 6 brush, make dry-brush marks over the foliage in the middle ground and foreground. Mix varying strengths of viridian and yellow ochre to produce light and dark effects.* Bottom: *Spatter Hooker's green light over the vines.*

Drybrush marks combine with spatter to produce a range of textural effects.

The vines appear to be receding into the middle ground, due to the successful use of linear perspective.

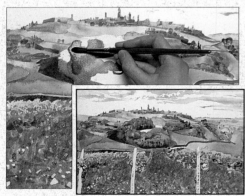

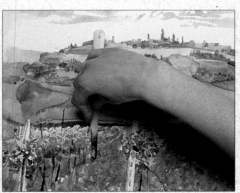

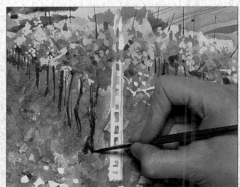

12 *Using the no. 6 brush, apply wet-into-wet washes of viridian, cadmium yellow, and burnt umber to develop the center of the grove.* Inset: *When the center of the grove is dry, develop more intricate detailing around the edges, using viridian.*

13 *Rub off the masking fluid from the vines and foreground fields. Soften bright areas with yellow ochre, cadmium yellow, and Hooker's green light. Mark the vine stems with the edge of a plastic palette knife in a Payne's gray/yellow ochre mix.*

14 *Once the grove is dry, fill in the final field in the middle ground with a light wash of yellow ochre. Refine the vine stems with a no. 4 brush, using a Payne's gray, raw umber, and cobalt blue mix. Use the same mix to reinforce shadows.*

The Finished Painting

This complex landscape demonstrates four of the most attractive characteristics of water-color painting: subtle touches of wet-into-wet paint in the sky; rich, overlaid tones in the middle ground; a variety of texturing effects in the vineyard and earth in the foreground; and the restrained use of masking fluid to allow the white of the paper to shine through.

Linear perspective leads the viewer's eye along the rows of vines into the grove in the center of the painting.

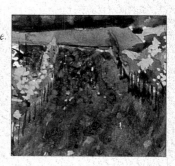

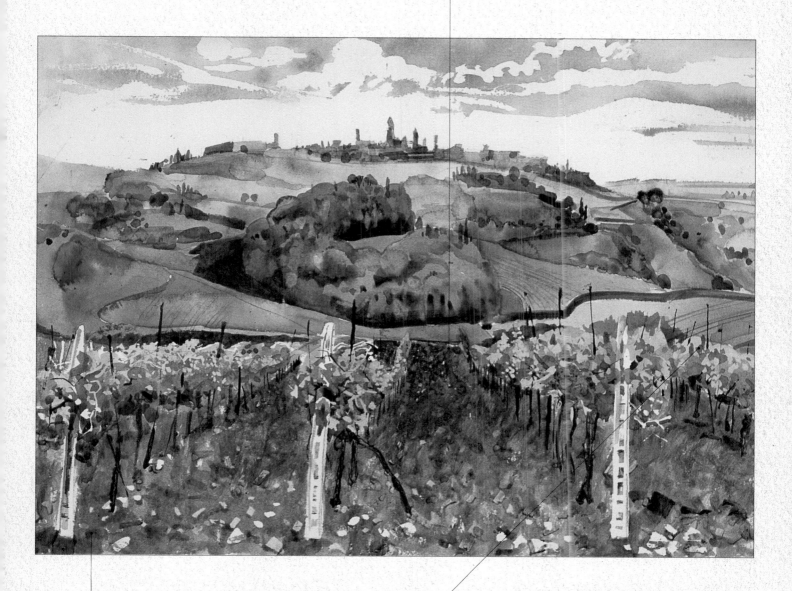

Using a range of the texturing techniques such as spattering, drybrush, and scraping with a plastic palette knife you can produce rich and varied textures in the landscape.

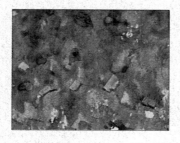

Gum arabic in the foreground alters the quality of the watercolor paint. White masking fluid is left on the paper to add highlights and texture.

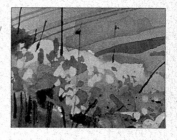

STILL LIFES:
Arranging a Still Life

A STILL-LIFE PAINTING is composed of inanimate objects, arranged either formally or informally. The still life is one of the most popular subjects for artists. Unlike portraits or figure painting, for which you need to persuade someone to sit for you, or landscapes, which require a suitable location, still lifes give you the opportunity to select your subjects by looking around your home. Objects that at first glance might not seem to have much potential may turn out to offer the perfect shape or color for your arrangement. Informal arrangements often work best: an array of fresh vegetables, a collection of perfume bottles, or ornaments on your mantelpiece are all equally suitable.

Deciding how to arrange the objects in order to create a harmonious composition is more difficult. Initially, determine what role you want each object in your still life to play. Which one is going to take center stage, and how are you going to balance colors and shapes? Try to make your color combinations harmonious, with the color becoming more intense toward the center of interest. At the same time remember to create balance, making sure that one area of the composition is not overloaded with activity while another is devoid of interest. Use the principles discussed earlier under Composition (pp. 34-37). It doesn't matter whether you are painting a landscape or a still life: the same guidelines apply.

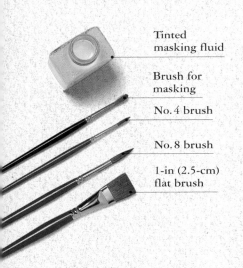

Tinted
masking fluid

Brush for
masking

No. 4 brush

No. 8 brush

1-in (2.5-cm)
flat brush

Sketches
Make sketches to work out the most interesting composition. In the first sketch (top right), the footwear is arranged in a straight line; in the second (bottom right), it is in a triangular formation to lead the viewer around the picture.

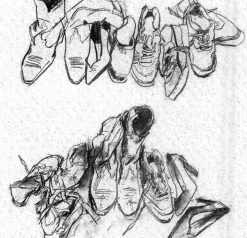

Paints	
Payne's gray	*Sepia*
Raw umber	*Cadmium orange*
Alizarin crimson	*Burnt umber*
Raw sienna	*Burnt sienna*
Cobalt blue	*Yellow ochre*
	Viridian

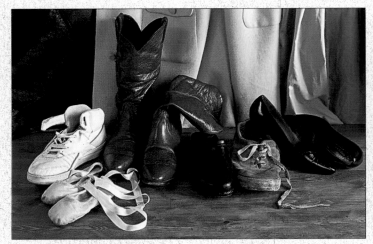

The Arrangement
This grouping, which appears random, was carefully arranged to exploit contrasts of color, material, texture, and size. The shoes are laid out formally in a triangular composition, with the white sneakers on either side providing balance.

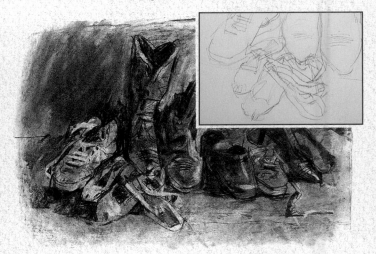

1 *Make a preliminary charcoal drawing to help ascertain the tonal relationships between each object. Inset: From this, make a light sketch in HB pencil, indicating the main objects and areas of light and shade.*

YOU CAN LEARN a great deal about the contents and arrangement of successful still-life groups by studying the works of master painters. Don't simply look at paintings by artists who have specialized in the subject: look for still lifes within other pictures. Diego Velasquez, Pierre Bonnard, and Jean-Baptiste Chardin all incorporated beautiful still lifes within their paintings.

The best way to decide whether your composition works visually is to make several drawings of the objects you have selected, in various arrangements, before you pick up your brush and start to paint. Making a preliminary sketch forces you first to concentrate and look hard at your composition. When you look at your drawings, think about how much space there is between the various objects. If you leave too much space, the composition may lack unity; too little and it may appear cluttered. Don't forget to relate your still life to the edges of the paper, too. Just as there should be interesting negative and positive shapes within the still-life group, so there should be interesting shapes around it. Experiment with filling the paper with your subject: too much space around the objects will make them seem lost and the background will then become too dominant.

One common mistake is to try to include too much in a painting or to try to tell a complete story. Do not hesitate to edit, or remove, some objects if they detract from the composition. In this exercise, for example, some of the shoes in the set-up lack their mates.

Think, too, about the mood you want to create. Is your aim a formal or an informal composition? Perhaps you want to evoke a domestic setting, as with the jumble of shoes and boots in this exercise. Maybe you would prefer to use traditional still-life materials such as fruits, colored glass, and metal objects, to create a more obviously staged grouping. Experiment with subjects in compositions that concentrate on spatial relationships, colors, and the effect of light on the selected objects. All these factors play a crucial role in the successful arrangement of a still life.

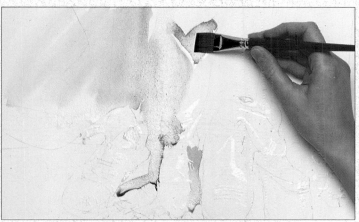

2 Mask out fine details, such as the bright light areas on the folds and laces of the shoes, then load a 1-in (2.5-cm) flat brush with Payne's gray, and lightly overlay wet-into-wet washes on the background.

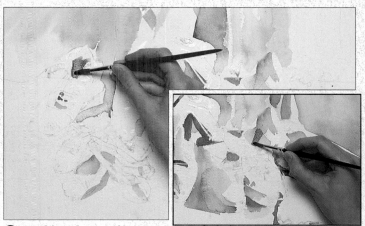

3 Build up layers of variegated washes of Payne's gray, using a no. 8 brush to fill in the shadow areas with less dilute paint. Inset Do not let the paint drift into the areas allocated to the shoes and boots. Use a small brush such as a no. 4 to control the flow of the paint if necessary.

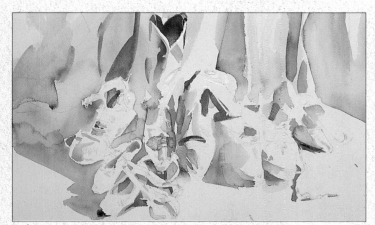

4 Create general areas of light and dark tones, especially in the folds of the coats behind the shoes. Squint your eyes to make it easier to differentiate between light and dark areas clearly. Refer to your charcoal drawing to double-check that the tones are right.

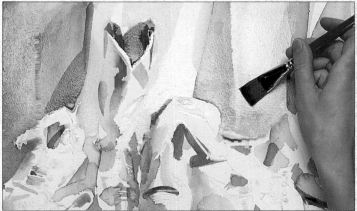

5 Allow the underpainting to dry. Using the 1-in (2.5-cm) flat brush, lay a wet wash of raw umber on the coat on the left, allowing the paint to drift slightly. Use a very wet wash of alizarin crimson over the middle coat.

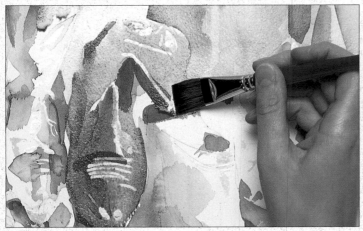

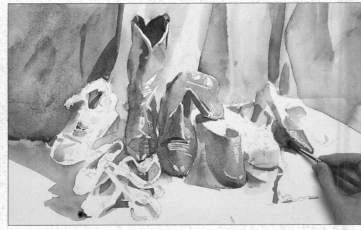

6 *Make up a rich, wet mix of raw sienna. Using the flat brush, begin to build up color on the boots, using the edge of the brush to create hard lines and the flat surface to fill in blocks of color. Remember to leave light areas white.*

7 *Using the no. 8 brush, paint the clog with a mix of cobalt blue and Payne's gray and the upright black shoe with a mix of dark sepia and cobalt blue. Add touches of pure cobalt blue around the rim of the clog and the curves of the shoe.*

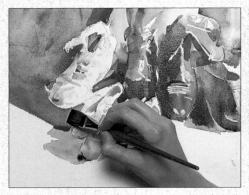

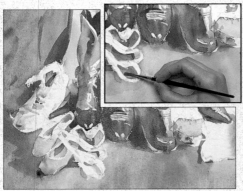

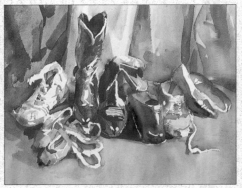

8 *Using the flat brush and a dark mix of cadmium orange and burnt umber, add shadows around the base of the shoes on the left. Work carefully, making sure that the paint does not drift into any of the objects. With a more dilute version of the same mix of colors, wash in the paler shadows falling to the right.*

9 *Dampen the foreground with water. Using the flat brush, apply a wash of cadmium orange and burnt sienna. Add a mix of cadmium orange and yellow ochre to the ballet shoes. Inset: Use the no. 4 brush to get into the tight areas of the foreground between the shoes. Note how the color of the foreground wash lightens as it dries.*

10 *Allow the image to dry completely, then rub away the masking fluid to reveal the bright whites. They will add sparkle and vitality to the image. Now assess which elements within the composition need further detailing and refining. The boot and the tennis shoe, in particular, require additional work.*

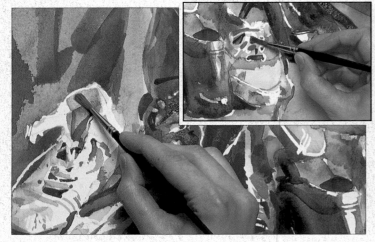

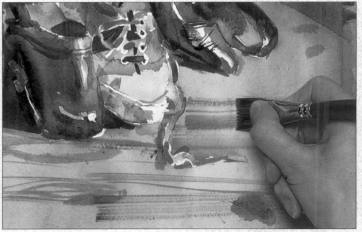

11 *With the no. 4 brush, define light and shaded areas on the sneaker, using a mix of cobalt blue and Payne's gray for the dark tones. Inset: Paint the shoelaces with alizarin crimson and viridian. Add touches of both colors to the ballet shoes to give them a soft texture.*

12 *Use the flat brush to create a textured surface in the foreground wood, in the same way as in the exercise on light (pp. 90–91). Use an intensely colored mix of raw sienna and cobalt blue, as the paint will look paler when dry.*

The Finished Painting

The whites give vitality to this still-life scene. Because light falls across the bottom corner of the composition on the left side, the viewer's eye follows the movement and shapes of the objects from left to right. The juxtaposition of light forms against darker ones adds interest, and the abstracted shapes of the coats in the background increase the sense of depth and color.

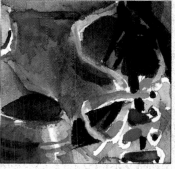

The patent-leather shoes are shiny and dark, in contrast to the flimsy fabric of the adjoining tennis shoe. The sharp heel of the dress shoe is inserted into the heel of the tennis shoe, creating a link between the two objects.

The loose ribbons are suggested by the slightest hint of color: cadmium orange mixed with yellow ochre. The whites provide a positive shape against the colored ground. The loose curl of the ribbons contrasts sharply with the tough boot leather behind it.

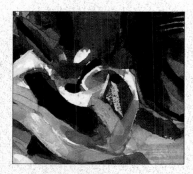

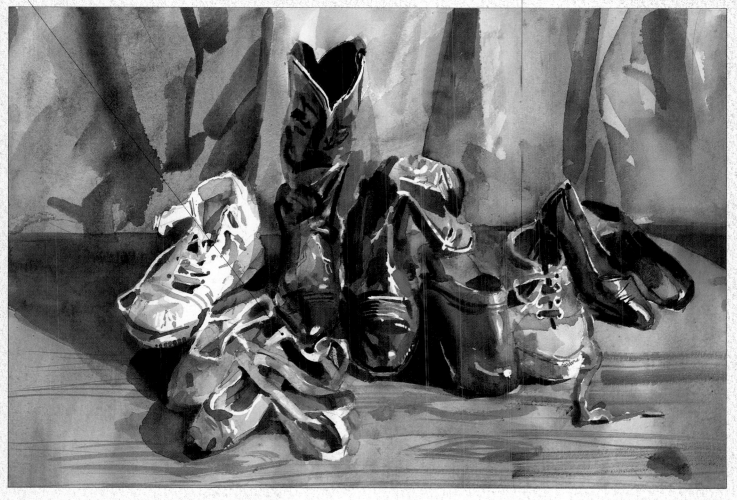

STILL LIFES:
Metal Objects

LIKE GLASS AND WATER, metal has a reflective surface that creates an exciting artistic challenge. Unlike glass or water, however, metal is opaque: every metal object has a color of its own, and you must pay as much attention, if not more, to this aspect of your subject as you do to any reflections contained within it. Different metals are made up of different colors. Silver objects, for example, are made up of cool neutral grays, and stainless-steel ones of blue-gray tones. Brass objects contain warm yellow tones, including such colors as raw sienna, raw umber, and sepia. By contrast, copper objects contain a combination of the warm and cool tones – warm reds and oranges alongside cooler blues and greens. Before you start to paint, look at your subject and work out which colors, both real and reflected, are visible on its surface.

Reflections in the surface of any metal object can be made up of a wide range of colors, although the exact colors will, of course, depend on the colors of the objects that are being reflected. Always make sure that the color of the metal object itself predominates. Even if the reflections of surrounding objects comprise many colors, concentrate on the main ones so that the reflections do not become a more important part of your painting than the metal. Remember, too, that the real-life object should always look sharper and less distorted than its reflection.

One of the most noticeable things about metal is the bright highlights that bounce off the surface. Depicting these highlights accurately is the key to a convincing representation, as they give you clues about the direction of the light and the form (curved or angular) of the metal object that you are painting. Mask out the main highlights in the early drawing stages, so that you can leave those areas free of paint and exploit the whiteness of the paper. Sometimes you may need to refine the white paper highlights after the masking fluid has been removed. You may find that you have have applied too much masking fluid and that the white areas are not integrated into the picture. Often a weak wash of color is sufficient to overcome this problem. Stand back frequently to make sure you retain the mood you have carefully worked for.

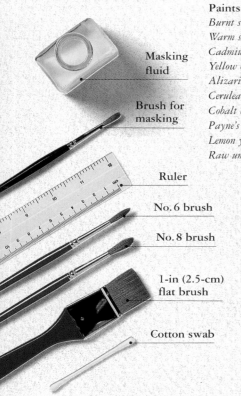

Masking fluid

Brush for masking

Ruler

No. 6 brush

No. 8 brush

1-in (2.5-cm) flat brush

Cotton swab

Watersoluble pencils

Paints
Burnt sienna
Warm sepia
Cadmium yellow
Yellow ochre
Alizarin crimson
Cerulean blue
Cobalt blue
Payne's gray
Lemon yellow
Raw umber.

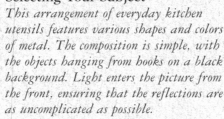

Selecting Your Subject
This arrangement of everyday kitchen utensils features various shapes and colors of metal. The composition is simple, with the objects hanging from hooks on a black background. Light enters the picture from the front, ensuring that the reflections are as uncomplicated as possible.

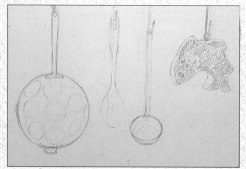

1 *Space the utensils equally. With an HB pencil, lightly sketch the four objects, indicating where the main highlights fall. Count the number of scales on the fish-shaped copper mold, and make sure that they are accurately rendered.*

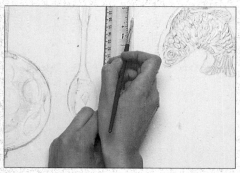

2 *Paint the main highlight areas with masking fluid and an old brush. Balance the brush against a ruler to mark in straight lines of highlight along the handles of the colander, spoon, and ladle. Wash the brush immediately after use.*

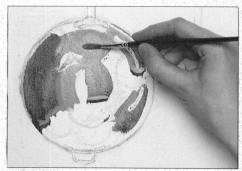

3 *Fill in the main shape and colors of the colander using a no. 8 brush. Choose a strong burnt sienna and warm sepia mix for the dark areas and a cadmium yellow and yellow ochre mix for the lighter areas, allowing the colors to spread and merge.*

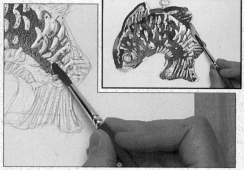

4 *Drop in small areas of the same colors on the fish-shaped mold, allowing them to merge. Inset: Put a paler wash of cadmium yellow and yellow ochre on the underbelly of the "fish" and a touch of alizarin crimson and cerulean blue around the gills.*

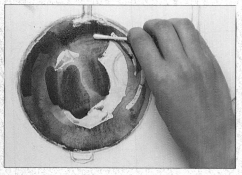

5 *Alternating between the colander and the fish mold, overlay various mixes of the same hues. Use a cotton swab to blend the paint as it begins to dry, making sure that the colander's surface looks rounded but smooth.*

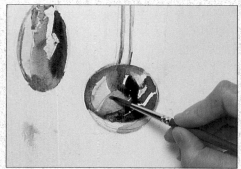

6 *Now start building up color on the stainless-steel spoon and ladle. Using the no. 8 brush and the cool tones of cobalt blue and Payne's gray, work the two colors wet into wet to build up the shapes and light and dark areas.*

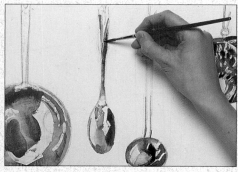

7 *Alternating between all the objects, add touches of the same colors to build up the tonal contrasts between light and dark areas. Paint the handles of the ladle and spoon with a mix of Payne's gray and burnt sienna.*

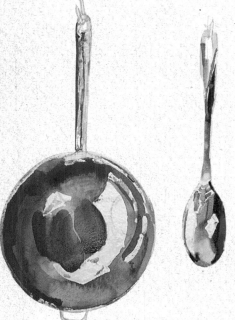

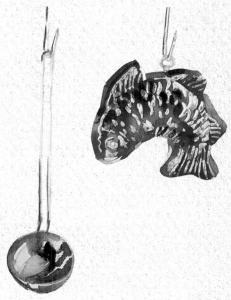

8 *Add some lemon yellow and burnt sienna to the colander handle. The utensils are beginning to take shape. Let the painting dry before continuing so that you can gauge how intense the hues will be once dry.*

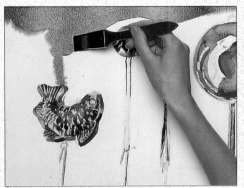

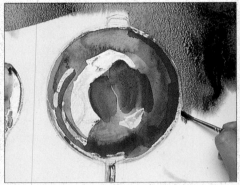

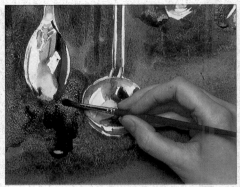

9 *Turn the board upside down and dampen the background of the painting. Using a 1-in (2.5-cm) flat brush, apply a wash of raw umber mixed with Payne's gray. Make sure the paint does not run onto the already painted utensils.*

10 *Make up a less dilute mix of raw umber and Payne's gray. Using a no. 6 brush, carefully fill in the spaces between the utensils. If any paint drifts onto the metal objects, quickly blot it off with a paper towel.*

11 *Turn the board the right way up again, and continue until the whole background is covered. The wash should not look flat. Paint shadows to the left of each utensil using the no. 8 brush loaded with a darker mix of Payne's gray and cobalt blue.*

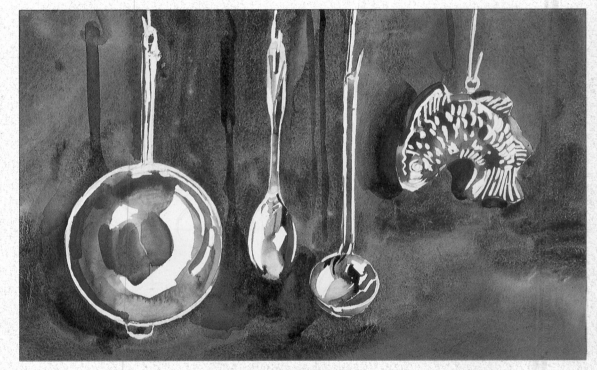

12 *Let the image dry completely. Now remove all the masking fluid. The unpainted areas stand out brightly, creating a sparkling and shining contrast to the intense surrounding hues.*

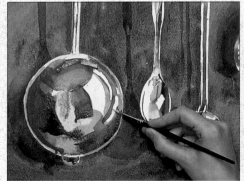

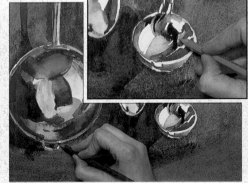

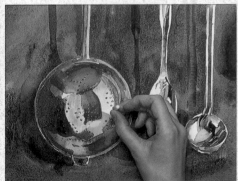

13 *Overlay further colors as necessary to build up the contrasts between light and dark areas on the surface of the utensils. Using the no. 6 brush, paint a curve of lemon yellow around the rim of the colander to emphasize its reflective quality.*

14 *Now use watersoluble pencils (vermilion, blue, scarlet, orange, ochre, brown, black, white, and cerulean) to define each utensil's shape. Use warm colors on the copper colander and mold. Inset: Use cool colors on the stainless-steel utensils.*

15 *Cut a cotton swab in half and use the cut end to stipple in the holes in the colander, using a thick mix of burnt sienna and sepia. If necessary, refine the highlights with more white watersoluble pencil marks.*

The Finished Painting

The image comprises a series of successful contrasts. The neutral gray tone of the background contrasts dramatically with the warm and cool tones of the utensils, as well as with the bright highlights where the paper was left free of paint. The warm colors of the colander and fish-shaped mold play against the cooler tones of the stainless-steel spoon and ladle, but the image is unified by the touches of burnt sienna contained in all objects.

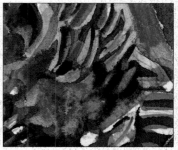

The fish-shaped mold is made up of a series of indentations with many reflections bouncing off its raised surface. All the warm colors in the palette are used to achieve this effect.

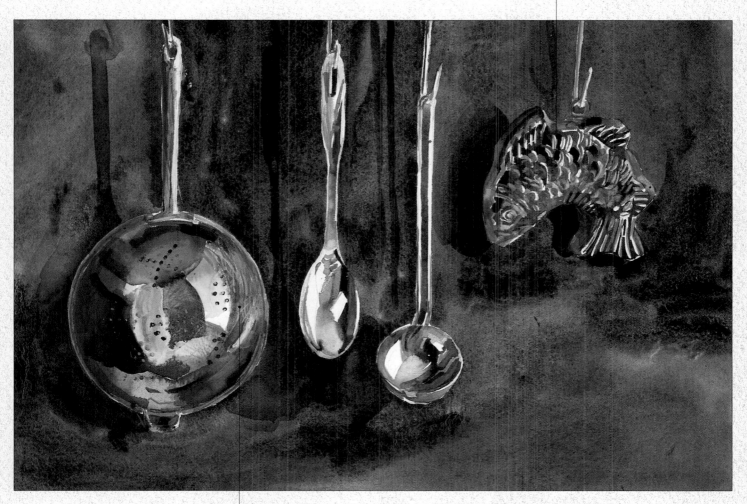

The contrasts between cool and warm hues, blending together on this utensil, give the impression of a shiny copper surface. Curved brushmarks and stippling in the holes enhance the rounded shape of the colander.

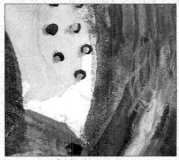

STILL LIFES:
Glass

COLORED GLASS, with the light glowing through it, seems tailor-made for the use of layer upon layer of thin, transparent watercolor washes. It complements the translucent quality of the paint in a way that opaquely colored objects can rarely match. The impression of translucency can be enhanced by skillful use of the white paper and masking fluid or tape to pick out highlights. Masking is also an easy way to obtain crisp, sharp edges. Using additives (see pp. 68–69) is another useful technique for painting glass. Gum arabic, for example, not only extends the drying time but also gives the paint a glazed appearance when dry, emphasizing the translucency of the subject. Honey and glycerin also extend the drying time of the paint and add a shine to its surface. All these additives give you longer to work into the paint and use techniques such as sgraffito (see pp. 76–77).

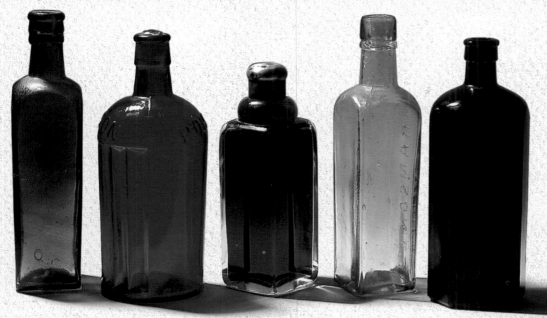

Glass Bottles

Take a selection of glass bottles of different colors, shapes, and sizes, and position them at different angles to each other to create an interesting composition. Remember to look at the spaces between them, as these too contribute to the composition. Light them with a spot lamp to create dramatic shadows.

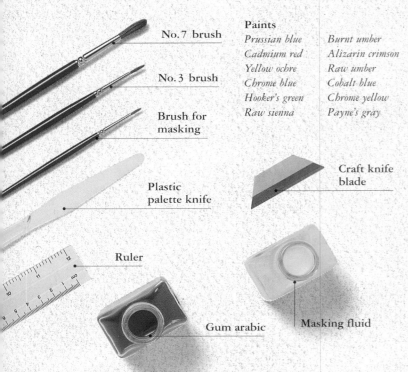

No. 7 brush

No. 3 brush

Brush for masking

Plastic palette knife

Ruler

Gum arabic

Craft knife blade

Masking fluid

Paints

Prussian blue	*Burnt umber*
Cadmium red	*Alizarin crimson*
Yellow ochre	*Raw umber*
Chrome blue	*Cobalt blue*
Hooker's green	*Chrome yellow*
Raw sienna	*Payne's gray*

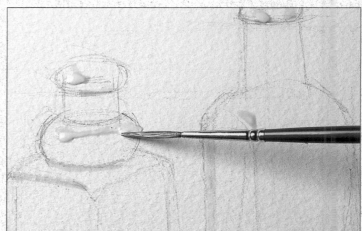

1 *Before you begin painting, lightly draw the outlines of the bottles with an HB pencil, accurately indicating the distance between each bottle. Make a mental note of the direction of the light and the position of the resulting shadows. Mask any areas of intense highlight precisely in masking fluid, using an old brush.*

126

THERE ARE MANY types of glass. Clear glass objects take on the color of objects around them. Always paint the background and surrounding objects first, as this gives you the base color from which to build up an impression of the subject itself. In this respect, painting glass is much like painting water and reflections.

Colored glass comes in many hues and can be clear or clouded. Glass that has been hand blown may have air bubbles within it and inconsistencies in its color and texture. Some glass objects are smooth and rounded in shape while others have sharp edges and indentations. Cut crystal glass has countless sharp edges and highlights reflecting in all directions, and to paint it well you will need to adopt one of the highlighting techniques demonstrated on pp. 62–63.

The position and strength of the light source have a tremendous effect on the appearance of glass. This is especially true of colored glass, which produces startling shadows when spot-lit – think, for example, of the impact of a stained-glass window in a church when the light shimmers through it.

When two pieces of colored glass throw shadows that cross one another, a third, fourth, and sometimes even a fifth color appears in the shadows. Whenever you paint shadows, make sure that they are slightly duller in tone than the color you use to paint the glass so that they do not appear more solid than the glass.

Before you start painting, think about where the highlights, midtones, and dark areas fall, and whether the glass creates shadows or stands stark against its background. Look carefully at the color of the glass and at the color of any objects that are near by. Don't worry if you seem to be spending more time looking at your subject than painting it – it will be time well spent.

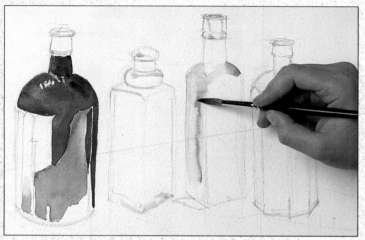

2 Take a no. 7 brush and fill in the dark area of the blue bottle with a wet wash of Prussian blue. Block in the paler area with a diluted purple mix made from Prussian blue and cadmium red. Now add yellow ochre to the base. Paint the hard edge of the green-blue bottle with a mix of chrome blue and Hooker's green.

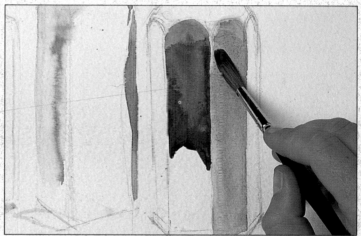

3 Paint the shaded side of the bottle on the right with a variegated wash of raw sienna, burnt umber, and alizarin crimson, and the light side with raw umber and cobalt blue. Make the contrast between light and shade far more marked than they are in reality, as the colors will lighten when dry.

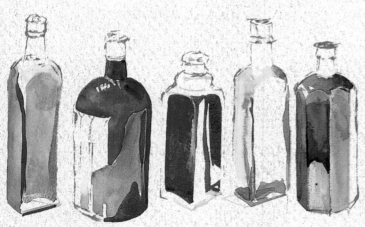

4 The bottle on the left was painted with a yellow ochre and burnt umber mix, and the edge and base defined with a dark umber line. Alizarin crimson mixed with a little cadmium red was dropped onto the middle bottle and allowed to spread. Each bottle now has its own distinct color.

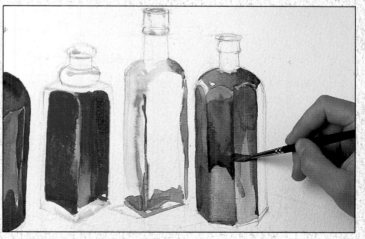

5 Begin to build up the tones by overlaying them, using the no. 3 brush to define details. The red bottle should incorporate touches of diluted alizarin crimson in the lightest areas. Paint the far right bottle with a mix of chrome yellow and raw sienna to build up the correct brown tone.

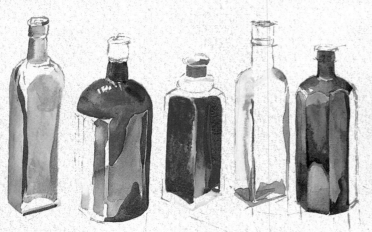

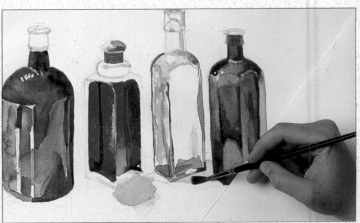

6 *The bottles are now beginning to take shape. The surfaces already appear glassy. Try to keep the colors clean and flat as you lay them in, and leave white spaces between them to emphasize their reflective qualities.*

7 *Paint the bottle tops and shadows in slightly paler hues of the main glass colors. For the brass cap of the center bottle, use raw umber for the light area and Prussian blue for the shadow. The pale crimson shadow shown here is not accurate but it will be corrected later in the painting process (step 11).*

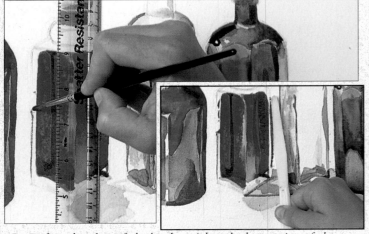

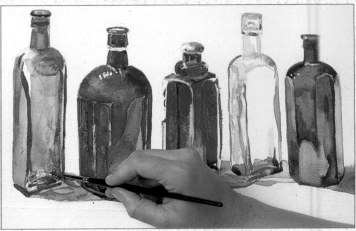

8 *Define the edges of the bottles with a darker version of the glass colors, using the no. 3 brush and resting on a ruler to get the edge straight. Inset: Once you have created the line, you can smudge and soften it by gently dragging a plastic palette knife across it while the paint is still wet.*

9 *The main bodies of the bottles should be dry, and you can return to them to build up further tones and develop color contrasts. On the first bottle use Payne's gray to create weight and shading at the base.*

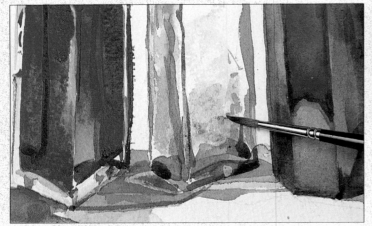

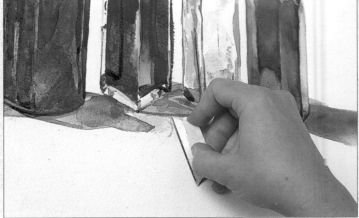

10 *Add a little gum arabic to a very pale chrome blue wash, and fill in the light area of the fourth bottle. The gum arabic has a glazed appearance when dry, and this emphasizes the rough surface of the bottle. As in earlier stages, leave some areas free of paint to create the impression of highlights.*

11 *To get rid of the pale crimson shadow, take a craft knife blade and gently scrape away the unwanted paint. Work slowly and gently so that you do not damage the surface of the paper. Then repaint the area in the correct color.*

The Finished Painting

Once the painting has completely dried, remove the masking fluid. The still life is simply composed, yet complex in color and tonal range. The depth of color in the blue, red, and dark brown bottles contrasts with the far paler and rougher green-blue bottle and the finer pale brown bottle to the left. Because the background is left white, the bottles appear more intense in hue. The sharp angles of the red bottle contrast effectively with the smooth rounded glass of the adjacent dark blue bottle. Although each bottle is a separate entity, the shadows intermingle to link the group. The differing heights and shapes add interest to the composition, as do their varying slants. The final brown bottle casts a shadow that leads the eye out of the picture.

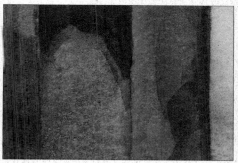

A yellow ochre and raw sienna mix was painted over the initial green wash to create a brown tone. This adds a sense of transparency and depth to the glass.

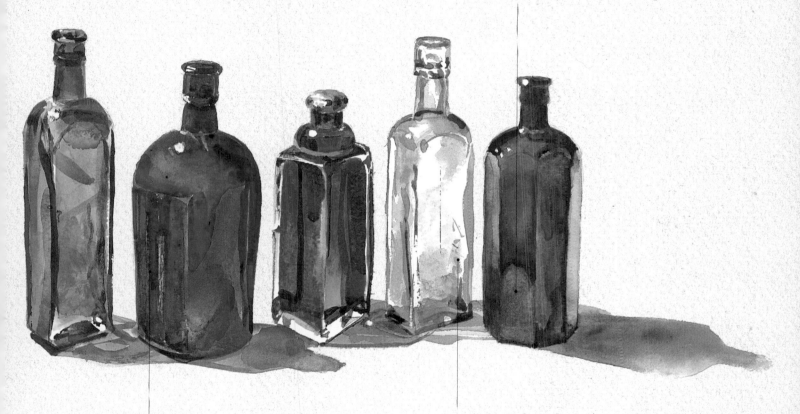

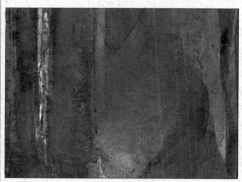

Dark, angular lines that emphasize the shape of the bottle create an impression of cut glass.

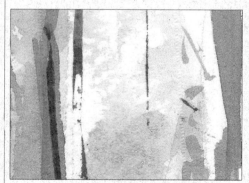

The white of the paper is used as a color in its own right. The surrounding area is colored with chrome blue, Hooker's green, and a little gum arabic to define the edge of the bottle and the shadow areas.

STILL LIFES:
Combining Your Skills

Combining Still-Life Subjects

This exercise combines glass, metal, and fabric in an elaborate still life. It includes distinct contrasts of color and quality: note, for example, how the opaque surface of the white china fruit bowl contrasts with the clear blue wineglass, and how the angular shapes of the cheeses counterbalance the round forms of the fruit and nuts piled above them.

No. 8 brush
No. 6 brush
No. 3 brush
1-in (2.5-cm) flat brush
1/2-in (12-mm) chisel brush
Cotton swab
Brush for masking
Masking fluid
Watersoluble pencils

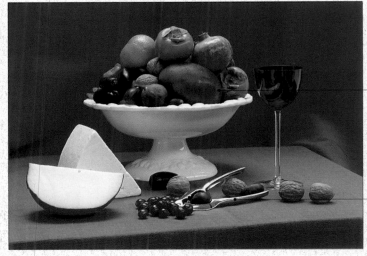

The bowl contains a rich array of textures and colors; arranging the various elements satisfactorily within it is an interesting challenge.

The clear blue wineglass and the shiny nutcrackers provide an effective contrast to the opaqueness of the bowl and fruit.

Paints

Hooker's green light	Cadmium yellow	Yellow ochre
Alizarin crimson	Cobalt blue	Cerulean blue
Cadmium red	Raw umber	Payne's gray
	Burnt sienna	Chinese white gouache

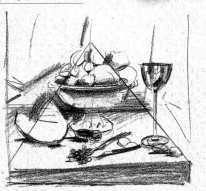

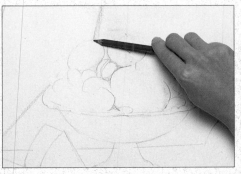

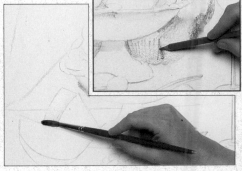

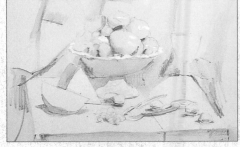

1 *Make a preliminary sketch in HB pencil to determine the composition's structure. The arrangement is triangular, with the fruit bowl as the pinnacle. The glass to the right adds an asymmetrical element, creating a change of pace.*

2 *On a piece of watercolor paper, draw the outlines of the objects in blue water-soluble pencil. Use the side of the pencil for thick lines and the tip for hard edges and angles. The blue pencil will merge into the painting when water is applied.*

3 *Dampen a no. 8 brush with clean water, then use it to blend and dissolve the pencil lines so that they soften on the paper. Inset: Take the pencil again and crosshatch areas of dark tone. You can then blend these with the brush.*

4 *The under-drawing is complete. Some areas, like the folds in the background fabric, are shaded to give a three-dimensional impression; the lighter areas are defined by pencil outlines and left white to be filled with paint later.*

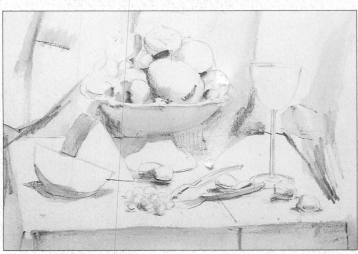

5 *The bright highlight areas need to be protected with masking fluid. Use an old brush. Curved strokes of masking fluid are required for the fruit, a large block for the white cheese and fruit bowl stand, and light touches for the nutcrackers and glass.*

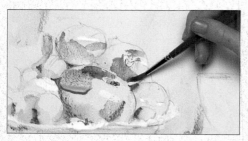

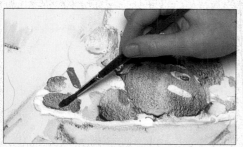

Progress Report

The fresh colors of the summer fruits have mixed wet into wet, creating a three-dimensional effect. The masking fluid allows you to control the placement of highlights. By this stage, you can see how important an underdrawing is in helping you to retain balance and proportion.

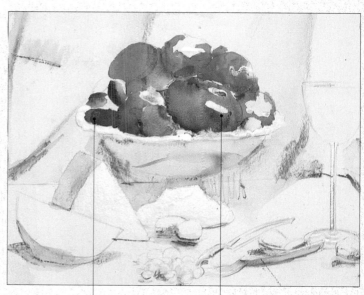

6 Top: *With a no. 6 brush, drop Hooker's green light and alizarin crimson over the mango, and cadmium red and cadmium yellow onto the pomegranate and sharon fruit. Bottom: Wash pale cobalt blue over the figs. Paint the chestnuts in the dish with a raw umber and burnt sienna mix.*

The combination of cool blue and warm brown and orange on the different fruits creates a fresh and lively mixture of colors.

Hooker's green light and alizarin crimson blend to create the three-dimensional form of the mango.

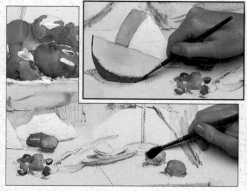

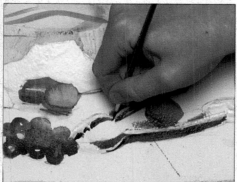

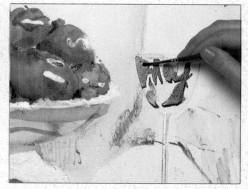

7 *Paint the chestnuts with raw umber and burnt sienna. Inset: Use a no. 3 brush to paint the white cheese rind with cadmium yellow and Hooker's green light. Drop pale yellow ochre onto the Edam cheese. Paint the rind in cadmium red and alizarin crimson.*

8 *Paint the nutcrackers with a mix of cobalt blue and raw umber. Fill the inner curves with cobalt blue, a cool blue to give the impression of a shiny surface. Paint in the cranberries with a mix of cadmium red, cadmium yellow, and alizarin crimson.*

9 *Lay a pale wash of cerulean and cobalt blue, mixed with alizarin crimson, over the blue wineglass, creating a deep plum color. Use a darker mix of the same colors to build up tonal variation within the glass and form a curved shape.*

Progress Report

Once the fruits were dry, they were overlaid with the same colors to develop their shape and depth. The richer hues make the contrasts between warm reds and cool yellows and greens stand out more. In order to develop further depth in the foreground, a mix of burnt sienna and Payne's gray was used to paint in very short, dark shadows under the chestnuts and cranberries.

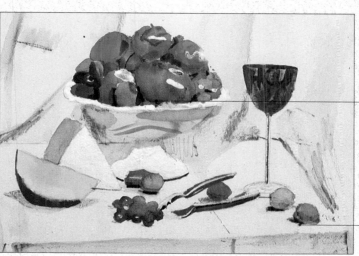

The contrast between the cool green and the warm orange helps to create an impression of three dimensions.

The dark shadows under the chestnuts throw them into sharp focus by making them stand out from the background.

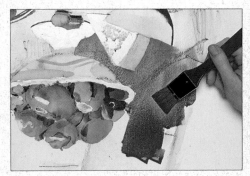

10 Turn the board upside down and, using a 1-in (2.5-cm) flat brush, paint the background fabric wet into wet with a thick mix of cadmium red and burnt sienna, allowing the colors to blend into each other.

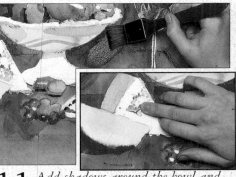

11 Add shadows around the bowl and across the fabric by dipping the flat brush into very dilute cobalt blue and letting the blue blend into the underlying orange wash. Inset: When this is dry, rub away the masking fluid.

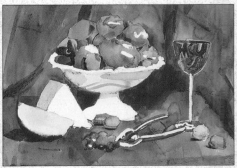

12 To develop the off-white color of the bowl, a few simple sweeps of very dilute yellow ochre are brushed lightly across its surface. With a no. 8 brush, touches of Payne's gray, yellow ochre, and cerulean blue are added around the base.

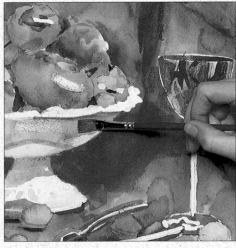

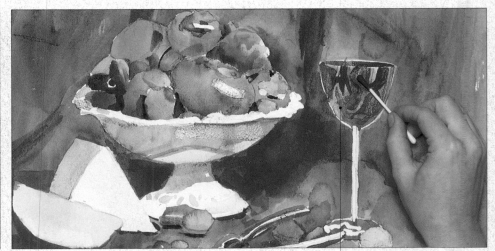

13 Using a ½-in (12-mm) chisel brush, blend the colors on the fruit bowl with a light wash of Payne's gray. This will help to integrate the bright white into the colored areas that surround it.

14 With a dampened cotton swab, blend the colors on the surface of the glass so that the highlights are reduced. Tonal contrasts within the glass help to make it appear transparent, yet too great a contrast between light and dark looks artificial.

When the bright high-light areas are blended into the surrounding colors, the transparency of the glass seems more pronounced.

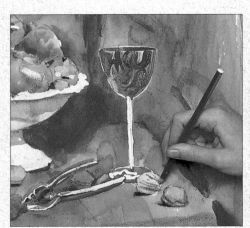

15 Add details and highlights with colored watersoluble pencils. Cross-hatch the chestnuts with a dark brown watersoluble pencil to create texture.

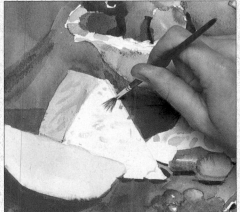

16 Using a no. 3 brush and the dry-brush technique, make yellow ochre, Payne's gray, and cadmium yellow marks on the white cheese to give it texture. Feather the bristles of the brush by pressing down quite firmly as you work.

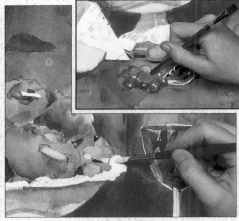

17 The fruit bowl has receded too far. To bring it forward, redefine the rim of the bowl using the no. 6 brush dipped in Chinese white gouache. Inset: Dip the end of the brush in the paint, and dot opaque white highlights over the cranberries.

The Finished Painting

The watersoluble pencil marks create further detail and help to define the different elements within the composition. The contrast between the cool tones of the cheeses and wineglass and the warm peach-colored background produces interesting tonal variations within the painting. Within the fruit bowl itself, the cool greens and warm oranges provide a rich array of color and form.

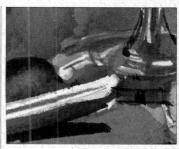

The close proximity of the glass, chestnuts, and metal nutcrackers creates a stimulating interplay of different textures.

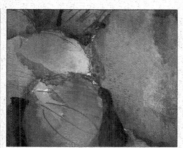

The fruit colors have blended together to produce a rich mix of warm and cool tones.

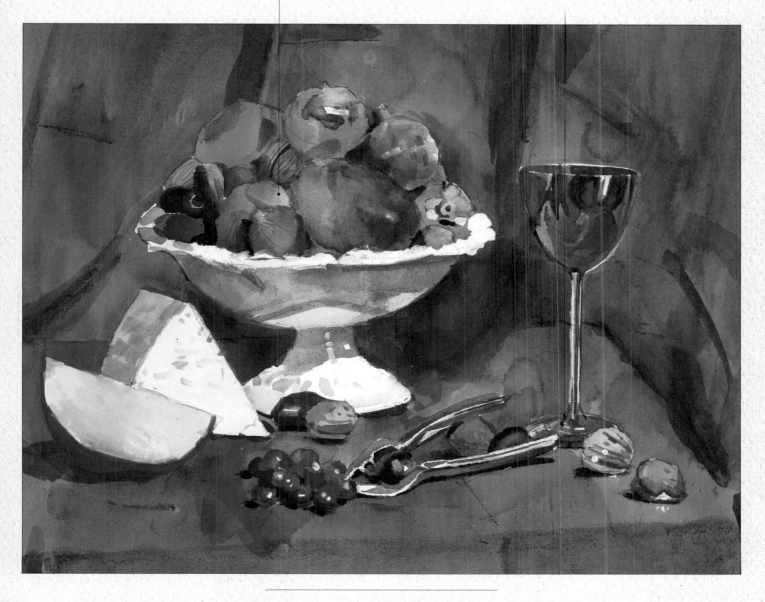

PAINTING PEOPLE:
Basic Figure Painting

FOR YOUR FIRST ATTEMPTS at painting the figure in watercolor, make a light pencil sketch of your subject before you start to paint in order to get the limbs and torso in proportion. Without an underdrawing, it is easy to lose sight of the overall shape of your subject once you start applying paint. A sketch can also help you work out where you need areas of dark and light tone in your painting. Remember, however, that it is intended to underpin your painting; you do not need to make a detailed drawing. Erase the pencil marks as you progress, or use water-soluble pencils which will leave no trace when water is applied to the picture.

Once you feel confident about drawing the figure, you can begin to apply watercolor, using the paint at first to fill in the shapes and then continuing to build them up layer upon layer until you have a full-fledged painting.

Watercolor is an excellent medium for building up skin tones in this way and for creating the impression of soft fabrics and layers of clothing (see pp. 138–141). As your skills develop, you can employ a wider range of techniques to produce more detailed figure paintings in both formal and informal poses. Pen-and-ink lines, masking, and Chinese white gouache will all help you to create highly detailed portraits in watercolor.

No. 4 brush

No. 6 brush

Steel-nib pen

Black India ink

Black water-soluble ink

Paints
Payne's gray
Burnt sienna
Cerulean blue
Cadmium yellow
Alizarin crimson
Cobalt blue
Lemon yellow

The Pose
This uncluttered pose – a three-quarters profile in simple lighting – enables you to concentrate on the shape and angle of the body and the tilt of the head, avoiding any complications such as dramatic shadows or foreshortening. The strong-colored clothes are built up by means of repeated overlays of paint.

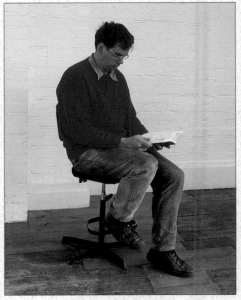

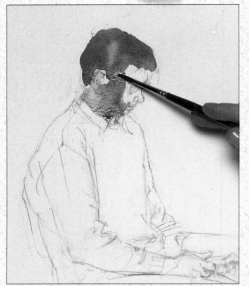

1 *Make a light HB pencil sketch. Paint the hair with a no. 4 brush and a Payne's gray and burnt sienna mix, allowing the colors to merge. Add depth with a little cerulean blue. Paint a dilute mix of cadmium yellow and burnt sienna across the face.*

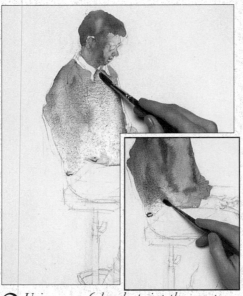

2 *Using a no. 6 brush, paint the sweater with a wet alizarin crimson/burnt sienna mix. Let the colors drift across the paper. Inset: Add cerulean blue to provide tonal variation. Deepen the folds with more cerulean blue, using the no. 4 brush.*

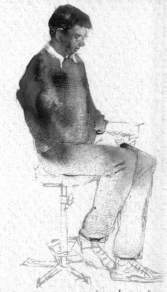

3 *The trousers were painted wet into wet with a dilute Payne's gray wash. This allowed the paint to flow naturally to enhance the soft quality of the fabric. More burnt sienna was added over the darker areas of the hair to suggest depth.*

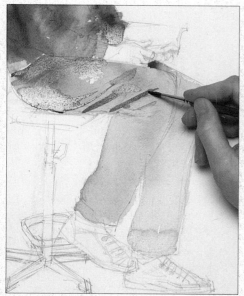

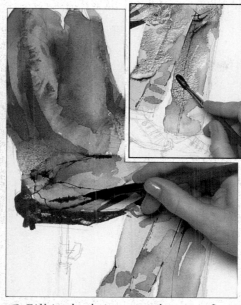

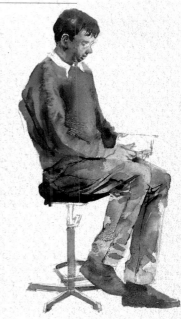

4 While the paint is still damp, paint strong lines in the folds of the trousers with the thicker solution of the Payne's gray and the no. 4 brush. This enables you to suggest the shape of the legs beneath and create a three-dimensional effect.

5 Fill in the chair seat with a mix of alizarin crimson and cobalt blue. Use a steel-nib pen and black water-soluble ink to emphasize the folds in the trousers. Inset: Soften the pen marks by blending the ink with the damp no. 4 brush.

6 The shoes were painted with a rich mix of Payne's gray and burnt sienna. Flesh tones were added to the hands, using lemon yellow mixed with burnt sienna. The metal chair stand was painted with a pale wash of Payne's gray and cerulean blue.

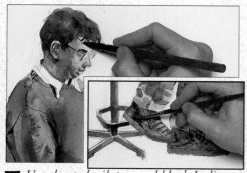

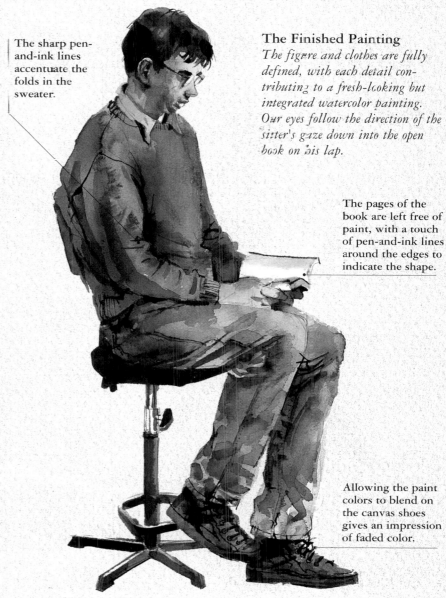

7 Use the steel-nib pen and black India ink to define the facial features and glasses, adding fine hair lines around the forehead. Inset: Using the no. 4 brush, build up the shape of the shoes with a mix of Payne's gray and Hooker's green light.

The sharp pen-and-ink lines accentuate the folds in the sweater.

The Finished Painting
The figure and clothes are fully defined, with each detail contributing to a fresh-looking but integrated watercolor painting. Our eyes follow the direction of the sitter's gaze down into the open book on his lap.

The pages of the book are left free of paint, with a touch of pen-and-ink lines around the edges to indicate the shape.

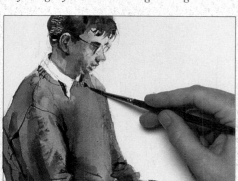

8 Refine the details of the shirt cuffs and the ribbing in the sweater with light pen-and-ink marks. With an emerald-green mix made from Hooker's green light, cadmium yellow, and lemon yellow, fill in the collar using the no. 4 brush.

Allowing the paint colors to blend on the canvas shoes gives an impression of faded color.

PAINTING PEOPLE:
Flesh Tones

WATERCOLOR IS an excellent medium to use for painting flesh tones as it has a natural affinity with the subject: both are made up of translucent layers and the best way to render skin tones in watercolor is to apply successive layers of paint.

Keep the applications of paint thin and light, as it is more difficult to lift off colors that have been applied thickly. Allow the work to dry between applications, either naturally or by using a hair dryer. Work layers of wet washes over dry paint to avoid producing muddy flesh tones. You must keep the paint fresh, so change your water supply regularly and wash out your brushes between each application.

Paint skin tones slightly darker than you perceive them to be, as they will dry to a paler tone. Don't let any preconceived ideas you might have about the color of skin affect how you render the subject. Although there is no set formula, certain color mixes work better than others. For pale skins, yellow ochre and burnt sienna are closer to the pink tones than rich cadmium yellow, for example. For darker skins, burnt sienna and raw umber are useful base colors and blues should be applied in areas of shade. Shadows on a face may appear as anything from green to dark blue, depending on the color of surrounding objects and the level and direction of natural light.

Tanned, Pale Skin

Pale flesh tones rely on the use of the white of the paper to provide the brightest highlights – as here. When painting pale flesh, don't be tempted to mix Chinese white gouache with orange to achieve pale pinks: instead, use very pale layers of yellow ochre, Venetian red or rose madder to build form and color simultaneously.

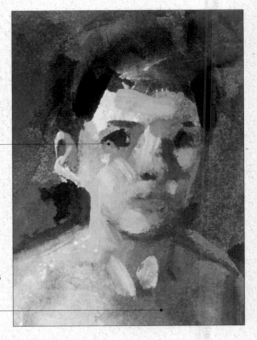

Warm shadows around the eye are built from burnt sienna and yellow ochre.

Yellow ochre and cerulean blue tones create dark and light contrasts on the cheek and shoulder blade.

Pale Skin, Rosy Cheeks

This woman has pale skin with a delicate rosy glow on her cheekbones, and high contrast between light and dark areas is crucial in depicting it accurately. The face is sculpted with areas of burnt sienna against yellow ochre. The profile is left almost white, to emphasize the strength of the light falling across the face. The variegated cobalt blue wash over the background enhances the skin tones. The hair is painted in yellow ochre and Venetian red washes, unifying the whole image.

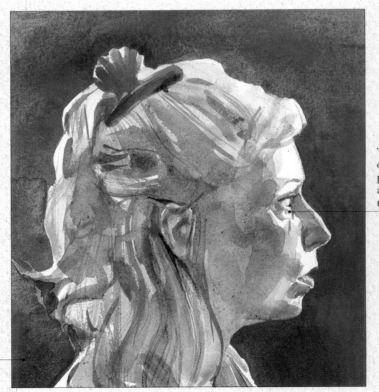

The eyes are left free of paint, the white paper acting as an additional color in this highlighted area.

There are marked temperature contrasts between the lights, darks, and mid tones, all of which are affected by the cool blue background.

136

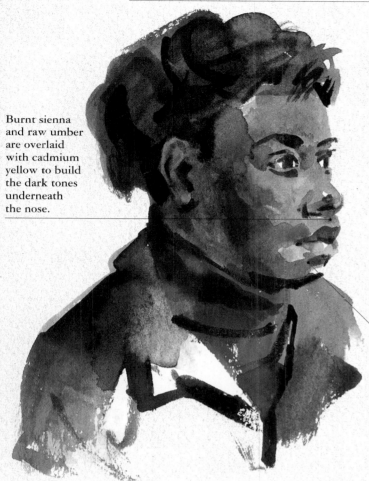

Burnt sienna and raw umber are overlaid with cadmium yellow to build the dark tones underneath the nose.

Dark Skin

Very rich dark tones enhance the deep colors of this young woman's skin. The style is sculptural, with slabs of color shaping the face. Burnt sienna and raw umber are used to establish the main skin tones, and cobalt blue is added to areas of dark shadow. The flesh tones are also enriched by the strong color of the woman's sweater. Cadmium yellow and cadmium red are used down the side of the face to break up the browns and add tonal interest.

The face is shaped with flat areas of browns, reds, and yellows. their contrasting angles producing depth and form.

Fair Complexion

This image combines a graphite pencil underdrawing with watercolor washes, letting the pencil define the shape of the face and the watercolor washes blend the lines into the flesh tones. This technique enables you to develop fine details without laboring the point. The pale skin tones are rendered in light washes of yellow ochre and rose madder, with the bright highlights picked out in Chinese white gouache.

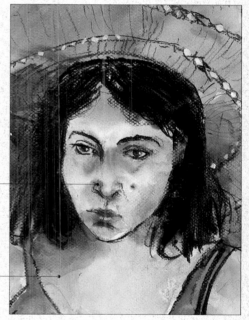

The nose is drawn precisely with charcoal to add depth and definition to the face.

Light washes of ochres and browns are overlaid wet on dry to build the subtle skin tones.

The eyes are detailed in water-soluble pencil and then overlaid with color washes to provide depth.

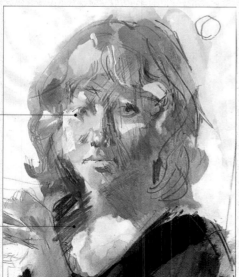

Further graphite pencil work is applied on top of dry underwashes to add detailing.

Olive Skin

Sometimes it helps to draw the details of a face with a dry medium, such as charcoal or water-soluble pencil, before you begin to build up the flesh tones. Here, charcoal serves this purpose. This Indian girl has an olive skin, which is rendered by a combination of light washes of yellow ochre and burnt sienna. The hair is a mix of Payne's gray and burnt sienna, which contrasts with the mix of cadmium yellow and yellow ochre used in the hat.

PAINTING PEOPLE:
Formal Dress

PAINTING A FIGURE wearing elaborate or very formal clothes requires a slow and steady buildup of colors and shapes. To produce a detailed portrait you will need more than one sitting: for the painting demonstrated on the next four pages, the sitter returned to pose on three occasions. Make a series of sketches before you start to paint. This will help you to get the proportions of the figure right. It will also force you to look at where folds fall in the fabric and how the light touches the subject. Quick sketches can also help you to capture fine details, such as facial features and hair.

Develop your painting slowly and methodically in order both to capture the likeness of your sitter and to build up the rich colors and fine details of the clothing he or she is wearing. Folds in fabric should be treated in the same way as any other light and dark areas on a textured surface. Use overlays of watercolor paint, wet on dry and wet on damp, in a slow and systematic manner, to develop the colors and textures of the materials. Allow one layer to dry completely before you apply the next. You may find it helpful to use masking fluid to define the outline of your figure or to protect fine details that will be painted in the final stages. Apply thin layers of watercolor, using small brushes, so that the paint doesn't drift into unwanted areas.

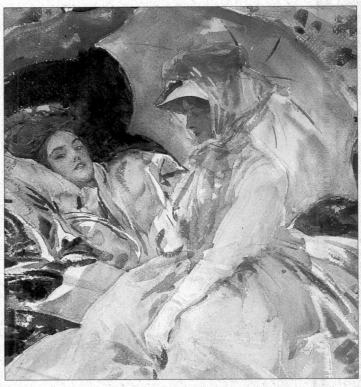

Ladies Reading, John Singer Sargent (1856–1925)
Sargent used angular brushmarks to develop folds and to imply voluminous layers of fabric in this light, fresh-looking watercolor.

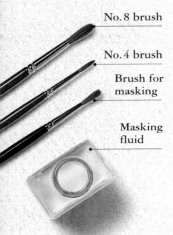

No. 8 brush

No. 4 brush

Brush for masking

Masking fluid

Paints
Cadmium red
Alizarin crimson
Cobalt blue
Cadmium yellow
Yellow ochre
Raw umber
Burnt umber
Hooker's green light
Chinese white gouache

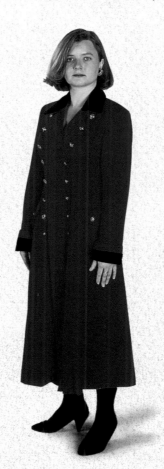

The Pose
Get your sitter to adopt a comfortable yet formal stance to show off the shape and fall of the clothing. Here the model stands at a slight angle to the viewer so that the dress and one arm are clearly visible, with her head turned toward the artist.

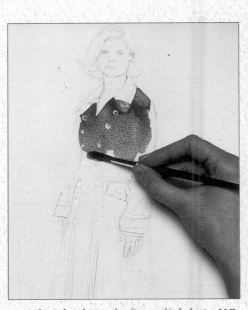

1 *After sketching the figure lightly in HB pencil, mask out the buttons on the dress with masking fluid and an old brush. Using a dilute mix of cadmium red and alizarin crimson, begin to wash in the general shape of the dress with a no. 8 brush.*

2 Overlay cobalt blue mixed with alizarin crimson on the damp red paint to emphasize areas that lie in shadow. To enhance the lighter areas on the main body of the dress, add cadmium yellow mixed with cadmium red. This should begin to define the folds that lie in the surface of the fabric.

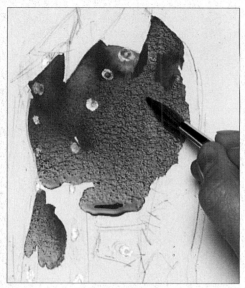

3 Continue to use the no. 8 brush to build up layers of cadmium red mixed with a small touch of cadmium yellow over the entire dress. Overpaint with a mix of cobalt blue and alizarin crimson to create cool tones where necessary. Allow the colors to blend together, wet into wet.

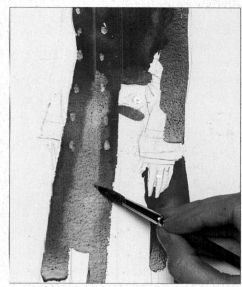

4 Let the paint dry. Now begin again, repeating the previous technique over the entire dress. These overlays of color help to create an impression of depth and shape within the body of the dress. Continue to build up the colors until you feel that they are the right density.

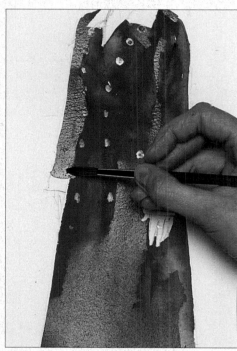

5 Long, straight brushstrokes applied with the no. 8 brush suggest fabric falling weightily downward. The shape of the body should dictate the direction of your brushstrokes — in toward the waist and out toward the bottom of the skirt.

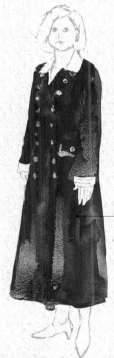

Areas of the dress that are bluer in tone appear cooler than those enhanced with cadmium yellow. By exploiting these different temperatures, you can suggest the folds in the dress.

6 Using a no. 4 brush, apply a mix of yellow ochre and a touch of alizarin crimson to begin shaping the flesh tones in the face and hands. Work in flat blocks of color. Inset: Paint the hair in a variegated wash of yellow ochre and raw umber.

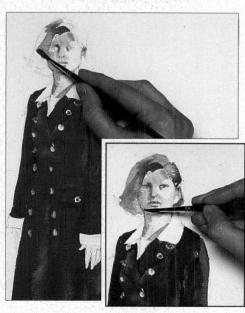

7 Paint the shoes, ankles, and legs with a mix of burnt umber and cobalt blue, using the no. 4 brush. Don't worry if the paint dries to a paler finish than required at this stage, as you can build the tones by overlaying more color once the initial wash has dried.

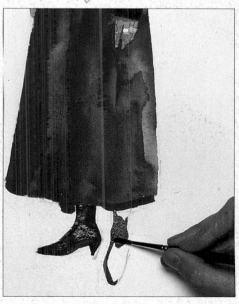

8 *Using the no. 4 brush, paint the cuffs and collar in a mix of raw umber and cobalt blue. Now gently rub away the masking fluid and paint in the brass buttons on the coat and the woman's rings using cadmium yellow.*

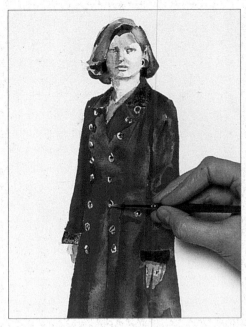

9 *Assess how far the portrait has developed. You may decide to alter certain elements to make sure, for example, that the proportions are well balanced and the colors accurate. In this instance, the tonal values on the dress are not strong enough, and the face lacks tonal variation.*

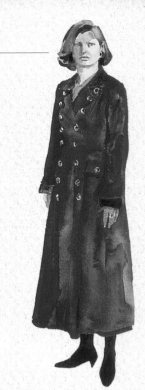

10 *Load the no. 8 brush with water and wet the surface of the fabric, then add further layers of a mix of cadmium red and cadmium yellow over the dress to enhance its rich and subtle textures. Remember to retain cool tones in the shaded folds by using a touch of cobalt blue mixed with alizarin crimson.*

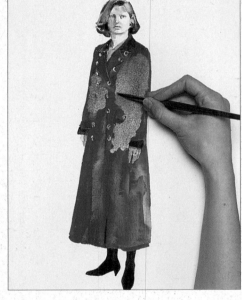

11 *As you add water to the paint, you can move it around on the paper and reshape the dress. Note how the figure is taking on a more curved appearance as the brush relocates the red paint on the arms and around the waist.*

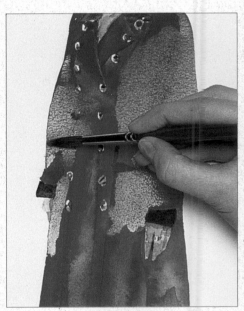

12 *Using the no. 4 brush, develop the tones on the face and hair, using variegated washes of raw umber and yellow ochre, washed in wet into wet. Add a touch of Hooker's green light to the right side of the face to make it appear cooler. Inset: Add more raw umber and yellow ochre to build the hair tones.*

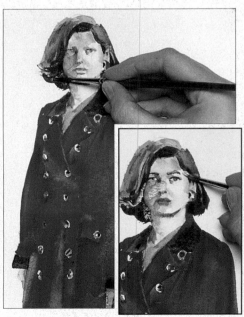

13 *Use Chinese white gouache to block out areas that need to be repainted. Allow these areas to dry, then rebuild the original tones to produce a richer color. This is particularly necessary on the dress, where the colors look too pale and flat when dry.*

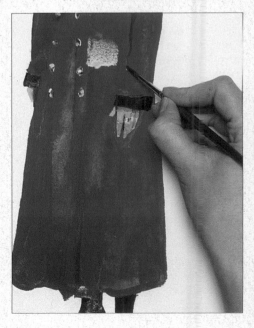

The Finished Painting

*Using only one main watercolor technique —
overlaying layers of paint wet into wet, wet
into damp, and wet over dry — you can
produce a fully developed figure in elaborate
dress. It is worth spending time and exercising
careful control to achieve such a rich result.
There is, however, a danger of overworking
an image that requires a gradual buildup
of color. Always retain freshness and
spontaneity as you work.*

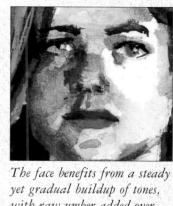

*The face benefits from a steady
yet gradual buildup of tones,
with raw umber added over
the original washes of yellow
ochre and alizarin crimson in
the later stages. Cadmium red
on the lips, together with
subtle green mixes in the skin
tones, enhance the features.*

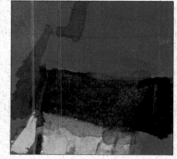

*Further applications of raw
umber and cobalt blue build
up to develop the rich tones of
the collar and cuffs.*

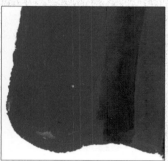

*Any unwanted splotches of
paint around the edges of the
figure can be scratched out
using the edge of a craft knife
blade, ensuring that the sharp
and formal quality of the
clothing is retained.*

PAINTING PEOPLE:
Combining Your Skills

Mother and Child

This portrait of a mother and her child combines many of the elements studied over the previous eight pages – poses, diverse skin tones, clothing, and setting. Young children are almost guaranteed not to sit still for you as you work. Unlike the previous projects, here your challenge is to capture the essence of the scene rather than to make a perfect copy of one moment in time. Your task is to capture the intimacy of the pair.

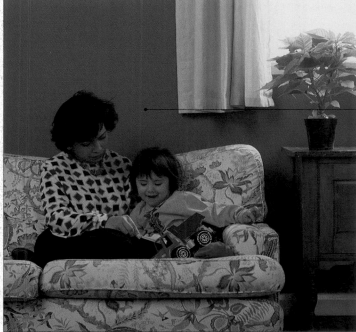

The bond between mother and child is evident from the way they snuggle up to each other. The intimate mood of the scene is reinforced by the relaxed poses.

Steel-nib pen

No. 3 brush

No. 8 brush

Black India ink

Brush for masking

Cardboard

Household candle

Masking fluid

Watersoluble pencils

Paints

Burnt sienna
Yellow ochre
Cadmium red
Cobalt blue
Burnt umber
Cerulean blue
Payne's gray
Viridian
Alizarin crimson
Chinese white gouache

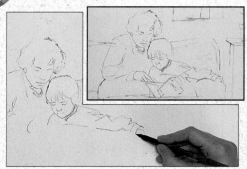

1 *Make an underdrawing using a steel-nib pen and diluted black India ink. Inset: Continue until you have completed the basic structural lines.*

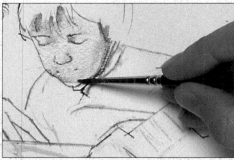

2 *Using a no. 3 brush, paint the child's skin with burnt sienna, yellow ochre, cadmium red, and cobalt blue mixes. Define the chin and cheek bones in burnt umber.*

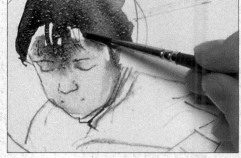

3 *Paint the child's hair wet into wet in a mix of burnt umber and cobalt blue. Try to maintain the angles you originally drew, even though the child is constantly moving.*

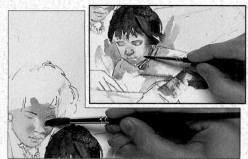

4 *Use a no. 8 brush to paint the mother's face with a yellow ochre and burnt sienna mix. Use cerulean blue washes on the child's shirt. Inset: Define the child's jaw with Payne's gray, using a no. 3 brush.*

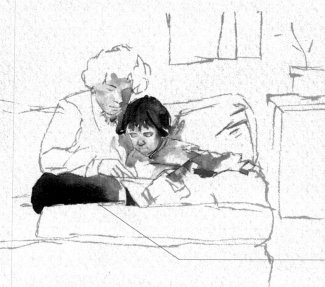

5 *A little viridian has been added to the child's hair, and the tones on the mother's face built up with burnt sienna. Her trousers were painted wet into wet, with a Payne's gray and cobalt blue mix.*

Overlays of color in the trouser folds help to suggest the form beneath.

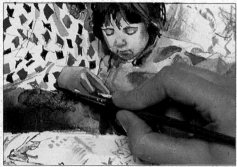

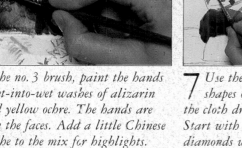

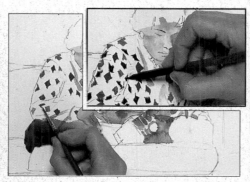

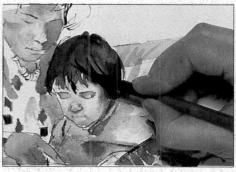

6 Using the no. 3 brush, paint the hands with wet-into-wet washes of alizarin crimson and yellow ochre. The hands are darker than the faces. Add a little Chinese white gouache to the mix for highlights.

7 Use the variations in the diamond shapes on the mother's shirt to show how the cloth drapes over the figure. Inset: Start with cadmium red, then define the diamonds with pen-and-ink outlines.

8 Define the child's hair, using the steel-nib pen and black India ink to mark in wispy lines and overall shape. You can also emphasize the areas of light and shade by smudging ink into the darker areas.

The hair is painted with a wet-into-wet mix of Payne's gray and burnt sienna.

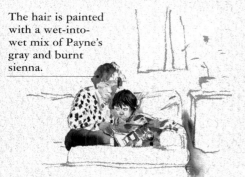

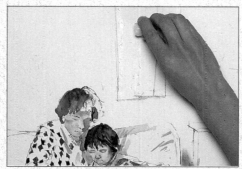

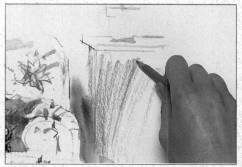

9 Various details have now been refined. Cobalt blue and cadmium red define the shape of the toy truck. Cobalt blue overlaid on the dry cerulean blue of the child's shirt defines the shape of her arm and shoulder.

10 Rub a household candle lightly over the area of the curtains. The wax adheres to the raised parts of the watercolor paper and will act as a resist, preventing paint from being absorbed in these areas.

11 Roughly color the cupboard with an orange watersoluble pencil, and begin to mark in the pattern on the sofa with semirandom pink, blue, and orange watersoluble pencil lines.

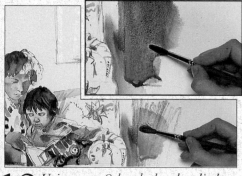

Once the mother's hair dries, you can define the fine hairs with pen-and-ink lines.

12 Using a no. 8 brush, brush a little water over the orange cupboard so that the watersoluble pencil lines create a rich, warm wash of color. Inset: The orange will dry to a paler tone, so add yellow ochre and burnt sienna on top of it.

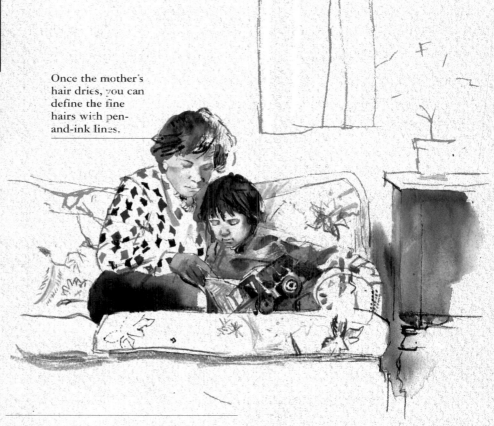

Progress Report

The painting is now beginning to take shape, and the main features are evident. Build layers of paint to create depth and contrast between areas of light and shade. Use pen and ink and watersoluble pencils to reinforce the creases on the clothes.

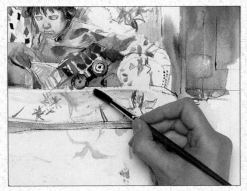

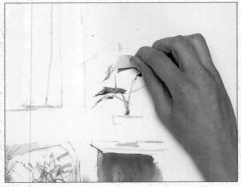

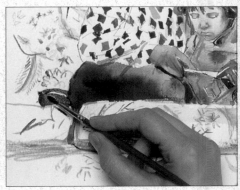

13 *Rinse your no. 8 brush, then brush a little clean water over the sofa area. The watersoluble pencil marks will blend together, making the pattern recede and appear less dominant in the composition.*

14 *Dip the edge of a piece of cardboard into a wet solution of viridian and mark the plant's leaves and stem. When dry, do the same with a wet yellow ochre solution. The two colors will blend slightly.*

15 *Using a no. 3 brush, paint the mother's boot with burnt sienna, making sure the paint does not run outside this area. Leave a line of white to give the impression of a highlight on the leather.*

Progress Report
Touches of Chinese white gouache are mixed into cadmium red to make the toy truck appear more intense in hue. More touches of Chinese white are added to the cupboard. A line of yellow watersoluble pencil creates a highlight area on the cupboard door.

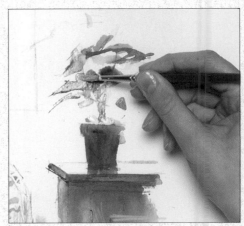

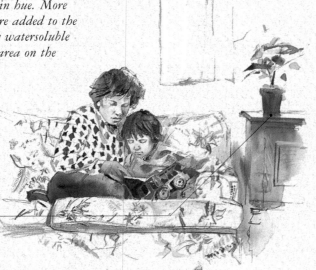

The flower pot is painted wet into wet with Payne's gray mixed with cobalt blue.

16 *Using an old brush, paint the plant's leaves with masking fluid. This will protect them from being splashed with the background color. Wash the brush in warm, soapy water immediately after use.*

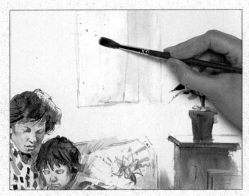

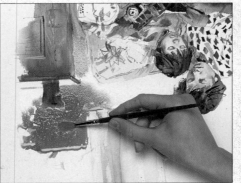

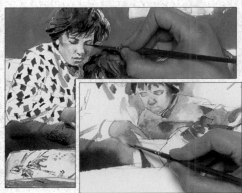

17 *With a no. 8 brush, paint yellow ochre wet into wet over the curtain. The paint will remain in the "troughs" of the paper but will not adhere to the raised areas treated with candlewax in step 10. The curtains will therefore look textured.*

18 *Turn the image upside down and, with a no. 8 brush, wash a mix of cadmium red, Chinese white, and yellow ochre over the wall. The plant is protected by masking fluid, but be careful not to paint over the pot.*

19 *Using the no. 3 brush, paint in the eyelids with a dark line of Payne's gray or a watersoluble pencil if you prefer. Inset:* Build up the shapes of the hands, using Chinese white mixed with yellow ochre and Payne's gray around the cuffs.

The Finished Painting

The painting retains a great degree of freshness. Without overemphasizing details, you can create a finished image that retains a sense of life and vitality. Areas of light pattern in the sofa and shirt contrast with opaque colors in the background, hands, and dark hair. The interaction between the two figures is intimate and sensitively portrayed. Their coloring is similar, and their absorption in the book they are reading enhances their familiarity with each other. Even though the figures moved while they were being painted, it is possible to capture an impression of stillness.

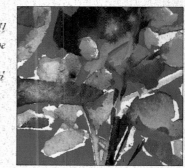

Once the paint over the background wall is dry, rub away the masking fluid to reveal the colors and crisp shapes of the plant's leaves.

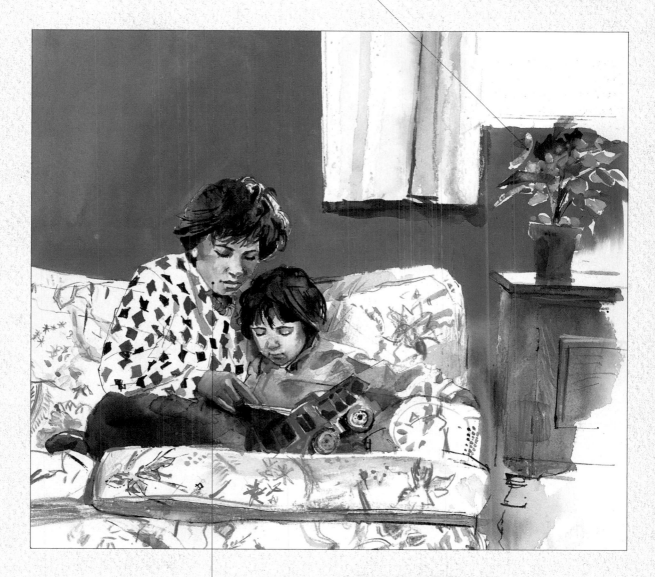

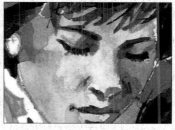

The facial details are more carefully refined than the rest of the painting as the expressions are essential in conveying the relaxed mood.

Rescuing Lost Causes

THERE ARE BOUND to be times when you make what seems to be an irreversible mistake, but you may still be able to save your watercolor painting. This section looks at a number of common problems and some simple ways of putting things right.

The immediate temptation is to cover up a mistake by applying more paint. Resist this impulse: more often than not you will end up with a muddy mess. Keep in mind that watercolor is translucent – so however hard you try to cover up an error, the paint underneath will still show through. If you want to rescue a wet run of color, try to mop it up immediately with a cotton swab or a rag. But if the paint is already being absorbed into the paper, you must wait for it to dry completely before you attempt to get rid of it. Patience is a virtue.

Sometimes you may get three-quarters of the way through a painting before you realize that the tones are wrong or that one feature inappropriately dominates all the others. One method of remedying such mistakes is to turn your picture upside down to find out whether an alternative pictorial approach suggests itself to you. This may sound like a rather eccentric approach to creating a work of art, but it often helps.

A mistake may be located in one specific area and therefore not affect the entire painting. In the most extreme circumstances you can cut the unwanted area of paper out, replace it with a new piece of paper glued to the back of the original, and then continue to paint. This method works best when you have a clearly defined area, such as an entire object to cut around.

Problem: The Colors Have Run

Solution: Wash the Colors Together and Start Again
When painting on location, a number of factors can disturb your work – none more so than a sudden downpour. In this instance the rain began to fall unexpectedly, causing the paint to run and ruin the painting.

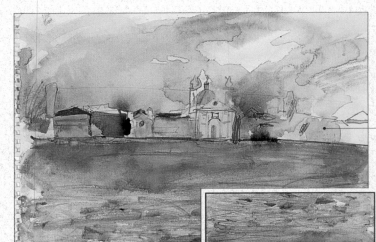

The colors in the painting are pale and uniform and can easily be blended together into a wash that will form the basis of a new painting.

Turning the paper upside down makes it easier to put the original composition to the back of your mind and come up with new ideas.

The Corrected Painting
The colors were washed together with a wet sponge to create a pale-colored ground, and the paper was left to dry. Then a new image was painted on top. The position of the original horizon line is still apparent, and its line was followed in the new painting to produce the curve of the river bank. The colors of the water and sky retain their different temperatures: warmer in what is now the water and cooler in the sky. The water from the original image was not tampered with greatly, as the colors make an equally realistic sky. The accident forced a more creative and imaginative response.

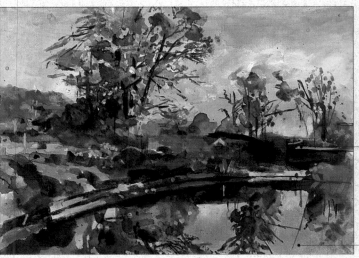

The slightly curved horizon line of the original suggests a convincing line for the river bank to follow. This provides a way to lead the eye into the middle ground.

The river was originally painted as the sky, but it is equally convincing in its new role.

Problem: One Area is Too Dominant

Solution: Cut Out and Replace

In this example the painting fails because the plate on which the plant is standing is tonally incompatible with the rest of the picture. It draws the viewer's attention toward it, rather than to the plant's leaves and out to the garden beyond. In order to redress this imbalance, some extreme action is needed. Using acrylic or gesso to cover the blue plate would create a change in texture over a large area of the painting (see p.148). In this instance it is preferable to cut out the offending area and attach a new piece of paper, which can be repainted.

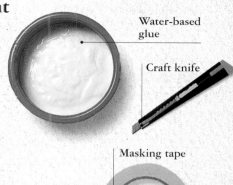

Water-based glue

Craft knife

Masking tape

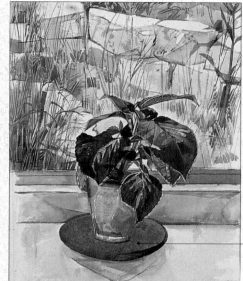

The blue plate creates an area of intense color in an otherwise subtly hued painting.

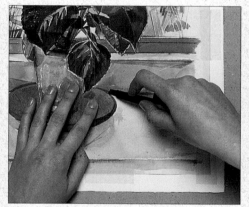

1 *Take a piece of watercolor paper identical to the original, and attach it to the back of the painting with masking tape. Cut around the plate with a craft knife, cutting through both pieces of paper.*

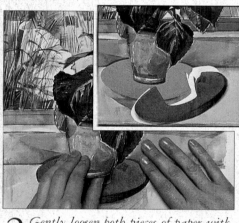

2 *Gently loosen both pieces of paper with your fingers. Inset: Carefully remove them. The cleaner your cuts, the easier this will be. Do not leave any rough areas.*

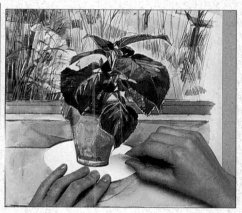

3 *Attach a rough piece of paper behind the painting with masking tape. Now glue your template piece of watercolor paper down in the space like the missing piece of a jigsaw puzzle.*

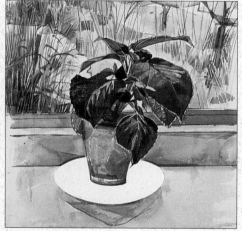

4 *As you can see, the blank piece of paper fits perfectly. You can now paint over the area again with fresh watercolor.*

The Corrected Painting

By leaving the plate white and adding only a few subtle washes of Payne's gray for the shadows, you can give the impression of an unpainted china plate. This is the perfect solution in this instance, as our focus is redirected from the plate onto the plant and out of the window toward the garden.

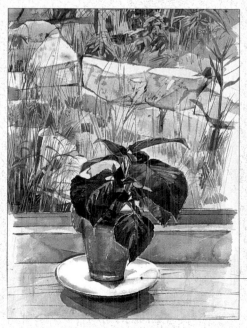

The plate now balances far more effectively with all other elements in the painting. There is no sign of the correcting work that has taken place.

THERE ARE TWO LESS RADICAL ways of creating a new, clean paper surface on which to paint. Both enable you to repaint specific, localized areas on your original paper without having to worry about underlying colors showing through. With both methods you need to make sure that the colors and tones you use when you repaint integrate perfectly into the original painting.

The first method is to cover the affected area with an opaque material that completely obscures the underlying watercolor paint. White acrylic paint and gesso can both be used in this method, though acrylic paint is generally easier to use. You must, of course, wait until the acrylic or gesso is dry before you start to repaint. Acrylic paint has good covering power and dries quickly. You need only one layer of paint, whereas if you use gesso, you should apply two or even three very thin layers, letting each dry completely before you apply the next. Dilute acrylic paint

with a little clean tap water first; otherwise that part of the painting may look as if it has a slightly raised surface. Acrylic paint also dries to a hard finish, so it is advisable to break the surface by rubbing it gently with pumice or fine sandpaper to give it a slight "tooth," similar to the watercolor paper on which you are painting.

The second method is carefully to remove the top layer of paper on which the paint sits. Once your painting is dry, scratch the paper surface with a craft knife or razor blade, or rub it gently with sandpaper. Be careful not to dig deeply into the paper, or rub it hard, as you may tear the paper. Blow or shake off any paper dust or flakes of paper, then repaint. One disadvantage of this method is that scratching into the paper surface can affect the texture of the finished painting, and so – unless that is the effect you want to achieve – it is best not to use this technique over a large area of paper.

Problem: An Area of the Painting is Too Dark

No. 4 brush

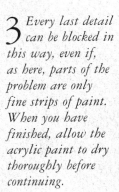

White acrylic paint

Solution: Create a New Ground Using White Acrylic Paint
Here, the tools the shipbuilder is using are so darkly painted that no detail is visible. This is a common problem for watercolorists, as the translucency of the paint dictates that you work from light to dark. If you work the other way around, the color of the overlying washes will be absorbed by the darker tones underneath.

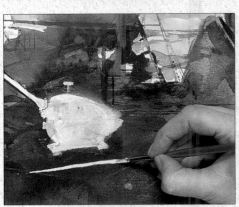

1 *Allow your painting to dry completely. Then, using a no. 4 brush, paint slightly diluted white acrylic paint over the area you wish to reclaim. Do not to allow the acrylic to spread into other areas of the painting.*

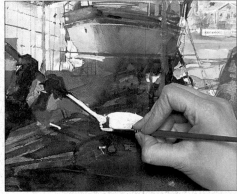

2 *Continue until the offending area of the work has been completely covered. The paint should be thick enough to block all traces of watercolor work underneath but still give a smooth finish.*

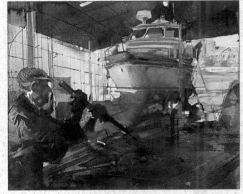

3 *Every last detail can be blocked in this way, even if, as here, parts of the problem are only fine strips of paint. When you have finished, allow the acrylic paint to dry thoroughly before continuing.*

The Corrected Painting
Because acrylic paint is opaque, any watercolor added on top of it will sit on the surface as if you were painting directly onto the paper. The fine details of the machinery have now been added.

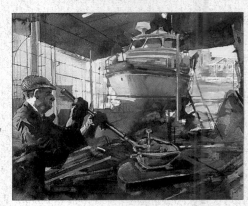

Problem: The Painting Looks Unbalanced

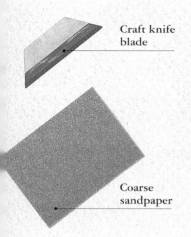

Craft knife blade

Coarse sandpaper

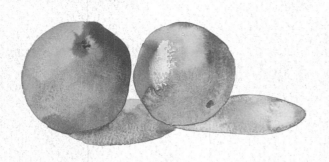

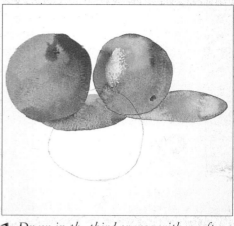

Solution: Add to the Composition
This composition looks unbalanced. You can improve it by removing the shadow and adding a third orange in its place.

1 *Draw in the third orange with a soft graphite pencil. The area it covers touches on the shadow beneath the two existing fruits, so this will have to be removed.*

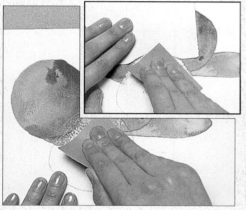

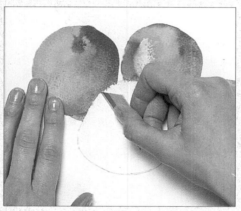

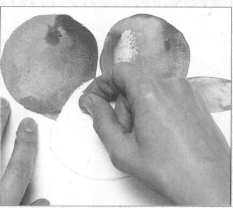

2 *Use coarse sandpaper to rub away the shadow. Rub in a circular fashion, breaking down the paper surface. Inset: Place paper over areas that you do not want to touch to protect them.*

3 *Once you have rubbed off most of the particles of paint, remove the protective paper. Using the flat edge of a craft knife blade, scrape away any remaining traces of paint from within the shadow area.*

4 *Use your fingernail to burnish the area, smoothing down the paper and removing any unwanted particles of paper or paint that may be sticking to the surface.*

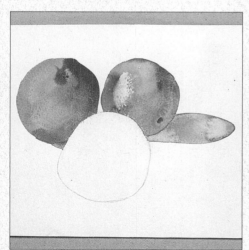

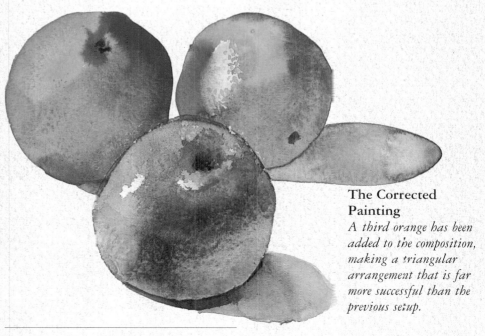

5 *You now have a clean area of paper over which you can paint a third orange. The surface of the paper has been broken down, but it is still suitable for wash work.*

The Corrected Painting
A third orange has been added to the composition, making a triangular arrangement that is far more successful than the previous setup.

FINALLY, IF YOU really cannot see a way to correct a picture, and you have worked it over too much to re-wet the paper and start again, you can try a severe remedy. Use a sponge to wash all the colors together on the paper, then lift as much out as possible with a rag or a second sponge. Remember, watercolor paper is made to absorb lots of water, so don't be afraid to flood the paper when you want to wash out a whole area. Restretch the paper and then repaint the surface with a thick wash of new color or colors in order to block out much of the original painting that lies beneath.

The most permanent pigments may stain the paper, and you may not be able to blend or wash off these colors as well as their less color-fast counterparts. Often you will still see traces of your former composition through the later layers of color. If this happens, make sure that you incorporate them into the design of your new painting. If you cannot completely cover your previous picture, take time to analyze what remains. Perhaps the line of a river running through a landscape can be reused to create the shape of a tree trunk. Turning your picture upside down or on its side may help you to come up with new compositional ideas, as it takes you one step farther away from your original painting. Alternatively, you may be able to use the existing shapes and colors as the basis for an abstract picture that expresses your mood. This can be an exciting way to approach painting: it forces you to think creatively and to search for new approaches to what might have begun as a fairly mundane piece of work.

The one golden rule is never give up on what may seem a lost cause. Instead, stand back and analyze exactly what needs to be done before you set to work correcting your mistake. Not only is it a shame to stop in the middle of a creative flow, but it is a waste of expensive materials and your time, too. It is very rare indeed to find that you cannot rescue your picture by one means or another.

Problem: You Are Dissatisfied With the Finished Painting

Solution: Wash Off the Old Painting and Start Again

In this example, the composition is uninteresting and the tonal values are uninspiring. The reflections of the bridge in the water are equally ineffective. A fresh wash over the entire painting is necessary.

Mop brush

Synthetic sponge

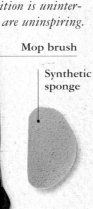

Paints
Hooker's green light
Cadmium yellow
Cerulean blue

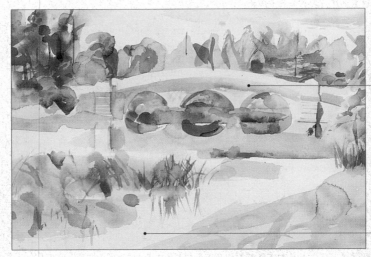

The tonal values of the bridge are weak and watery. They can easily be washed out with water.

Much of the paper remains white, so paint does not have to be removed before reworking begins.

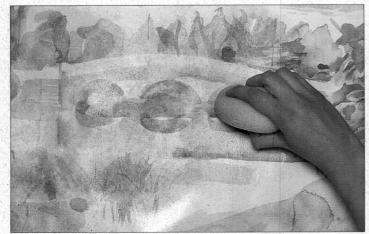

1 *Begin by dislodging the existing paint with a dampened synthetic sponge. Roughly rub the sponge over the paper in a circular fashion to dislodge even the most embedded particles of paint. As you work, the paint colors will run together and start to produce a subtle ground.*

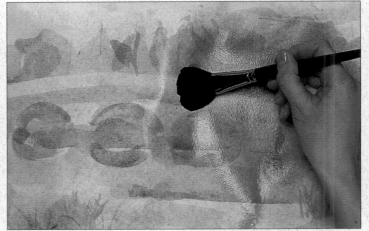

2 *Using a large mop brush, paint over the surface of the wetted paper with a series of variegated washes. Apply a mix of Hooker's green light and cadmium yellow, wet into wet, to begin to block out the underlying image.*

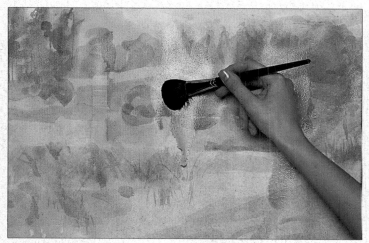

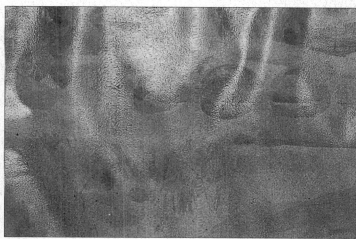

3 Add lots of water to the paper as you work across it. Now lay some cerulean blue washes onto the existing cadmium yellow and Hooker's green light, to cool the tone slightly and introduce some variation. The image should begin to disappear.

4 Because it has been saturated with water and paint, the paper is buckling. Watercolor paper is designed to hold a lot of water, so you do not need to be afraid that it will tear. However, you do need to restretch it while it is still wet.

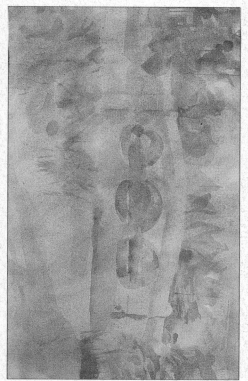

Some color still remains when the image is washed off. The new blue-green ground color is used to full advantage in the new painting, becoming an integral part of both the sky and the foliage.

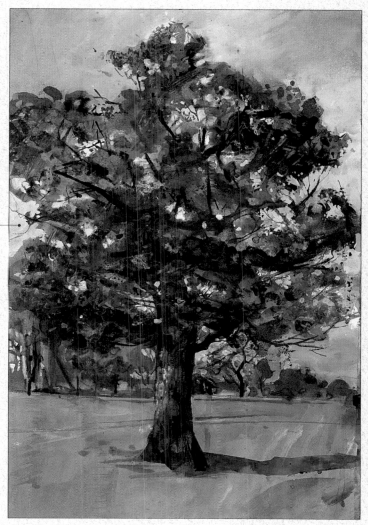

5 Let the paper dry before you paint over it again to create a new image. Traces of the underlying picture still show through, although it is quite subtle in appearance. Turning the paper on its side may help to suggest a new composition to you.

The Corrected Painting
The new picture bears no relation whatsoever to the underlying image. It was turned on its side and reworked extensively. The underlying colors of the washed and sponged paper were carefully analyzed and subtly incorporated into the new composition.

Matting and Framing

Awatercolor is never truly complete until it has been matted and framed. But how do you know which mat and frame to choose? It is as easy to ruin the look of a work by framing it inappropriately as it is to enhance it by choosing well. To many artists this is the most difficult stage.

Finding a frame that suits your picture is, of course, largely a matter of personal taste, yet there are some basic principles that will make your choice easier. Always allow the picture to dictate the frame, not the other way round. The frame and mat should complement what is housed inside, but the viewer's eye should go straight to the image, regardless of what surrounds it.

There are various ways to go about getting your pictures framed. You can ask a professional framer to do the work for you, you can buy ready-made framing kits and assemble the frame yourself, or you can buy the various materials needed and start from scratch. It is probably best to wait until you have some experience before attempting this last option.

If possible, take your painting with you when you go to buy a mat or a frame. This makes it much easier to visualize the finished result. Framers will give you examples of mats to hold against your work, enabling you to select a color that complements the tones in your painting. When it comes to the frame, the job is more difficult, as there are so many styles to choose from. Watercolors are so subtle and delicate that large, heavy frames can easily detract from them. Watercolors also need protection from the elements and light, so they should always be framed behind protective glass.

You also need to think about the size of the mat and frame. There are no hard-and-fast rules, but you should make sure that the painting does not look cramped. Small watercolors often look good in a large mat; with a bigger painting you can generally get away with a smaller proportion of mat to picture. Traditionally more space is left at the bottom of a mat than at the top, as this gives a better balance to the picture. A good framer will be able to advise you on all these points.

Walnut Frame and Wash-Lined Mat

Choose a frame that picks out one of the colors in your painting, enhancing the image. Here, a plain walnut frame was selected. It is simple in design, yet the wood has an interesting texture in its own right. A cream mat is often a sensible choice for watercolor paintings, as it does not shout for attention. This mat is decorated with a simple beige wash line, helping to draw the eye into the image. Note that slightly more space was left at the bottom edge of the mat than at the top, ensuring balance.

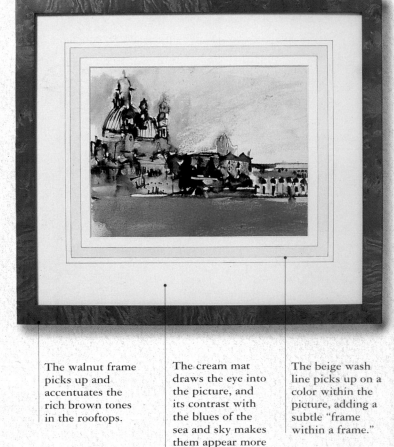

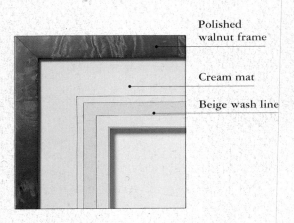

Polished walnut frame

Cream mat

Beige wash line

The walnut frame picks up and accentuates the rich brown tones in the rooftops.

The cream mat draws the eye into the picture, and its contrast with the blues of the sea and sky makes them appear more brilliant.

The beige wash line picks up on a color within the picture, adding a subtle "frame within a frame."

Gold-Leaf Frame and Lined Mat

There is sometimes a good reason to frame watercolors ornately, as long as your choice is not overelaborate. This gold frame has beveled edges, which add depth and substance to the frame, yet the frame is relatively fine and does not weigh heavily around the picture. The gold color enhances the beige touches of watercolor in the painting. The cream mat, once again, provides a subtle introduction to the richer colors in the painting. The mat is decorated with simple blue ink lines close to the picture, which draw the eye into the sea and sky of the painting.

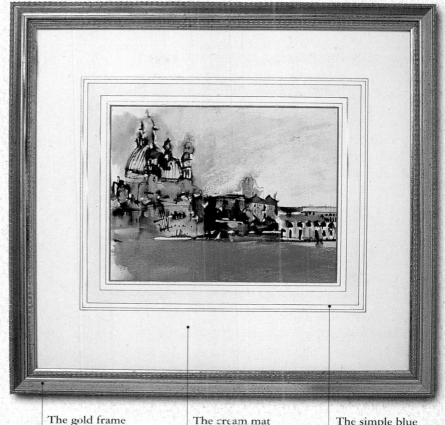

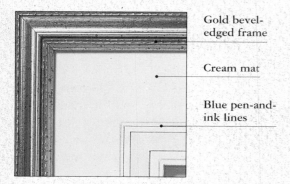

Gold bevel-edged frame

Cream mat

Blue pen-and-ink lines

The gold frame enhances the beige tones in the painting.

The cream mat invites the eye into the richer tones of the picture.

The simple blue pen-and-ink lines draw attention to the blue of the sea and sky.

Black Painted Frame and White Mat

Some artists prefer a minimalist approach to their work and frame their paintings with the utmost simplicity. Black frames can deaden a painting if there are no black or intensely dark tones within the work of art, but they can also help to define the linear qualities in a painting. In this instance the pen-and-ink work in the watercolor is enhanced by the simple frame.

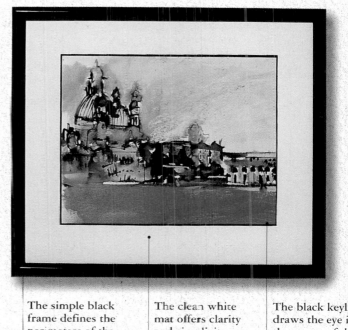

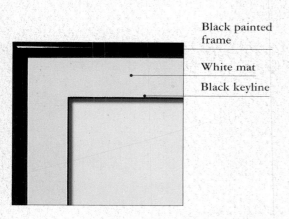

Black painted frame

White mat

Black keyline

The simple black frame defines the perimeters of the painting without adding fussiness to the finish.

The clean white mat offers clarity and simplicity.

The black keyline draws the eye into the center of the mat and so into the painting.

Glossary

Accelerator: A substance added to paint to speed up the drying time.

Acrylic: A quick-drying water-base paint bound with synthetic resin. Unlike watercolor, acrylic is available in transparent and opaque colors.

Additive: Any one of a number of substances that can be mixed into paint to alter properties such as drying time and viscosity.

Atmospheric effects: *See* Perspective, aerial.

Bleach into ink: A technique in which diluted bleach is used to remove areas of ink. The ink-free area can then be painted with watercolor, or any other type of paint, leaving the ink-stained area as a dense, boldly colored background.

Body color: *See* Gouache.

Brushes: There are many types of brushes, but the three listed below are the most useful for watercolor painting.

    Chisel: A brush with a flat ferrule in which the hairs are arranged in a straight line to give a flat edge. Chisel brushes are sometimes referred to as one-stroke brushes.

    Mop: A full brush with a round ferrule and therefore a rounded head of bristles, often used to apply a wash to a large area.

    Round: A useful general-purpose brush with a round ferrule on which the hairs come to a fine point. Round brushes are available in a wide range of sizes.

Color

    Complementary: The term used to describe colors that lie opposite each other on the color wheel – red and green, for example.

    Cool: A color from the blue and green side of the color wheel, thought to suggest coolness.

Primary: A color that cannot be made by mixing other colors. There are three primary colors: red, yellow, and blue.

Secondary: A color made by mixing together two primary colors.

Tertiary: A color made by mixing a secondary color with any other color.

Theory: The scientific principles of color analysis.

Warm: A color from the red and orange side of the color wheel, thought to suggest warmth.

Wheel: A method of visually arranging the primary and secondary colors to demonstrate the relationships between them.

Composition: The placement of separate elements and colors within a painting, usually creating a sense of balance and harmony.

Craft knife: A safety knife with a retractable blade used for cutting around fine, small areas. The blade is easy to change when blunt. A craft knife is also useful for some special watercolor techniques, such as sgraffito.

Distressing: The technique of roughening the surface of the paper to create interesting textures and tones. The altered texture of the paper surface is very evident when paint is applied. Several methods can be used to distress paper: rubbing with sandpaper, scratching with the edge of a craft knife blade, and crumpling paper in the hands are the most common.

Drybrush: A technique in which paint is applied with an almost-dry brush carrying very little paint.

Gesso: A substance traditionally made with whiting and animal glue, now available in acrylic form, that is used to create a painting surface on paper or poster board.

Gouache: An opaque water-base paint also known as body color. In watercolor painting one of the main uses of gouache is as a means of painting a light color on top of a dark one without any of the underlying particles of paint showing through.

Ground: The prepared surface – paper or canvas – on which the artist works.

> **Toned ground:** A ground that has been lightly tinted with a wash of color.

Highlight: The point on an object where the light strikes a reflective surface, often left as white paper in watercolor painting.

Horizon line: An imaginary line at the artist's eye level. Establishing the horizon line in a painting is an essential first step in establishing the perspective of a painting.

Hue: A term used to define a color, by which it is distinguished from another.

Interest, center of: The focal point of a picture, the point to which the viewer's eye is instinctively led. The center of interest is often, but not always, the main feature of the painting.

Masking: A technique in which part of the picture surface is temporarily covered to prevent paint from reaching it. Masking fluid and masking tape are the two most common and effective masks, but a simple piece of paper laid over the surface can also be used.

Matting: Placing a painting on a piece of cardboard prior to framing it. Traditionally, more space is left at the top of a mat than at the bottom since this gives a better balance to the painting.

Optical mixing: Placing dots or touches of different colors in close proximity to each other so that they appear to the viewer to merge together and form another color.

Overdrawing: A technique that involves drawing over an area on which a watercolor wash has already been laid.

Overlaying: A technique in which layers of watercolor paint are laid over washes that have already dried in order to build up color to the desired strength.

Palette:
> (1) The board or dish on which an artist lays out, mixes, and dilutes paint.
> (2) The colors selected by an artist that characterize his or her work.

> **Limited palette:** The use of very few colors in the making of a painting. A limited palette can consist of as few as five colors.

Pan: A small, rectangular, open container in which watercolor paint is sold.
> **Half pan:** A half-size version of the above.

Paper: There are three established types of paper in general use in watercolor painting. Each type is available in a range of weights.

> **Cold-pressed (CP):** This is the most popular and versatile type of paper. It has an even texture with good "tooth" and is suitable for many different styles of working. Cold-pressed paper is sometimes referred to as "NOT" - that is, paper that is not hot-pressed.

> **Hot-pressed (HP):** Hot-pressed paper is the smoothest type available. It is particularly suitable for delicate brushwork and over-drawing in pencil or pen and ink.

> **Rough:** Rough paper has the coarsest texture. The peaks and troughs can be exploited to great effect in loose, impressionistic work.

Perspective: A system of drawing or painting that enables the artist to create the illusion of spatial recession on a flat surface.
> **Aerial perspective:** A system in which tones and colors are used to suggest distance. Colors are generally paler toward the horizon.

Linear perspective: A system that exploits the fact that objects appear to be smaller the farther they are from the viewer in order to create an illusion of spatial recession.

Resist: A material that prevents one medium from touching the paper lying beneath it. This technique exploits the fact that certain substances repel others; wax, for example, repels water, and so a water-based paint will not adhere to the paper if it is applied on top of wax.

Retardant: A substance added to paint in order to slow down the drying time.

Sgraffito: A technique of scratching back into the paint surface, usually to reveal the paper or an underlying color, to create an interesting texture.

Shade: A color that has been darkened by the addition of another color, such as lamp black or Payne's gray.

Spattering: A technique in which paint is flicked onto the paper in order to create texture. The technique produces a semirandom effect.

Sponging: A technique in which colors are laid on the paper with a sponge rather than a brush in order to create texture. The same technique is also used in watercolor painting to dampen the paper with water.

Stippling: A technique of applying color to paper in dots, using the tip of the brush.

Temperature: The relative visual warmth or coolness of a color.

Tint: A color that has been lightened. In watercolor painting, this is achieved by adding water.

Tone: The relative darkness or lightness of a color.

Underdrawing: A technique of drawing the subject before applying paint. It can be used as a technique in its own right, to create a particular artistic effect, or as a guide to enable the artist to establish the correct size and shape of his or her subject before beginning to paint.

Wash: Varying dilutions of watercolor paint applied to the surface of the paper with a brush or sponge.

    Flat wash: A wash laid evenly across the paper.

    Gradated wash: A wash that gradually changes from light to dark in intensity.

    Variegated: A wash, often random, varying in intensity and color.

Watercolor: A translucent water-base paint consisting of pigment bound with gum arabic. Mixed with water to achieve the desired density of color, it is available in both tubes and pans.

    Concentrated watercolor: An intensely colored paint, available in liquid form.

Weight: The term used to describe the relative thickness or thinness of paper. Weight is usually expressed in grams per square meter (gsm) or in pounds per ream – a ream being 500 sheets.

Wet into wet: A technique of applying paint to a wet or damp surface so that colors blend together.

Index

Picture Credits and Acknowledgments

Picture Credits

The author and publishers are grateful to the following for their kind permission to reproduce copyrighted paintings and photographs:

Albertina, Vienna, 112; Boston Museum of Fine Arts, Charles Henry Hayden Fund, 138; British Museum /Bridgeman Art Library, 98; Christie's Images, 106; Jon Hibberd, 102; The Metropolitan Museum of Art, New York, 90; National Gallery of Scotland, 40; National Portrait Gallery, Smithsonian Institution/Art Resource, New York, 6; Tate Gallery, London, 102; Towner Art Gallery, Eastbourne/Bridgeman Art Library, 56; Ulm Museum, 33; Victoria and Albert Museum, London/Bridgeman Art Library, 7; Charlie Waite, 57, 98, and 114.

All other paintings are by Stan Smith.

Acknowledgments

The author would like to thank Kate Gwynn for research and assistance; Louie Rey-Edgar, Stephanie Edgar, Miranda Fellows, Kit Smith, and Tim Smith for acting as models; Emma Pearce for her invaluable advice; and Stuart Stevenson and Winsor & Newton for their very generous supplies of materials.